Beginning Android Tablet Programming

Starting with Android Honeycomb for Tablets

Robbie Matthews

Apress®

Beginning Android Tablet Programming: Starting with Android Honeycomb for Tablets

ISBN-13 (pbk): 978-1-4302-3783-9

ISBN-13 (electronic): 978-1-4302-3784-6

President and Publisher: Paul Manning
Lead Editor: Steve Anglin and Tom Welsh
Technical Reviewer: Stephen Bull and Peter Brownlow
Editorial Board: Steve Anglin, Mark Beckner, Ewan Buckingham, Gary Cornell, Morgan Engel, Jonathan Gennick, Jonathan Hassell, Robert Hutchinson, Michelle Lowman, James Markham, Matthew Moodie, Jeff Olson, Jeffrey Pepper, Douglas Pundick, Ben Renow-Clarke, Dominic Shakeshaft, Gwenan Spearing, Matt Wade, Tom Welsh
Coordinating Editor: Anita Castro
Copy Editor: Mary Ann Fugate
Compositor: Bytheway Publishing Services
Indexer: SPI Global
Artist: SPI Global
Cover Designer: Anna Ishchenko

Distributed to the book trade worldwide by Springer Science+Business Media, LLC., 233 Spring Street, 6th Floor, New York, NY 10013. Phone 1-800-SPRINGER, fax (201) 348-4505, e-mail orders-ny@springer-sbm.com, or visit www.springeronline.com.

For information on translations, please e-mail rights@apress.com, or visit www.apress.com.

Apress and friends of ED books may be purchased in bulk for academic, corporate, or promotional use. eBook versions and licenses are also available for most titles. For more information, reference our Special Bulk Sales–eBook Licensing web page at www.apress.com/bulk-sales.

The source code for this book is available to readers at www.apress.com. You will need to answer questions pertaining to this book in order to successfully download the code.

I dedicate this book to my family. Without your support and occasional nagging this book would never have been finished.

Robbie Matthews

Contents at a Glance

Contents

About the Author

 **Robbie** has been a programmer since the early 1980s, when a friend came home with a Commodore PET. He's been working with computers ever since, usually doing "the tricky bits."

He has worked on just about every aspect of computer programming you can think of. At one stage, he was the world expert on a computer language called Sybol, which no one remembers anymore, and wrote the firmware for some early GPS tracking devices.

His involvement in Android programming started when he began contributing to the Scripting Layer for Android (SL4A) project, which he is now maintaining. He's also an author and editor: he is the editor-in-chief for the *Andromeda Spaceways Inflight Magazine*, and in 2003 he won the Peter McNamara award for Publishing and Editing. In 2009, his collection of short stories, *Johnny Phillips: Werewolf Detective*, was shortlisted for an Aurealis Award.

He is married, has two adult children, and runs his household for the convenience of two small dogs (or so they inform him). In what spare time he has, he rides his bicycle, plays guitar, and likes role-playing games.

About the Technical Reviewer

 Steve Bull is a mixed-media technology artist and entrepreneur whose practice includes extensive software engineering experience. For the last ten years, he has created location-specific narratives and games that explore the social, technological, and creative possibilities of cell phones. He codes in Android, iOS, Asterisk, and most recently in Junaio 3D augmented reality. He's recently been commissioned to deliver 50 AR busts into a private Italian garden bordering the Mediterranean.

Acknowledgments

I'd like to thank the SL4A crew: I never would have gotten into this otherwise . . . I'd particularly like to thank Damon Kohler for starting SL4A in the first place: many of the techniques in this book were cribbed off his foundations. And I'd even like to thank Paul Ferrill, for dobbing me into Apress—without that, I may have had my weekends free!

Some Notes on Using the Downloaded Code

There is a significant amount of sample code in this book. The code is downloadable from the Apress web site: there will be a link from this book's individual page.

Navigate to the Apress web site, and look for "Beginning Android Tablet Programming." I would expect it to be here: www.apress.com/9781430237839, but links are subject to change. There will be a link to download the source code, and it will be in a single zip file, probably BA3TPSource.zip.

Setting Up Eclipse

All the coding examples (except those in Python) are written with Eclipse in mind. Chapter 1 will walk you through setting up your Eclipse environment. Go read it now and follow the instructions. I'll wait.

Importing the Example Projects

To import the sample projects, open Eclipse and click the following:

File ↗ Import ↗ General ↗ Existing Projects Into Workspace ↗ Next

Check "Select Archive File", and browse to wherever you've put BA3TPSource.zip.

A list of available projects should appear. You can either select the projects you are interested in, or just import all of them. Hit Finish, and let it do its stuff.

The Utilities Library

You may need to do some additional setup for the BA3TPUtils library. This is a set of utility functions that a number of the later projects share. It needs to know where to find the Android development files. To set this up, right-click BA3TPUtils, and then go to the following:

Build Path ↗ Add External Archive

Navigate to the following:

<wherever you installed the android-sdk>/platforms/<your preferred platform>/android.jar

For example, on my Windows computer, that is as follows:

C:\Program Files (x86)\Android\android-sdk\platforms\android-11\android.jar

Another problem you may find is BA3TPGps or BA3TPContacts2 complaining about either a missing BA3TPUtils or perhaps it can't find FileUtils, ListPicker, or MessageBox. This may mean you neglected to import BA3TPUtils in the first place, or that they can't find it.

The solution is to import BA3TPUtils according to the following instructions, and (if needed) tell the complaining projects where to find it.

Right-click the offending project, and go to the following:

Build Path ↗ Configure Build Path ↗ Projects ↗ Add ↗ BA3TPUtils ↗ OK

Then everything should work.

Python Examples

To save you typing, all the Python example files in Chapter 4 are included in the download. Look for the Python folder in BA3TPSource.zip. The file examples.txt provides a table of which listing corresponds to which source file.

CHAPTER 1

Getting Started

Welcome to the world of programming the Android tablet. In this chapter, I'll introduce you to the basics of setting up your programming environment. I'll walk you through your first Android program, and we'll even take a run through the world's quickest introduction to Java.

But first: a slightly self-indulgent history of the world of handheld computing.

A Short, Personal History of Portable Programming

Handheld computers have been around longer than you might think. For a lot of people, it was only yesterday that the iPhone appeared on the scene, and all the cool kids had to have one.

But I've been using such handheld devices on and off since the late 1970s.

My first introduction to something you could call a handheld computer was the Sharp PC-1210. This had a single-line display and a QWERTY keyboard, and could be programmed in BASIC. It was owned by a cousin of mine, and I wanted one so badly I could taste it.

Okay, not sure what I would have used it for—probably generating random encounters in D&D[1]—but it kicked off a mild obsession with cute handheld devices that persists to this current day.

I looked on with interest as the Apple Newton appeared in 1987, proudly announcing handwriting recognition. I also watched as it crashed and burned, a victim of its own marketing hype, which vastly surpassed its technical capability. However, it was probably my first encounter with a tablet computer.

Then the PalmPilot appeared in 1996, or thereabouts. I got me one of those. It's still kicking around the house somewhere. The Palm had handwriting recognition of a sort, but much less ambitiously implemented, and as a result, it worked quite nicely.

I loved that thing. The designers had paid a lot of attention to the Newton debacle, and kept a firm eye on what was achievable with the technology of the day. A handheld computer is, of necessity, quite a limited device compared to a laptop computer. Never mind that today's smartphones have more computing capacity than NASA had when they put a man on the moon; they're still much more restricted in terms of memory, processing power, and screen real estate than a desktop computer, and, by their very nature, probably always will be.

Therefore, Palm OS was not designed to do everything. It made the simplifying assumption that anyone with a PalmPilot would also have access to a computer, so they let all the stuff requiring heavy processing and storage capacity live on that computer. They then concentrated on maximizing what the user actually saw and used. They also invented the term that is used for this whole class of devices, a personal data assistant, or PDA.

And this is an important thing to remember about programming for a mobile device. Keep it simple, avoid bloat, and concentrate on usability. Pay attention, because this will appear on the snap quiz later.

---

[1] I was, and still am, a geek. And proud of it!

Then there were devices like the Psion. I've owned several models of these. They were particularly nice because they had a small but fully functional keyboard that you could actually touch-type on. The Psion had a simple programming language of its own, and ran the Symbian operating system. This is interesting because, although the Psion is long dead, the Symbian OS is alive and well and living in Nokia phones.

Then I got another Palm device, this time a LifeDrive. This was a PDA only a little thicker than a modern iPhone. It supported Wi-Fi and Bluetooth, and had a touch screen, a fairly comprehensive suite of user applications, and a 4 GB drive. In fact, apart from not actually having a phone built in, it was very close to the modern smartphone: about five years prior to the appearance of the modern smartphone.

The other side of the mobile device coin was, of course, the mobile phone.

In the late 1980s, my company put a car phone in my car rather than risk me being out of touch for more than five minutes at a time.

In the early 1990s, I got my first half-brick, and I've had one ever since, getting a new model every couple of years. And over that time, they've gotten cleverer, with bigger screens and more functions. Address books, calendars, calculators, games . . .

You see where I'm going here. The mobile phone and the PDA have been on a collision course since forever. And, for all intents and purposes, with the advent of the smartphone, they've arrived.

There have, of course, been other small, mobile devices in common use since at least the middle of last century—if you count cameras, even longer. (If you count watches, a couple of centuries.)

Transistor radios. Calculators. Cameras. Watches. Walkmen. MP3 players. DVD players. GPS navigators. eBook readers. They've all, one by one, been assimilated by either the PDA or the mobile phone, and now the PDA and the phone have assimilated each other.

Again, this trend is not as new as many people think. Combination mobile/PDAs were available a decade ago, in the form of the Kyocera 6035 (a Palm OS–based phone). There have been the Treo, the Blackberry, and various Windows CE platforms, to name but a few.

But for the most part, these were purchased by either your smart young executive or your die-hard tech geek. They were, when all is said and done, rather expensive and generally less functional than just buying the devices you needed.

With the release of Apple's iPhone, everything seemed to come together. Functionality, price point, and marketing push all combined to make the smartphone a must-have, mass-market appliance.

There is yet another branch of the mobile computing tree that I haven't mentioned—the laptop. The first hands-on experience I ever had with a laptop was the KayPro II (way, *way* back in 1982). This was a CP/M Z80–based machine with two floppy disks, and a built-in screen (a cathode ray tube). It wasn't a called a laptop. It was a "luggable" computer, in that it had a handle, and you could carry it, if you were fairly strong.

The next one I had access to was a Commodore-SX64, which was a Commodore 64, built into a box, with a floppy disk, a 5-inch screen, and a handle. I thought it was pretty neat.

Real laptops appeared after that, and have steadily become more powerful, smaller, and with better batteries. Touch screen models appeared about five or six years ago, but while nice, they didn't set the world on fire.

A few years ago, I got my first netbook—an extra small laptop with a solid state drive. I used this as my mobile device until recently, when I acquired my HTC Desire Android phone.

And then Apple announced the iPad, basically a big iPhone with a bigger screen, which neatly bridged the gap between the laptop and the smartphone.

This brings us down to two complementary mobile devices, the smartphone—something that fits into your pocket—and the tablet, something still light and portable, which has the screen size and peripherals to do serious work.

The Advent of Android

Nice as the iPhone and the iPad were technically, they were emphatically *not* open source. In fact, many people had issues with Apple's restrictions on what could and could not be put in your smartphone.

Plus, as I've just laid out, the smartphone has been arriving for quite some time, with at least three well-established mobile operating systems in the marketplace, so the iPhone was soon to have competition.

Android Inc. was founded in 2003, and acquired by Google in 2005. The Open Handset Alliance—a consortium of companies including Google, Motorola, HTC, and a bunch of other handset manufacturers and carriers—was announced in November 2007 (a mere two months after the launch of the iPhone). That same day, the Android platform was revealed.

Android was built on a Linux kernel, and is fundamentally open source (with some exceptions). Android apps are primarily written in Java. The Android version of Java runs on what is called the Dalvik virtual machine, which is optimized specifically for handheld devices.

Fast-forward a few years to 2011, which I like to call "the present." There have been a few Android tablets released, but these are still fundamentally upsized mobile phones as far as their operating system is concerned. It's only with the release of Android 3.0 (Honeycomb) that we have a version that takes full advantage of the expanded capabilities of a full-sized tablet.

Which brings us to the whole point of this book.

Figure 1-1. Programming tablets used to be much more difficult . . .

Let's get straight down to brass tacks. By the time you finish this chapter, you should be running your first genuine Android program.

Preparing Your Computer

You'll need a programming environment to start programming your Android tablet. This will involve downloading the Java Development Kit (JDK), the Eclipse IDE (Integrated Development Environment), and the Android Software Development Kit (SDK).

The Android SDK is written primarily in Java, although it does have a few native code extensions. If you don't like Java, there are some alternatives. You can actually get started much faster and more easily in, say, Python. I've got a whole chapter—Chapter 4—on that later in the book, which might suit you better if you just want to get stuck straight in. It also has the advantage that you can program straight on your Android—you don't need an attached computer.

However, the bulk of Android is written in Java, and therefore the bulk of documentation is aimed at Java. It's the language that allows you to get the most out of your device, so it will behoove you to come to an understanding of Java even if you end up doing your application development elsewhere.

Installing Your Development Environment

Here is the short version:

1. Go to this link: `http://developer.android.com/sdk/installing.html`

2. Follow instructions.

3. Start programming!

Actually, it is almost as simple as that, and, given the rate at which Android is being updated, you should take that as the definitive version.

However, while this is pretty simple, there are a few traps and tricks for young players, so I will expand.

1. Make sure your computer is up to spec. See `http://developer.android.com/sdk/requirements.html` for an up-to-date list. The SDK comes in versions for Windows, Linux, and Mac, which covers just about any personal computer out there these days. You should be able to find a version to suit you.

2. Make sure you have a recent copy of the Java Development Kit (JDK), currently here: `www.oracle.com/technetwork/java/javase/downloads`.

3. Install Eclipse, from `www.eclipse.org/downloads`.

4. Download the Android SDK from `http://developer.android.com/sdk/index.html`.

5. Start Eclipse. If you've done this in the right order, Eclipse should be able to find the JDK for itself. If not, you may have to tell Eclipse where to find it manually.

6. Install the ADT (Android Developer Tools).

   a. In Eclipse, go to Help ➤ Install New Software ➤ Add

   b. Enter **ADT Plugin** as the Name field.

   c. Enter `https://dl-ssl.google.com/android/eclipse/` into the Location field.

   d. Hit OK.

    e.   An Available Software dialog should appear. Check Developer Tools, and then click through Next until you get to Finish.

    f.   Let it load and then restart Eclipse.

7.   Tell Eclipse where to find the Android SDK:

    a.   Window ➤ Preferences ➤ Android

    b.   Browse to where you installed the Android SDK (i.e., `c:\program files\android\android-sdk` for windows, or `/Developer/android-sdk-mac_x86`)

    c.   Apply ➤ OK

8.   Load the platforms.

    a.   Window ➤ Android SKD and AVD Manager

    b.   Click Available Packages. There's no real reason not to just download everything under Android Repository, but as a minimum you'll want the Android SDK Platform-Tools, and Android Platform 3.0 or 3.1. Download the documentation as well.

That's it! We should be all ready to go. Here are a couple of extras that might be worth doing.

Creating an Emulator Instance

It's almost certainly faster to use an actual Android device hooked up to your computer via USB cable, but sometimes you don't have one on hand. In Eclipse, go to Window ➤ Android SKD and AVD Manager and choose Virtual Devices, and create yourself a new one. Choose API level 11 and give it a meaningful name, like **Honeycomb**. Give it a reasonable size for external storage: the 16 MB default is way too small. I usually set mine to 512 MB.

■ **Caution** The Android Emulator is *very slow*. The Honeycomb emulator is *even slower*. Be patient, go have a coffee while it starts up, and don't shut it down again until you are definitely done with it.

Some tips to make it go faster:

- The emulator is a single-threaded process. It will only ever use one CPU at a time. Therefore, you will get better performance on, say, a dual-core than a quad-core of similar specs, because the emulator can take advantage of more of your CPU power.

- You can also increase the Dynamic Ram Size to 1024 . . . but make sure this is less than your computer's physical memory, or it will backfire on you.

Setting Your Path

There are some powerful tools that come with the Android SDK. The one you are most likely to be using is adb, which is a command line tool. Make sure platform-tools is in your path before you try using it—for example:

- Windows: PATH=%PATH%;C:\Program Files\Android\Android-SDK\platform-tools

- Linux: export PATH=$PATH:~/android-sdk/platform-tools

- Mac: export PATH=$PATH:~/Developer/android-sdk-mac_x86/platform-tools

Your actual paths will depend on where you installed your Android SDK.

Your First Android Program

Let's get down to business . . . our first actual Android program.

Fire up Eclipse, and we'll create our first Android Hello World program. This is going to be pretty easy. File ➤ New ➤ Android Project should look something like Figure 1-2.

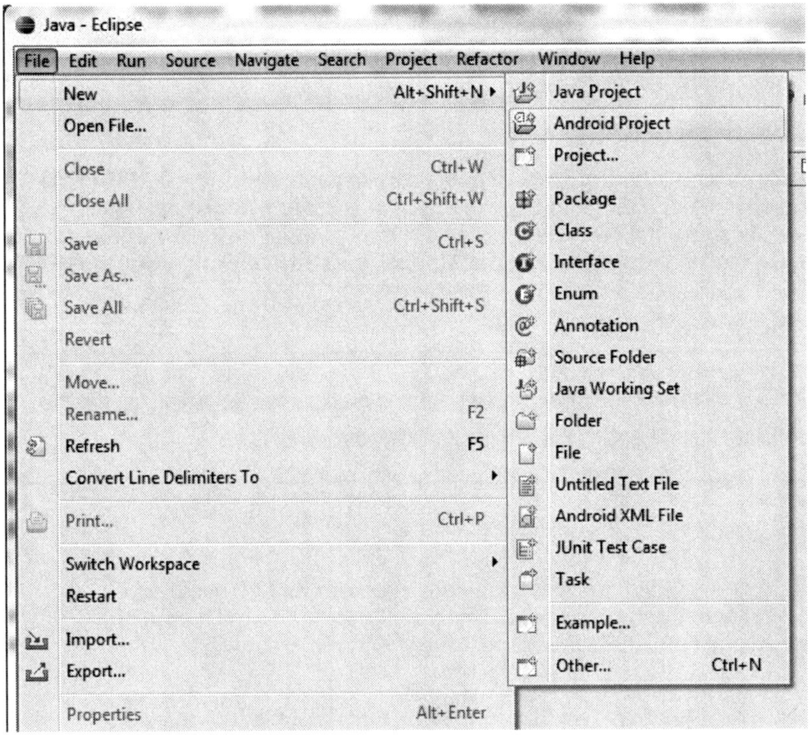

Figure 1-2. Creating a new Android project in Eclipse

■ **Note** On the Mac, the command is File ➤ New ➤ Project ➤ Android Project on Mac.

The next step is to give your project a name (I've chosen BA3TPHello for this exercise) and pick your target environment.

This will probably be Android 3.0 (Honeycomb), but for this exercise, any build target will do. You can change your mind later, too.

You need to supply a project name, an application name, and a package name.

If you look at my example in Figure 1-3, you'll see I've left Create Activity ticked, so that a default activity will be created.

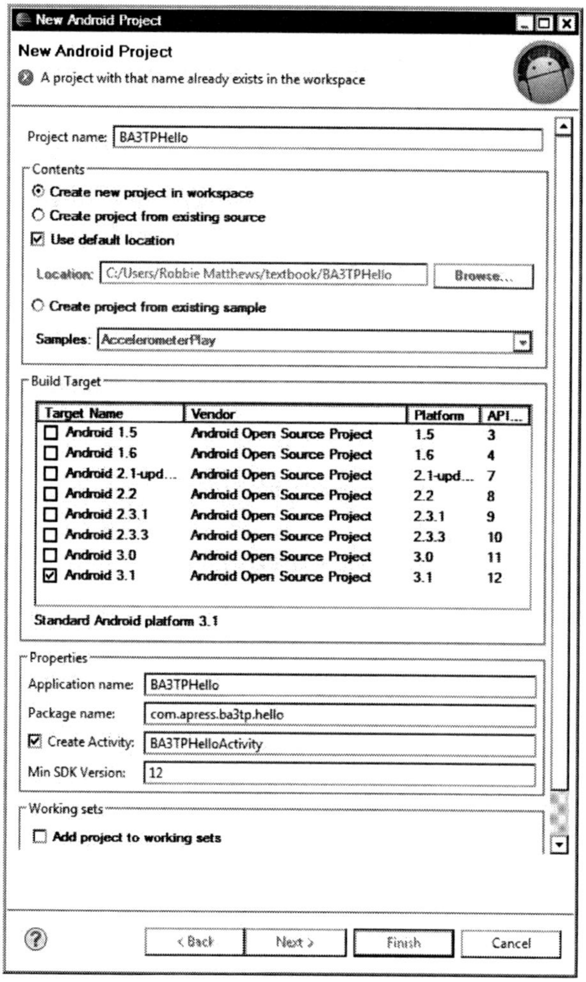

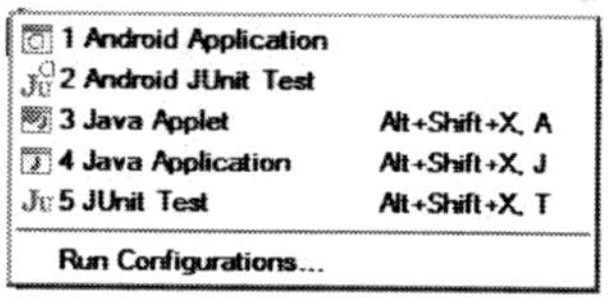

Figure 1-3. Android application settings

More on activities shortly. For the moment, we'll just let the Android SDK do all the work for us.

Make sure you've either set up an emulation or have your Android device plugged in. Hit Finish and then Run. If Eclipse seems unsure of what to run, right-click the project you've just created, and select Run As. When asked, tell it you want an Android application.

And, voila, you should see something like Figure 1-4.

Figure 1-4. Screenshot of Hello World program

Wait, I hear you say. How does it know I wanted Hello World? Well, the screen application automatically puts Hello World into your screen layout.

This may not be that satisfying. Look in the Package Navigator, under res ➤ layout ➤ main.xml. This should pop open a layout editor (Figure 1-5).

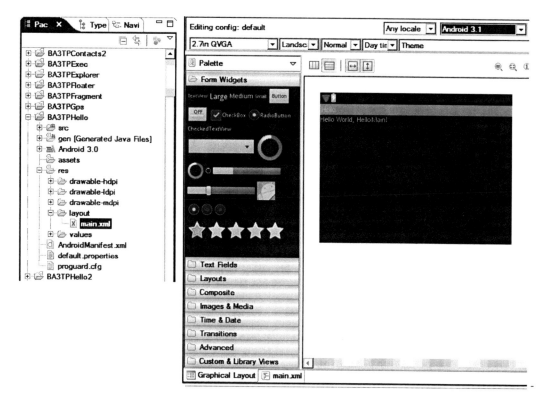

Figure 1-5. Layout editor

There's a lot of stuff in there, which we'll get to later.

For the moment, click the words Hello World to select the control, right-click, choose Show In ➤ Properties, and scroll down (a long way) until you find Text.

This should say:

```
@string/hello
```

This is actually telling the control to use the string resource "hello", which is defined elsewhere. I'll get to that later, too. For the time being, we'll ignore string resources and just type in the text we want to appear, such as the following:

```
Hello Universe
```

You should see this reflected in the layout screen. Save all, run, and watch the result.

Oh, No! Java!

If you're already familiar with Java, you can skip this bit. If you're a die-hard Java fanatic, you definitely should skip this bit.

This is for everyone else. You have been warned.

Yeah, not everyone is a fan of Java. I won't say it's a language that you love or hate. It's more like a language you can love *and* hate, both at the same time.

I've been involved in just such a relationship for years.

On the surface, it should be great. It's a multi-platform, object-oriented (OO) language with a clean syntax and a mass of tools. And you can download and use it for free!

But: It's slow to run, slow to compile, very wordy, and very fussy about its syntax. What's more, the extensive libraries are *so* extensive that a learner can get very lost, very quickly. Many of the libraries are bloated, quite are few of them are, frankly, not very good, and the examples can leave you even worse off than before. The graphical user interface components are horrible and unwieldy, and don't even get me started on layouts.

To top it off, the Java community seems to have evolved a jargon completely separate from the rest of the world.

And yet . . . it is, really, when you get down to it, quite an elegant language, once you get over the first hurdles. And it turns out to be a surprisingly good fit for mobile platforms.

This is perhaps less surprising than you might think. Java (originally called Oak) was actually first designed to run on a PDA. Don't believe me? Google it, I'll wait.

Of course, it was much too cumbersome to run on the hardware available at the time, but it has persisted and grown. And, as the hardware has improved, and the technology of virtual machines has matured, it has turned up in more and more mobile devices.

For example, many mobile phones will support Java ME (Java Platform, Micro Edition), which is a cut-down version of Java for mobile devices. When I started playing with it, I found the libraries had been stripped to a fairly compact core, and what was left was quite easy to navigate.

Java development environments have been steadily improved. The two major Java IDEs (Netbeans and Eclipse) offer many features to make programming in Java easier. Most common errors are detected early, and fixes suggested.

Why Java needs these extra features is a topic for another occasion.

Now, I've been programming for mobile devices for a long time. I've written applications for Palm devices, Java ME–enabled phones, and Windows CE. I've even built the complete firmware for customized handheld units in the deep distant past.

They all tended to have a few things in common: a fairly steep learning curve, limited libraries, and (for those used to desktop computing) odd screen handling routines.

Android is, without doubt, the nicest such OS. It was dead easy to get started and was well documented, and I was doing fairly complex tasks within a few hours of getting my system set up.

So it's worth persisting.

A Quick Guide to Java

This book is not going to try to teach programming from the ground up. In fact, I'm going to assume at least a basic understanding of programming techniques.

I'm not even going to attempt to teach Java from scratch. There are many excellent tutorials on the Web, or for a comprehensive treatment see *Learn Java for Android Development*, by Jeff Friesen (Apress, 2010). But I will try to hit some high points.

First, see our stock standard "Hello World" program in Java, in Listing 1-1.

Listing 1-1. *Hello World*

```
import java.io.*;

public class HelloWorld {
  public static void main(String[] args) {
```

```
    System.out.println("Hello World");
  }
```

Pretty simple, right? In fact, it maps quite closely to your standard C "Hello World" (Listing 1-2).

Listing 1-2. *Hello World in C*

```
#include <stdio.h>

int main(int argc, char *args[])
{
  printf("Hello World\n");
}
```

Pull in a definition of the I/O routines, declare a main function, and go wild.

It quickly becomes a bit more complex than that. I'm just going to hit some of the points that confused me at first. This is going to be a quick and dirty intro. Be warned.

Structure

If you are already familiar with C++, or any of C++'s descendants or admirers such as JavaScript or PHP, the basic structure of Java should already be familiar to you.

A block is defined with curly brackets ({}). They act exactly like begin and end in Delphi or Visual Basic: defining a logically related chunk of code.

Everything, and I do mean *everything*—every bit of code and all the variables—is declared in classes. In Hello World, there is one class (HelloWorld) declaring one static method, main.

Variables can be declared locally inside any block. Variables defined in the body of the class definition are known as fields.

And, with the exception of a handful of primitive types, *everything* is an object, which is a member of the class Object, logically enough.

Methods (or functions or procedures as they are also known) can return any type, or void for none, and are differentiated from variables by always having brackets. Listing 1-3 shows some examples.

Listing 1-3. *Some Examples of Methods*

```
public class ScratchPad {

  int classVariable;
  int myMethod(int argument) {
    int i;
    i=10+argument;
    return i;
  }

  // This one has no parameters.
  int anotherMethod() {
    return 99;
  }

  void myProcedure() {
    int ninetyNine = anotherMethod();
```

```
        System.out.println(myMethod(22));
    }
}
```

A method can have zero or more parameters. A method with no parameters still needs the round brackets "(" and ")" to tell Java it *is* a method. Methods return their values via a return statement, the exception being void, which doesn't return a value.

Primitives

No, not people living in grass huts. Java has a small selection of very basic types that are *not* objects, and out of which everything else is built.

- byte: 8-bit signed integer

- short: 16-bit signed integer

- int: 32-bit signed integer—your basic workhorse

- long: 64-bit signed integer

- float: 32-bit floating point; unless you have a compelling reason to keep storage down, use a double instead.

- double: 64-bit floating point

- boolean: True or false—that's it.

- char: Characters, like "A" and "Z"; they are actually Unicode characters, and 16 bits wide.

Observant readers will note there are no unsigned integer types. This is a design feature (annoyingly). There are ways around it, most commonly by moving up to the next sized integer. There are also some specific classes for handling unsigned bytes. Most of the time you shouldn't need to worry too much.

Avoid the temptation to use short and byte unless you are working with large arrays or storing to disk and need the space. They tend to get converted to int or long internally anyway, so you aren't really gaining anything by using them.

You may note that String is not a primitive. Strings are objects, albeit very well-supported objects. More on that later.

Flow Control

Listing 1-4 shows a quick précis of the flow control options.

Listing 1-4. Examples of Java Flow Control

```
public void testif() {
    boolean x=true;
    if (x) dostuff();
    else dootherstuff();
    int y = 3;
    if (y<3) dostuff();
```

```
    else if (y>3) {
      System.out.print("This is in a block");
      dootherstuff();
    }
    else {
      System.out.println("Dunno.");
    }

    y=1;
    while (y<10) {
      System.out.println("Hello"+y);
      y+=1;
    }

    for (int i=0; i<10; i++) {
      System.out.println("Hello"+y);
    }
  }
```

So, pretty much as per C or C++ or PHP or Javascript. Not wildly dissimilar to Pascal.
If you are not quite sure of how the for loop works, it's surprisingly simple. The for statement supports three arguments, separated by semicolons (;). The first argument is called once (to set the start conditions). The second argument is evaluated each time around the loop to see if it is still true. If not, the loop stops. The third argument is called after each loop, and is commonly used to increment a counter—so:

```
for(int i=0; i<10; i++) System.out.println("Hello"+i);
```
It is *exactly* equivalent to this:

```
int i=0;
while (i<10) {
System.out.println("Hello"+i);
  i++;
}
```

Almost every for loop can be written as a while loop, but it's more convenient.
You may have noticed I've declared int i *within* the loop itself. This is counted as declaring the variable i within the for block . . . so it is visible only inside the for loop.
i++ is a common shorthand for i=i+1. In Java, you can also use C-style shortcuts for operations, so i+=1 is also equivalent.
(Actually, i++ is not quite the same as i+=1. It's called a post-increment. It returns the value of i, then adds one to i. It's a cute and useful capability, but resist the temptation to overuse.)

Objects

Object-oriented programming (OOP) has been with us for many years now. Pretty much any language of any stripe supports it to some degree or another. An object may contain both data and code to manipulate that data. However, whereas most languages support objects to some extent or another, Java is *all* about objects. There is nothing else. Everything you do has to be in an object. And in Java, you define your objects as classes, i.e., public class HelloWorld.
The key words here are class and public.

▩ **Note** A class describes an object. Objects are created (or to use the technical term, *instantiated*) from classes. If you like, the class is the cookie cutter, and the objects are the cookies. Confused? Good, it means you're paying attention.

By common convention, and enforced by the compiler itself, each public Java class is defined in a Java file with the same name as the class, i.e., `HelloWorld.java`.

Java is case-sensitive. Be warned now.

Each class has members. A member can be a field (data) or a method (known as functions or procedures in other languages).

All the members of the class can be assigned various modifiers, some of which are more or less obvious:

- `public`: This member can be seen by everything.

- `private`: This member can be seen only from within this class.

- `protected`: This member can't be seen from the outside world, but can be accessed from with the package, class, or subclasses.

If there are no access modifiers, this member can be seen from within its own class and package.

Any OO language worth its salt includes methods for creating a new class from an existing class. In Java, this new class is referred to as a subclass. In some other languages, this would be a descendant.

`static` and `final` take a bit of explaining, and there are subtleties. A `static` member (be it a method or field) belongs to a class rather than an object. The difference is subtle, but important.

Most of the time, when you create a class, you would then create an instance (aka object) of the class using new, and work with that. Each instance has its own copy of its data.

Sometimes you want global variables or functions, something not attached to any particular instance. But Java doesn't even have the concept for a function or variable that is not contained in a class. That is where `static` comes in.

Let's say we build another, slightly more meaningful example in Listing 1-5.

Listing 1-5. Use of static

```java
import java.io.*;

public class SimpleExample {
  public static int staticVariable = 0;
  public int classVariable = 0;

  public void nonStatic() {
    classVariable += 1;
    staticVariable += 1;
    System.out.println("I'm a nonstatic method. Called: "+classVariable+" times.");
    System.out.println("I've been called in total: "+staticVariable+" times.");

  }

  public static void main(String[] args) {
```

```
    for (int i=0; i<5; i++) {
      SimpleExample simple = new SimpleExample();
      simple.nonStatic();
    }
  }
}
```

To compile and run this from the command line, do the following:

1. Paste the example into SimpleExample.java.

2. Run javac SimpleExample.java.

3. Run java SimpleExample.

You should see something like this:

```
I'm a nonstatic method. Called: 1 times.

I've been called in total: 1 times.

I'm a nonstatic method. Called: 1 times.

I've been called in total: 2 times.

I'm a nonstatic method. Called: 1 times.

I've been called in total: 3 times.

I'm a nonstatic method. Called: 1 times.

I've been called in total: 4 times.

I'm a nonstatic method. Called: 1 times.

I've been called in total: 5 times.
```

You'll see that the main method runs a for loop five times, creating a new instance of SimpleExample each time, and called its nonStatic method. The classVariable is a new for each instance, but staticVariable is linked to the class itself.

Just to make it clearer, I'm going to mix it up a bit in Listing 1-6.

Listing 1-6. Demonstrating the Differences Between Static and Normal Data

```
import java.io.*;

public class SimpleExample2 {
  public static int staticVariable = 0;
  public int classVariable = 0;
```

```
public void nonStatic() {

   classVariable += 1;
   staticVariable += 1;
   System.out.println("I'm a nonstatic method. Called: "+classVariable+" times.");
   System.out.println("I've been called in total: "+staticVariable+" times.");

}

public static void main(String[] args) {
   for (int i=0; i<3; i++) {
      System.out.println("new Object "+i);
      SimpleExample simple = new SimpleExample();
      for (int j=0; j<=i; j++) {
         simple.nonStatic();
      }
   }
}
}
```

This should give you the following:

```
I'm a nonstatic method. Called: 1 times.

I've been called in total: 1 times.

new Object 1

I'm a nonstatic method. Called: 1 times.

I've been called in total: 2 times.

I'm a nonstatic method. Called: 2 times.

I've been called in total: 3 times.

new Object 2

I'm a nonstatic method. Called: 1 times.

I've been called in total: 4 times.

I'm a nonstatic method. Called: 2 times.

I've been called in total: 5 times.

I'm a nonstatic method. Called: 3 times.

I've been called in total: 6 times.
```

What this slightly more complex example shows is that the classVariable is definitely associated with the instance of the class, whereas the staticVariable is associated with the class itself. Once the class has been loaded, it will stay in memory forever.

A keen-eyed observer will note that main is a static method. This means that it can be called directly without needing to create an instance of the class with a new call first.

To put it in terms of less purely object-oriented languages, static methods take the place of *non-object-oriented functions* or procedures, and static fields take the place of global variables—which leads us to final.

The keyword final had me puzzled for the longest time, not the least because it has subtly different meanings for methods and for fields. It doesn't help that it was often misused in example code.

If a method is marked as final in a class, it can't be overridden. If you extend that class, you can't create your own version of that method. In real life, the number of times this is desirable is fairly minimal. However, it does give a *very slight* performance boost. I emphasize *very slight*, because on a modern computer it's almost unmeasurable. You will see quite a bit of example code on the Web marking methods as final t inappropriately, so you can safely ignore that usage. Unless you have a compelling reason for stopping a subclass from overriding this method, don't use it.

For fields it has a related, but quite different, meaning. A final field can be set once, and only once. This is not all that useful for class fields, but comes into its own for static fields.

The public static final field is what, in other languages, you'd call a constant.

There are some subtle differences . . . you can use dynamic data to set them (once) at runtime, and they are typed, but for all practical purposes, they are constants. Think of them that way, and you won't go too far wrong.

Constructors, Initializers, and Overloading

Having defined your class, you'll want to create instances of these classes to do cool stuff with. The keyword here is new—for example:

```
ArrayList fred = new ArrayList();
```

Simple and straightforward. This creates a new instance of ArrayList, called fred. But sometimes, you'll see something like this:

```
ArrayList fred = new ArrayList(10);
```

Where did the 10 come from and why?

Well, when you define a class, you can also define how that class is constructed, by declaring constructors, which might look like Listing 1-7.

Listing 1-7. Various Constructors and Initializers

```
public class TestConstruct {

  private int notInitialized;
  private int simpleInitiazed=22;
  private int fromConstructor;
  private int fromInit;
  private int fromSecondConstructor;

  // Initialize routine. Always called before constructor.
  {
```

17

```java
      fromInit = 927;
  }

  // Simple, no argument constructor.
  TestConstruct() {
    fromConstructor=99;
  }
  // Single argument
  TestConstruct(int arg1) {
    fromConstructor=arg1;
  }
  // Two int argument.
  TestConstruct(int arg1, int arg2) {
    fromConstructor=arg1;
    fromSecondConstructor=arg2;
  }
  // String Argument
  TestConstruct(String string) {
    fromConstructor=string.length();
  }

  @Override
  public String toString() {
    return "Info: "+notInitialized+"-"+simpleInitiazed+"-"+fromConstructor+"-"+fromInit+"-
"+fromSecondConstructor;
  }

  public static void main(String[] args) {
    TestConstruct first = new TestConstruct();
    TestConstruct second = new TestConstruct(127);
    TestConstruct third = new TestConstruct(432,234);
    TestConstruct forth = new TestConstruct("Hello.");
    System.out.println(first);
    System.out.println(second);
    System.out.println(third);
    System.out.println(forth);
  }
}
```

Since constructors are all about initializing your object, I've shown a few of the many ways of skinning this particular cat in Java.

If you look at the various fields in Listing 1-7, you'll see you can just include an "= value" as part of the definition. Looking a bit further down, you can see what looks like a function without a name or type, just a set of curly braces. This is called an initializer. It will be called every time the class is constructed, and you can use it for more complex initializations than the single-line approach.

Next we come to the constructor itself.

A constructor is a special method. You can tell a constructor because it has the same name as the class, and does *not* return a type.

You will note you can have more than one constructor in a class. This is because Java supports overloading.

With overloading you can declare a method (and a constructor is just a special kind of method) multiple times, as long as the number and/or type of arguments is different.

As a further example, Listing 1-8 demonstrates this in the form of methods.

Listing 1-8. Overloaded Methods

```java
public String mymethod() {

  return "?";
}

public String mymethod(int arg1) {
  return "Arg1="+arg1;
}

public String mymethod(String arg1) {
  return "Arg1="+arg1+"(string)";
}

public void mymethod(Object o) {
  // Do nothing, return nothing.
}
```

All these declarations of mymethod are legitimate. Java will work out which one to call based on the number and type of arguments. In fact, what uniquely identifies a method in a class is the combination of name and arguments. This is called a method signature.

Note that the mymethod can return different things . . . in the last example, mymethod is a void. The return type is *not* part of the method signature.

Where's "Free"?

Keen-eyed observers will note that in my SimpleExample class, I'm cheerfully creating new objects all over the place, but nowhere am I freeing them. If you're a C++ or Delphi (or just about any other non-managed OOP language) programmer, this should be making you twitch. It certainly made me twitch.

Java takes care of freeing its own objects. Once you are done with them, Java will come along and tidy them up.

This can take a bit of getting used to, but after a while, you get used to just lying back and enjoying.

When in doubt, just create another object, and Java will take care of the rest. Creating new objects is even pretty efficient, so don't worry about it on that score.

There are only two caveats.

1. Objects that use system resources will normally have a method to explicitly release those resources. You should always use them when you are done—for example:

```java
FileInputStream mystream = new FileInputStream("readme.txt");
mystream.close();
```

The close will release the file handle and do other system-related tidying up. It doesn't *free* the mystream object directly, but now it's not consuming system resources you might need elsewhere.

2. Make sure you don't leave references to created objects floating around. The garbage collection works by counting references to an object. Once nothing more is interested in it, the object will be tidied up.

You can still have memory leaks occurring by leaving references to them. Local variables (those inside methods) are disposed of after you've left the methods. Class fields hang about until the containing object goes away. static fields will stay forever (or until the application ends, anyway)—so:

```
static List myListOfEveryObject = new ArrayList();

void addNewObject() {
  Object o = new Object();
  myListOfEveryObject.add(o);
  o=null;
}
```

Every object there will hang about forever. Even though you've set the original reference to null, another reference will be sitting in that list forever.

Of course, clearing the list will take care of that:

```
myListOfEveryObject.clear();
```

String Handling

Also bewildering is the number of classes apparently available for string handling, and the documentation can be confusing.

String handling is actually very straightforward and intuitive if you're used to almost any other language.

```
String mystring = "Hello";
String world = "World";
mystring = mystring + " there.";
mystring += world;
int myinteger = 5;
mystring = "I have " + myinteger + " marbles.";
```

Most of that will work the way you'd expect. There's a gotcha, though:

```
if (world=="World")
```

This won't work. Actually, it will work, but only because Java reuses its string constants. It won't work if you are comparing two arbitrary strings.

What you need is equals:

```
if (world.equals("World"))
```

It has to do with comparing identity and value.

There are situations where StringBuffer or StringBuilder would be more efficient, but there's no need to rush into it. In fact, StringBuffer (a modifiable string) is much less useful than you might think.

■ **Note** StringBuffer and StringBuilder both do fundamentally the same job. However, StringBuffer had a few problems, so StringBuilder was presented as a newer, shinier, more efficient tool. But by the time the Java community worked this out, there was an awful lot of code out there using StringBuffer, so StringBuffer has stayed around. This is the same reason you have the near-identical HashTable and HashMap. And yes, it can be confusing.

Packages

Obviously, when writing a program of even moderate complexity, you don't want to be putting everything in one class. You'll want multiple classes, for code reuse, and just organizing stuff into logical bits. The Java compiler tends to reinforce this behavior.

You can override this behavior if determined, but doing so would probably be counter-productive. Therefore, we can arrange code into packages. This is done by simply adding the following into the top of your code, in each Java file:

```
package mypackagename;
```

Then Java knows that all these files are logically grouped and can talk to each other, and probably belong in the same application file when you eventually get around to releasing the code into the wild.

So far so good. In theory, you can use any name for a package. In practice, everyone uses a name derived from an Internet domain. For example, this book is being written for apress.com, and I've decided to group all the example code under ba3tp (Beginning Android 3 Tablet Programming). Therefore I'm going to call my first package hello.ba3tp.apress.com. Right?

Well, actually, no. I'm going to call it:

```
package com.apress.ba3tp.hello;
```

Yes, you do it backward. It sort of makes sense. This means that the fully qualified name of my Hello class would be com.apress.ba3tp.hello.Hello. If you want to access that class from a different package, you'd need to either type in the full name, or include an import clause at the top of your code.

Now, according to the documentation, packages do not have to be arranged hierarchically. In practice, pretty much every compiler or development environment out there assumes it is.

What's more, they insist on storing the source code hierarchically. So com.apress.ba3tp.hello will end up in src/com/apress/ba3tp/hello.

Coming from another programming environment, I found this horribly different from anything I'd used before. I suspect I'm not the only one. You can fight it if you're determined, but frankly, it's probably not worth the aggro. Lie back and think of England—it'll soon be over.

Fortunately, Eclipse has a fairly reasonable package navigator and search functions. You'll soon get used to it. Probably.

Now, some further notes about packages:

Classes within the same package can access anything else in classes from the same package unless they are explicitly marked private. You also don't need to use import or the fully qualified name of the class to refer to it.

Lists and Maps

Anything resembling a computer language has to have something to manage lists. Java has a bewildering array of such lists, from your basic, primitive array, to some quite complex List and Map objects.

An array is the simplest of these. Every language supports arrays in some form or another—just lists of contiguous data that can be accessed by a numeric index.

They exist in Java, and work pretty much the way you expect. The syntax is something like this:

```
String[] mystrings = new String[10]; // Create an array of 10 strings
int[] myints = new int[5]; // Create an array of 5 integers
int myint = myints[3]; // Access the integer stored in position 3 (zero based)
String[] things = {"brown","paper","packages"}; // Handy shortcut for creating initialized
arrays.
```

And so forth. Java arrays are of a fixed size, which can't easily be changed.

So we have lists. Lists can grow and shrink quite readily, and store any object.

Somewhat disconcertingly, there are multiple lists to choose from.

```
List mylist = new ArrayList();
List mylist = new LinkedList();
List mylist = new Vector();
```

. . . to name only a few. They are all different implementations of the same interface, meaning that while the back end is quite different, they can be manipulated the same way.

For most practical purpose, I'd use ArrayList, unless you know it's going to be growing a lot from one end, in which case LinkedList may be faster. Vector is very similar to ArrayList, but older. And it's synchronized.

Then we have maps. Maps are like lists, except that you access them with a key. The key can be any object (not just an integer) and need not be contiguous. PHP would call this an associative array, Python a dictionary.

This has an even more bewildering choice of options:

```
Map mymap = new HashMap();
Map mymap = new Hashtable();
Map mymap = new IdentityHashMap();
Map mymap = new TreeMap();
Map mymap = new WeakHashMap();
```

Which to choose? Well, for most intents and purposes, HashMap is your go-to mapping type. It's the fastest, although Hashtable is close. But Hashtable is older and synchronized, which slows it down a bit. Unless sharing an object between threads, it need not be synchronized, and you can do it explicitly if you need to.

The Hash maps will store data in any order that takes their fancy. If you want your data ordered, use TreeMap. IdentityHashMap is fairly specialized, in that it uses an object's *identity* rather than its value. Listing 1-9 may help to clarify this.

Listing 1-9. *Some of the Subtle Differences Between Types of Maps*

```
Map myidmap = new IdentityHashMap();
Map mymap = new HashMap();
String string1 = new String("Hello World"); // One instance
String string2 = new String("Hello World"); // Another instance with the same value
```

```
mymap.put(string1,someobject);
mymap.put(string2,someotherobject);
myidmap.put(string1,someobject);
myidmap.put(string2,someotherobject);
```

A normal map will end up with one item in it, because string1 and string2 have the same value: Hello World.

IdentityHashMap will have two entries, because string1 and string2 are different objects.

WeakHashMap is a little weird, in that it will allow its keys to be garbage collected. You probably won't use this in normal operation.

A nice thing about lists is that recent versions of Java support a foreach loop (a la Python or PHP):

```
for (Object o : mylist) {
  System.out.println(o);
}
```

This will run through every item in mylist, setting o to that item each time. It will work on any list, and is much more compact than some of the other methods you might use.

Generics

Sooner or later—probably sooner—you'll run into the Java concept of generics. Since these are almost identical to C++ templates, I will often refer to them as such.

They'll look something like this:

```
List<String> mylist = new ArrayList<String>();
```

Gosh, what are all those angle brackets doing there? What do they mean? Panic!!!

Okay, that was my reaction. Maybe you'll be calmer.

Again, the concept is pretty simple. Whereas your plain List or Map works on objects, which can be anything, typically you'll have a limited number of types you want to play with.

Let us assume you want to build a Map containing File objects, keyed with a String. Using plain maps, you'd do something like Listing 1-10.

Listing 1-10. Using a Map Without Generics

```
public void testmap() {
  Map mymap = new HashMap();
  mymap.put("file1", new File("file1.txt"));
  mymap.put("file2", new File("file2.txt"));
  mymap.put("readme", new File("README"));
  // Later....
  File workfile = (File) mymap.get("readme");
}
```

Note the (File) notation. This is known as a cast. It tells Java that this object is actually a File. But there's nothing to stop you adding a String. Or a Uri, or any other object you can think of to your map. Which is fine and dandy for a small program, but if your program starts going up in complexity, mistakes happen. If you do make a mistake, that cast will throw a runtime exception, which can be annoying.

With generics, you can write boilerplate code, and then at compile time tell Java what classes you want them to operate on—allowing you to rewrite the foregoing to the following:

```java
public void testmapTemplate() {
  Map<String,File> mymap = new HashMap<String,File>();
  mymap.put("file1", new File("file1.txt"));
  mymap.put("file2", new File("file2.txt"));
  mymap.put("readme", new File("README"));
  // Later....
  File workfile = mymap.get("readme");
}
```

You've told Java that this map is keyed with Strings and contains Files. The compiler then takes over to make sure that only Files and Strings can be used. Also, you don't have to use a cast on the get later, because the compiler already knows what should be there.

Inheritance and Interfaces

In OOP, classes can be built from other classes, allowing you to add extra capabilities, or change behavior. This is done using the extends keyword. See Listing 1-11 for some examples.

Listing 1-11.Some Examples of Inheritance

```java
private class AnotherClass {
  int x;
  int y;

  @Override
  public String toString() {
    return x+","+y;
  }
}

private class NewClass extends AnotherClass {
  int z;

  @Override
  public String toString() {
    return super.toString()+","+z;
  }
}
```

AnotherClass is a simple class that contains x and y values, and will print them nicely if asked.
toString() is a method that *every* object has, and will be automatically called whenever an object has to be treated like a String.
@Override is an annotation. It's not strictly necessary, but informs the compiler that you do know what you are doing and deliberately changing the way this method behaves. It will also throw a warning if what you're attempting to override isn't in your base class, which is a common form of hard-to-trace programming error.
NewClass is descended from AnotherClass, and has all its fields and methods, plus some new ones.
Note the super keyword in NewClass. This tells it to call the toString() method in the parent class (AnotherClass), and then it adds its own twist.
But a class can be extended only from one parent. What if we want more?

Java has the concept of interfaces. An interface is the *promise* to implement certain minimal methods and behavior, as in Listing 1-12.

Listing 1-12. Using an Interface

```java
interface MyInterface {
  void onClick(View v);
}

private class NewClass extends AnotherClass implements MyInterface {
  int z;

  @Override
  public String toString() {
    return super.toString()+","+z;
  }

  @Override
  public void onClick(View v) {
    System.out.println("Clicked");

  }
}

private void doInterfaceStuff(MyInterface anInterface) {
  anInterface.onClick(null);
}
```

If you look at doInterface, you'll see it is working off an interface rather than a full class. All it knows is that the object—wherever it came from—will have an onClick method, which it can call. This is handy when you want to implement something to work off a whole range of different objects with similar behavior.

Annotations

You'll see these popping up a lot. When I was learning Java, I found these more confusing than not.
   An annotation will look like this:

```java
@Override
@Rpc(name="callMe",description="more detailed information")
@Deprecated
```

Annotations are a way of adding extra information into your program, and are used in many different ways. They can be used to add metadata to a class, method, field, or parameter.
   This can be queried at runtime or compile time, and used as hints or additional information to allow third-party products to do fancy stuff with existing code. The Java compiler can use it to hide or issue warnings.
   There are a bunch defined in Java itself, and you can build your own if you really want. For now, just know that they are used in the same place and way that static, public, private, and final are used—as a modifier. So they do *not* have semicolons after them.
   Some examples you might come across:

- `@Override`: Tells the compiler you are deliberately overriding this method; otherwise it may issue a warning.

- `@Deprecated`: Throws a warning at compile time that this code is obsolete

- `@SuppressWarnings("unused")`: Tells compiler to stop complaining about unused code

And Many More

I think that just about covers it. In many ways, though, it just brushes the surface. There is thread handling and synchronization and file handling, which I haven't even mentioned yet. I'll get to them as they come up. Hopefully this chapter will have given you a bit of a kickstart into the world of Java programming.

And with those thoughts, let's get our hands dirty.

Summary

In this chapter, you have come to grips with installing a development environment onto your computer.

You've been given a quick and dirty overview of Java—enough to get you started, anyway.

You should now have at least an idea of what I'm talking about when it comes to constructors and methods and fields.

You should even be starting to get an idea of some of the clever things Java can do.

You should have created your first simple Android program, and be well on your way to programming your Android tablet.

Actually, you should be well on your way to programming non-tablet Androids, too: at this stage of proceedings, there's not a lot of difference to see.

And you've also been treated to an informative (if brief) history of handheld computing.

Exciting, isn't it?

CHAPTER 2

How Android Works

This chapter will attempt to explain the basic structure of an Android application: how it all fits together, what an `Activity` is, what `Intents` are, and why to use them.

Figure 2-1. The internals of Android are not for everyone . . .

Basic Structure of Android Programs

One of the big issues with any sort of programming for mobile devices is that they are relatively limited. Limited memory, limited (or no) disk space, limited processing power, limited screen space, limited keyboard access. You just don't have the luxury to waste memory or screen real estate, or even assume you're going to have a keyboard or mouse.

It's also desirable to maintain, or at least encourage, similar behavior and user interfaces.

A tablet has fairly decent screen space compared to a phone, but even so, the rest of the limitations still hold sway.

A desktop computer, with a large screen, keyboard, mouse, AC power supply, high-speed processor, large chunks of memory, and huge disk space, means that the programmer and the OS can afford to be fairly casual about resource use. A desktop computer can have hundreds of processes running at any given time, and if it runs out of memory, it just uses the disk for swap space.

An Android device does not have these luxuries.

Having said that, a decade ago I was working on computers that would look pretty weedy compared to your average smartphone, so it's all a matter of perspective.

Fun little factoid: The Apollo 11 guidance computer, which took men to the freaking *moon*, had 2 KB of RAM, and 32 KB of ROM, and ran at a dizzying 1.024 MHz. Not gigabytes of memory, not megabytes, but *kilobytes*. Not gigahertz, but megahertz, and not many of them either.

Heck, the computer I learned to program on had 8 KB of RAM and a cassette tape for data storage. And when you tell the kids that these days, they just *don't* believe you. (I've also used a punchcard in anger. Once. But I digress.)

The point here is that an Android phone or tablet still has a whole heap of grunt, but it's not a desktop and never will be. As a result, there are certain ways of behaving that will differ from your desktop paradigm.

The biggest example is going to be screen space. A modern desktop will allow you to open dozens of windows at once, each doing something different. A smartphone really doesn't have that sort of room.

So an Android phone has things pretty firmly organized around the concept of a screen, or View. This is less of an issue on a tablet—indeed, most of the new features in Honeycomb have to do with taking advantage of this screen space—but still, the View is where the user is going to be doing most of his interacting, and you are going to be doing most of your code.

ANDROID AND FOOD

Every version of Android OS to date has had an OS number, an API level, and a code name. The code name has always been a sweet food of some kind. I can only assume that Google doesn't feed its coders enough.

Versions of Android

Version	API	Code name
1.5	3	Cupcake
1.6	4	Donut
2.1	7	Éclair
2.2	8	Froyo
2.3	9	Gingerbread
2.3.3	10	Gingerbread (also)
3.0	11	Honeycomb
3.1	12	Honeycomb (still)

A typical Android application will contain one or more Activities, each possessing one or more Layouts, which will be expressed as Views.

An Activity represents a unit of code and data that is used to interact with the user. In the old days, we would call this a *program*. An application can have more than one Activity. It can also have Services and Providers, but I'll get to them later.

Android knows which bit of your application to access based on the AndroidManifest.xml file, which you'll find at the top level of your project.

Let's start with a simple example—a more complex version of our Hello World program. This will have a Button. Be very excited!

■ **Tip** You can download the source code for all these examples from the Apress web site, if you don't feel like typing.

Let's start with a new project: File ➤ New ➤ Android Project.

```
Project Name:     BA3TPHello2
Build Target:     Android 3.0
Application Name: Hello2
Create Activity:  Hello2Main
Finish
```

You should end up with a new project. If you open it up with the Package Navigator, it should look a bit like Figure 2-2.

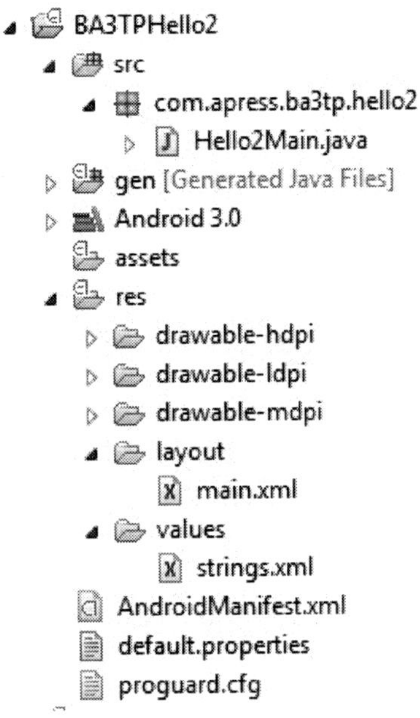

- BA3TPHello2
  - src
    - com.apress.ba3tp.hello2
      - Hello2Main.java
  - gen [Generated Java Files]
  - Android 3.0
  - assets
  - res
    - drawable-hdpi
    - drawable-ldpi
    - drawable-mdpi
    - layout
      - main.xml
    - values
      - strings.xml
  - AndroidManifest.xml
  - default.properties
  - proguard.cfg

***Figure 2-2.** The Eclipse Package Navigator*

What the bits are:

Everything in src is Java source code, organized in a package hierarchy.

Hello2Main.java is the Activity we just told the Android Project wizard to create.

gen is a folder maintained purely by the Android toolkit (ADT), and it contains helper code to keep track of all your resources.

assets contains files that can be included as part of your package, which is sort of what res does, but files in assets have specific library functions to help you access them as files, even though they are compressed.

res is a standard Java folder, and into that you put all your resources that aren't code. These will typically contain things like icons, images, media, and string tables. Android applications will also contain layout files.

What I'm going to do here is have you create a button, which when clicked will pop up a message on the screen.

You do this by opening the main.xml file (double-click), finding the button icon, and dragging it onto the screen.

It should end up looking something like Figure 2-3.

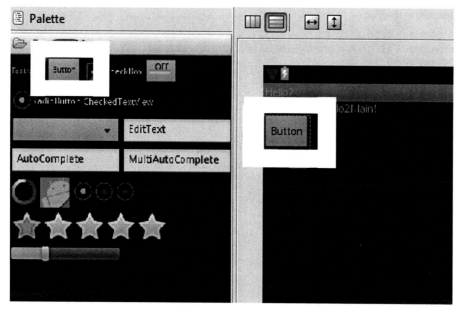

Figure 2-3. Adding a button for a layout in the layout editor

Now, on the button you've just created, right-click ➤ show in ➤ properties.
This should bring up a lengthy properties list.
Scroll down until you find the Text property, and change the Value to something of your own, such as **Press Me**. You should see the caption on the button change.
Then scroll up until you find On Click. Set the Value to **onPressClick**.

■ **Note** All the identifiers in Java are case-sensitive. Upper- and lower case *do* matter. Get very used to checking that you have uppercase and lowercase correct. You'll note that I'm using mixed case quite a lot. This is referred to as CamelCase, and is used to make the variables and methods more readable. It's not enforced by the language, but it is a very commonly used convention.

If you are familiar with Delphi, or Visual Basic, or Visual C++, this should feel right at home. If you are not familiar with this technique, we are controlling what our button does by setting properties. You'll get used to it.
What we've just done is tell Android what we want displayed on our button, and to call a method named onPressClick when clicked.
All this is stored in main.xml. You can have more than one layout; in fact, you almost certainly will. And the main layout does not have to be called main; it's just a convenient placeholder that the Android wizard created for you.
The layout editor will have a tab at the bottom marked main.xml.

It should look something like this:

```xml
<?xml version="1.0" encoding="utf-8"?>
<LinearLayout xmlns:android="http://schemas.android.com/apk/res/android"
    android:orientation="vertical"
    android:layout_width="fill_parent"
    android:layout_height="fill_parent"
    >
<TextView
    android:layout_width="fill_parent"
    android:layout_height="wrap_content"
    android:text="@string/hello"
    />
<Button android:id="@+id/button1" android:layout_width="wrap_content"
android:layout_height="wrap_content" android:text="Press Me"
android:onClick="onPressMe"></Button>
</LinearLayout>
```

LinearLayout is the first and simplest layout handler available. It allows you to drop buttons and text boxes and what have you on the form, and will keep them visible (or at least accessible) regardless of zooms and flips and so forth.

The TextView was another automatically created control that contains static text. In this case, it's set to @string/hello. This is a reference to a string table. If you open up strings.xml, you'll see that it contains a couple of strings. "hello" is set to Hello World, Hello2Main! You can edit this to something more useful.

Unlike Delphi or the others, Android does not conveniently set your event handler code for you. You'll need to put that in yourself, which brings us to—*gasp*—actual coding.

Open up Hello2Main.java, and you should see something like this:

```java
package com.apress.ba3tp.hello2;

import android.app.Activity;
import android.os.Bundle;

public class Hello2Main extends Activity {
    /** Called when the activity is first created. */
    @Override
    public void onCreate(Bundle savedInstanceState) {
        super.onCreate(savedInstanceState);
        setContentView(R.layout.main);
    }
}
```

You'll see that our new Activity is, in fact, descended from (extends) Activity, which is the default Android Activity class. It has lots of useful methods, but for the moment, we are interested in only one, onCreate. There are a number of *onSomethings* that are called at various points in the Activity life cycle. You override these to put your own handling in.

Since this the first time we've looked at actual Android code, I'm going to take this line by line:

```java
package com.apress.ba3tp.hello2; // This is our package name.

import android.app.Activity;
import android.os.Bundle;
```

The import lines tell the compiler what packages we want to pull our classes from. They are not absolutely necessary, but they save typing. We can now just refer to "Activity" as "Activity". Otherwise we would need to put in the fully qualified name, `android.app.Activity`, every time we referred to it.

■ **Note** When you first look at the import section, you'll probably see just a single `import` line, with a (+) next to it. Because Java very rapidly accumulates boilerplate code, most Java editors will automatically hide this extra guff under what are called `folds`. You can expand it by clicking the (+), but most of the time you won't need to. Eclipse is quite good at sorting out which imports you need or don't need.

```
// This is our class definition. Note we're extending Activity

'public class Hello2Main extends Activity {
/** Called when the activity is first created. */
    @Override
    public void onCreate(Bundle savedInstanceState) {
```

`Bundle` is a handy Android class that contains, well, a bundle of data. When `onCreate` is called, it passes a `Bundle` of information that you could have stored when you exited the `Activity`. This is handy, because the OS may decide to arbitrarily kill your application to make room for another one. The `savedInstanceState` bundle allows you to pick up where you left off, more or less transparently to the user.

```
super.onCreate(savedInstanceState);
```

`super` is the Java keyword that refers the ancestor class, in this case, `Activity`. This calls the standard startup routines, and then you can add your own.

```
setContentView(R.layout.main);
```

And this will tell the `Activity` to load up the `main.xml` layout, incidentally creating the various controls it needs, and displaying it on the screen.

This brings us to R. A few pages back, I referred to the gen folder that the ADT generates for you. What this does is go through all the resources in the res folder, and creates a Java class (called `R.java`) that contains the IDs of all the resources.

At this stage, it should look a lot like this:

```
package com.apress.ba3tp.hello2;

public final class R {
    public static final class attr {
    }
    public static final class drawable {
        public static final int icon=0x7f020000;
    }
    public static final class layout {
        public static final int main=0x7f030000;
    }
```

```
public static final class string {
    public static final int app_name=0x7f040001;
    public static final int hello=0x7f040000;
}
}
```

You can then pass these IDs to various methods to retrieve those resources.

The advantage with generating R rather than managing your own IDs is that mistakes have a much higher chance of being picked up at compile time—always good. It also makes it easier to read.

Now back to Hello2Main.java, to our onPressClick event.

Below onCreate, add the following chunk of code:

```
public void onPressClick(View v) {
    Toast.makeText(this, "You pressed me!", Toast.LENGTH_SHORT).show();
}
```

Toast—so called because it "pops up" messages—is the simplest form of communication with the outside world, and just flashes up a little box containing the text you've just passed to it. You may notice Eclipse warning you that it doesn't know what a View is, and you will see the word View underlined with a little red squiggle. This is because we haven't included an import for View.

If you move your mouse over View, a drop-down box should appear, containing several suggestions for resolving the problem. The top one should be "import View". Click it. Ditto for Toast, if it's needed.

If you go look at the imports section, you'll see the following two lines added:

```
import android.view.View;
import android.widget.Toast;
```

There's nothing to stop you adding these manually, but Quick Fix is a handy tool.

Save, Run → As Android Application, and look at the results. There is a Console tab, on which you can watch progress. It should be saying something like the following:

```
[2011-04-03 00:35:11 - BA3TPHello2] Android Launch!

[2011-04-03 00:35:11 - BA3TPHello2] adb is running normally.

[2011-04-03 00:35:11 - BA3TPHello2] Performing com.apress.ba3tp.hello2.Hello2Main activity
launch

[2011-04-03 00:35:11 - BA3TPHello2] Automatic Target Mode: Unable to detect device
compatibility. Please select a target device.

[2011-04-03 00:35:17 - BA3TPHello2] Launching a new emulator with Virtual Device 'honeycomb'

[2011-04-03 00:35:19 - BA3TPHello2] New emulator found: emulator-5554

[2011-04-03 00:35:19 - BA3TPHello2] Waiting for HOME ('android.process.acore') to be
launched...

[2011-04-03 00:36:28 - BA3TPHello2] WARNING: Application does not specify an API level
requirement!
```

```
[2011-04-03 00:36:28 - BA3TPHello2] Device API version is 11 (Android 3.0)

[2011-04-03 00:36:28 - BA3TPHello2] HOME is up on device 'emulator-5554'

[2011-04-03 00:36:28 - BA3TPHello2] Uploading BA3TPHello2.apk onto device 'emulator-5554'

[2011-04-03 00:36:30 - BA3TPHello2] Installing BA3TPHello2.apk...

[2011-04-03 00:37:33 - BA3TPHello2] Success!

[2011-04-03 00:37:35 - BA3TPHello2] Starting activity com.apress.ba3tp.hello2.Hello2Main on
device emulator-5554

 [2011-04-03 00:41:22 - BA3TPHello2] ActivityManager: Starting: Intent {
act=android.intent.action.MAIN cat=[android.intent.category.LAUNCHER]
cmp=com.apress.ba3tp.hello2/.Hello2Main }
```

And, all going well, you should see our "Hello" screen, with a button, which you can press. And a little message will pop up.

Note the complaint about not setting a minimum SDK level. This is true, and we don't care yet. This is a simple program that will run as cheerfully on a phone as a tablet. As we move onto more complex examples, this will change.

What you should see is something like Figure 2-4.

Figure 2-4. The first of our applications that actually does something

You may see Figure 2-5, instead.

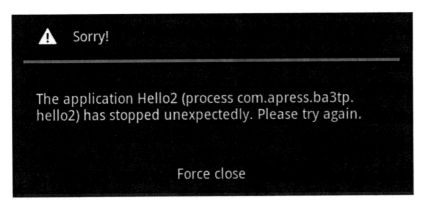

Figure 2-5. *Our first real application crashing and burning*

This will happen from time to time. It means you have an uncaught exception. I'll get on to exception handling in a bit. In the meantime, gosh, it would be nice if Android would tell us what we've done wrong.

Well, there is a handy facility called Logcat. Window → Show View → Other → Android → Logcat will open a window showing all sorts of useful debugging info. The bit we are interested in is the following:

```
04-03 02:14:03.473: ERROR/AndroidRuntime(30066): FATAL EXCEPTION: main

04-03 02:14:03.473: ERROR/AndroidRuntime(30066): java.lang.IllegalStateException: Could not
find a method onPressMe(View) in the activity class com.apress.ba3tp.hello2.Hello2Main for
onClick handler on view class android.widget.Button with id 'button1'
```

Looks like I failed to match up the name in the layout file to the name in the Java file.

In this case, it was a deliberate[1] error on my part, but it's easy to get it wrong. The name needs to match exactly (remember case sensitivity), the type needs to be a public void, and the argument needs to be a View. If any of these do not match, the onClick event won't work.

SOME MORE TIPS ON IMPROVING EMULATOR PERFORMANCE

The Android Honeycomb emulator is very, *very* slow, and frankly, at the time of writing, a little flakey. You may need to be patient and poke it a few times. Better yet, get an actual Android device and plug that in instead.

If you really need to use one, here are some handy hints to make life a little easier:

---

[1] For a given value of "deliberate".

- When creating your AVD (Android Virtual Device), make sure you give it ample memory—I suggest 1024 MB and 512 MB of SDCard.

- Reduce the screen resolution (I find 800 x 600 seems to work more or less).

- Enable snapshot to save it rebooting every time you start it.

- If possible, run on a dual- or single-core computer to get the most out of your CPU.

- Break down and buy an actual tablet device.

Another handy hint: Sometimes (especially when the emulator is waking up), you'll see the program get as far as "Starting activity" in the Console, and then hang. Hitting "Run" again will generally get past this.

When you've got as far as "ActivityManager: Starting: Intent", your application should be running okay.

Now, let's have a look at doing some more with our sample program.

I'd like to take advantage of our pregenerated "Hello World" TextView control. Drag another button onto your screen—it'll end up immediately under our existing button, because that's what a LinearLayout does—and set Text to "Press More" and OnClick to "onPressMore".

Click the TextView (which is currently displaying the text "Hello World, Hello2Main"), Show In → Properties, find "Id", and set that to the following:

```
@+id/textview
```

You could just enter any random number and use that to identify our control, but the "@+id/" syntax will be picked up by the ADT and popped into gen/R.java, from where we can refer to it later.

This id is the simple way to find the control at runtime to manipulate it.

Now, in Hello2Main.java, add the following code:

```
public void onPressMore(View v) {
  TextView tv = (TextView) findViewById(R.id.textview);
  tv.setText("I've been pressed too.");
}
```

What are we doing here?

Once a layout has been loaded (done here in our onCreate method), all the controls on that screen are available as Java objects to be manipulated.

The foregoing code is using findViewById to find our TextView. findViewById is a method of Activity, which, since our Hello2Main is descended from Activity, we can just go ahead and use without having to qualify it.

findViewById returns a View. And a View is any control that can be shown on the screen. You'll find that all your controls are descended from a View.

You may also notice that I've cast findViewById to TextView, because I want to access some specific properties belonging to a TextView.

Having acquired our View object (tv), I'm just going to set the Text property to something different.

PROPERTIES IN JAVA

If you're coming from Delphi, or VB, or a language like that, you'll be used to properties.

For various historical reasons, Java doesn't have properties as such. It does have considerable support for some property-like behavior, the use of standardized getters and setters.

For example, you already know that `TextView` and `ButtonView` have a `Text` property.

To set `Text`, you'll use the `setText` method. To get `Text`, you'd use the `getText()` method.

So all the properties you see in the Properties list can be accessed in that way.

This is a little cumbersome. However, you'll find that Eclipse has tools to simplify this process.

Lifecycle

The Android `Activity` has a distinct life cycle, which you can hook into to customize behavior.

Table 2-1. The Activity Lifecycle.

Method	Description	Killable?	Next
onCreate()	Called when the Activity is first started; use for general setup.	No	onStart()
onRestart()	Called after your Activity has been stopped, prior to it being started again	No	onStart()
onStart()	Called when the Activity is getting ready to start interacting with the user	No	onResume() or onStop()
onResume()	The Activity is now visible and ready to start interacting with the user.	No	onPause()
onPause()	The Activity is about to stop interacting with the user.	Interesting...	onResume() or onStop()
onStop()	The Activity is no longer visible.	Yes	onRestart() or onDestroy()
onDestroy()	The Activity is being disposed of.	Yes	Nothing

Note the Killable column. Anything marked No is guaranteed to be performed, assuming the previous step was achieved. The ones marked Yes *may* be called. There are no absolute guarantees that they *will* be called, because the OS may decide to kill the Activity dead before it gets there.

onPause() is interesting for a couple of reasons.

Firstly, it's the obvious and preferred spot to save anything that needs saving. But a warning: Whatever you put in there has to be pretty quick, because any lengthy processing will directly impact user responsiveness, and that will be bad.

Secondly, it's one of the significant differences between Honeycomb and previous versions, and has to do with Fragments.

Fragments are a new and exciting feature that makes use of the extra screen space available on a tablet, which I'll get onto in more depth shortly. They have their own life cycle that complements the Activity's life cycle.

However, for the moment, let's get a handle on the basics. One more play with Hello2, before we move onto other things. This should demonstrate some different parts of the life cycle, a user editable text box, and how to save your settings for later.

Let's put an EditText view onto our form (see Figure 2-6).

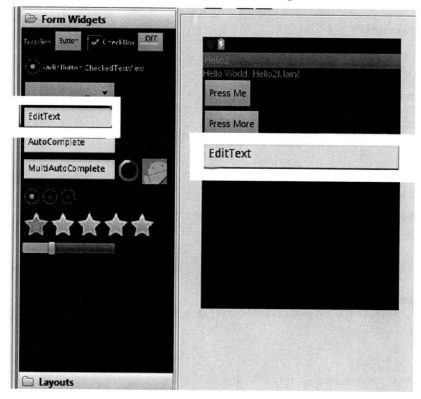

Figure 2-6. Adding an EditText to your layout

EditText is a box where you can edit Text (okay, stating the obvious).

A quick look at the properties will show this should already have an ID, @+id/editText1, which will do for our purposes. We'll leave the rest alone, because what I'm going to attempt to demonstrate is a little more detail in the life cycle of an Activity.

We're now going to add a few little bits of code:

```
package com.apress.ba3tp.hello2;

import android.app.Activity;
import android.content.SharedPreferences;
import android.content.SharedPreferences.Editor;
import android.os.Bundle;
import android.preference.PreferenceManager;
import android.view.View;
import android.widget.EditText;
import android.widget.TextView;
import android.widget.Toast;

public class Hello2Main extends Activity {
  EditText mEditText1;
  SharedPreferences mPreferences;

  /** Called when the activity is first created. */
  @Override
  public void onCreate(Bundle savedInstanceState) {
    super.onCreate(savedInstanceState);
    setContentView(R.layout.main);
    mEditText1 = (EditText) findViewById(R.id.editText1);
    mPreferences = PreferenceManager.getDefaultSharedPreferences(this);
  }

  @Override
  public void onResume() {
    super.onResume();
    mEditText1.setText(mPreferences.getString("myedit", "EMPTY"));
  }

@Override
 public void onPause() {
    super.onPause();
    Editor e = mPreferences.edit();
    e.putString("myedit", mEditText1.getText().toString());
    e.commit();
  }

  public void onPressClick(View v) {
    Toast.makeText(this, "You pressed me!", Toast.LENGTH_SHORT).show();
  }

  public void onPressMore(View v) {
    TextView tv = (TextView) findViewById(R.id.textview);
    tv.setText("I've been pressed too.");
  }
}
```

I've highlighted the changes, and it's worth addressing each bit.

```
EditText mEditText1;
SharedPreferences mPreferences;
```

Now, because using `findViewById` and so forth is boring, requires extra typing, and is thus more error-prone, and is also slower, I'm creating some class fields that I can initialize in `onCreate` and refer to later.

These types of fields are often referred to as `members`, and by convention start with an "m". This is *just* a convention, but it is used widely in the Android community.

```
mEditText1 = (EditText) findViewById(R.id.editText1);
```
This sets our previously declared member to the editText1 control.

```
mPreferences = PreferenceManager.getDefaultSharedPreferences(this);
```

Android has a nice feature for storing and retrieving `Preferences`. These are referred to as `SharedPreferences`, and allow you to read and write keyed chunks of data. They are not designed for massive storage—don't go trying to put an MP3 in there, for example—but are very handy for settings and so forth. You can created named and public `SharedPreferences`, but you automatically get one created for you by the system and returned by `PreferenceManager.getDefaultSharedPreferences(this)`.

■ **Java Note** You'll see there is no `new` keyword. This is because `getDefaultSharedPreferences` is a `static` method of `PreferenceManager`, and manages that sort of stuff for you. In fact, it most likely will return an object that it created earlier, but you don't need to know about those details. `this` is a keyword in Java meaning "this current object."

A lot of calls in Android require what is called a `Context`. A `Context` is a complex interface that tells the Android methods who is calling, and why. `Activity` supports the `Context` interface, and most of the time you will be passing the current `Activity` as a `Context`. Thus, this.

```
@Override
public void onResume() {
    super.onResume();
    mEditText1.setText(mPreferences.getString("myedit", "EMPTY"));
}
```

`onResume` is called when the `Activity` becomes visible. What we are doing here is pulling a string from our shared preferences keyed on "myedit", and displaying it in the `EditText`. If nothing has been saved in "myedit" before, it will default to "EMPTY".

Note the `super.onResume()` line. This is calling the inherited method, and is mandatory. If you fail to include this line in any of the lifecycle hooks, Android will throw an exception. Note that you don't have to call the super method for *every* override you ever do, but the lifecycle methods demand it.

```
@Override
public void onPause() {
    super.onPause();
    Editor e = mPreferences.edit();
    e.putString("myedit", mEditText1.getText().toString());
```

```
    e.commit();
}
```

Writing back to a SharedPreference is slightly more complex, but not very. When you want to make changes, call the edit() method. This will return an Editor object, which is what you use to make the changes. When you are done making your changes, you need to commit() those changes, or nothing will be saved.

Oh, and note the toString() after the getText(). getText() doesn't return a String, it returns an Editable object. This is because EditText can contain more than just a String. You can use it to manipulate different sections of your text in different ways.

But for the moment, all we want is the text, and toString() does that nicely.

Anyway, save and run, and off you go.

JUST LIKE AN INI FILE

In fact, Windows programmers will note that this is very much like using an INI file or using the registry. And so it is, with one significant difference:

INI files and such are hierarchical. With INI files, you can group values into sections, and registries support fully fledged trees.

Preference files are flat . . . one level of keys.

The Java approach to this—and you'll see it all over—is to use dot notation in the keys. For example, if we'd wanted to keep the value of the edit and the input type, we could use the following:

```
e,putString("edit.text", mEditText1.getText().toString());
e.putInt("edit.type",mEditText1.getInputType())
```

This is not essential, but works pretty well, and is yet another widely used Java convention.

Intents: What, Where, Why, and Are They Honorable?

You won't be able to play in Android very long without running into Intents. They scared the heck out of me when I first came across them, but the concept is, in fact, very simple.

An Intent is simply a class that tells Android what you want to do.

Instead of putting options on a command line and telling an executable to run, you build up your requirements and arguments in an Intent, and then tell Android to sort out what to do with it.

An Intent can be implicit or explicit.

An explicit Intent will open a specific Activity in a specific application.

An implicit Intent will give Android some hints, but will let it work out what to do with it.

Let's start with implicit Intents. One of the simplest is to open a web page in a browser. It'll look a lot like this:

```
public void onBrowseClick(View v) {
Intent intent = new Intent(Intent.ACTION_VIEW);
intent.setData(Uri.parse("http://google.com"));
startActivity(intent);
}
```

I'll assume you've worked out how to put a new button on the screen by now.

Intent.ACTION_VIEW is a standard action, one of quite a few, that simply works out which application on your device is designed to handle the type of data you've just passed it. In this case, it's a web page.

You'll note that data is always a Uri.

If that's all you ever use an Intent for, well, you're already well ahead of the game, but you can use it for many things in many ways.

There is a lot of extra information that can be added into an Intent. For example, let's say we want to open a PDF file that we previously downloaded. We might do something like this:

```
public void onPdfClick(View v) {
    Intent intent = new Intent(Intent.ACTION_VIEW);
    intent.setDataAndType(Uri.parse("file:///sdcard/Download/sample.pdf"), "application/pdf");
    try {
      startActivity(intent);
    } catch (ActivityNotFoundException e) {
      Toast.makeText(this,e.getMessage(),Toast.LENGTH_SHORT).show();
    }
}
```

There are several things demonstrated here.

I'm telling the Intent I want to view a PDF that I'd previously downloaded. For pretty much all Android devices, the default downloads directory is /sdcard/Download. (It may differ, and there are some calls you can make to confirm where it is on your actual device, but this will do for the moment.) The code also assumes you have a file called "sample.pdf" on your Android.

As well as the Uri of the file, I'm also passing the MIME type of the file (application/pdf), to let Android know that, yes, I want this treated as a PDF.

I've also added a try and catch, because your device may not know what to do with a PDF. If there is no PDF reader installed (there isn't on the emulator), your application will throw an exception, and if you don't handle it yourself, you'll get the dreaded "Force Close" message.

MORE JAVA NOTES: EXCEPTIONS

When something goes wrong with Java, it will throw an exception. On a desktop, this will typically display an error message and a stack trace, and then stop.

On Android, it throws the "Force Close" message, and writes the error message into Logcat. This is not terribly helpful for your average user.

But you can handle these exceptions yourself using the try…catch syntax.

This will look a lot like the following:

```
try {
  … code
} catch (AnExceptionType e) {
  … handle that exception, which in this case is returned in e.
  … like, display the error message returned in e.getMessage()
} catch (AnotherExceptionType e) {
  … handle the different exception
} catch (Exception e) {
```

```
… all exceptions are descended from the Exception class, so this can be used as a
… catch all. Make sure it's at the end, though.
}
```

There is also `try..finally`, which will make sure a chunk of code is *always* run—very handy for making sure you always run tidy-up code, regardless of what else goes wrong.

Note that while you are encouraged to be specific as to which exceptions you handle, there's nothing to stop you from just trapping on "Exception". If you've got a number of different exception types you know you may have to deal with in the same way, or you aren't completely sure which exceptions you may get, just drop back to "Exception".

Another way you can use Intents is as an explicit Intent.

Here is a simple use of Intent for switching between two Activities in the same application. (I've called it BA3TPIntents, downloadable from the Apress.com web site).

It consists of two Activities, each with a single screen (Figure 2-7).

Figure 2-7. Two remarkably similar Activity screens

All the buttons do is swap between the two Activities. The code in question looks like this:

```java
public class ActivityOne extends Activity {
    /** Called when the activity is first created. */
    @Override
    public void onCreate(Bundle savedInstanceState) {
        super.onCreate(savedInstanceState);
        setContentView(R.layout.activityone);
    }

    public void onSwap(View v) {
      Intent intent = new Intent(this,ActivityTwo.class);
      startActivity(intent);
    }
}
```

and

```java
public class ActivityTwo extends Activity {

    @Override
```

```
public void onCreate(Bundle savedInstanceState) {
    super.onCreate(savedInstanceState);
    setContentView(R.layout.activitytwo);
}

public void onSwapBack(View v) {
  Intent intent = new Intent(this,ActivityOne.class);
  startActivity(intent);
  }
}
```

What we are doing here is creating an Intent with a specific class . . . in this case, the other class in this package. There is another thing I had to do, which was add an entry into AndroidManifest.xml.

```
<activity android:name=".ActivityOne" android:label="@string/app_name">
        <intent-filter>
                <action android:name="android.intent.action.MAIN" />
                <category android:name="android.intent.category.LAUNCHER" />
        </intent-filter>
</activity>
<activity android:name=".ActivityTwo"></activity>
```

Each Activity has to be declared in AndroidManifest.xml—fair enough.

activity android:name is the name of the class we want to run. Note the "." prefixing the name. This is shorthand for "this current package," otherwise you'd need to put in the fully qualified class name: com.apress.ba3tp.testintents.ActivityOne.

The Intent filter is a bit trickier. This is for use with implicit Intents, in this case, the action: *android.intent.action.MAIN* and the category: *android.intent.category.LAUNCHER* tell the Android apps screen that this Activity is the main Activity for this application, and can be called from the application launcher.

You can have multiple Intent filters for each action. More later.

Because ActivityTwo has no actions or categories attached to it, it can be accessed only explicitly. Now, let's mix it up a little.

```
<activity android:name=".ActivityOne" android:label="Activity One">
        <intent-filter>
                <action android:name="android.intent.action.MAIN" />
                <category android:name="android.intent.category.LAUNCHER" />
        </intent-filter>
</activity>
<activity android:name=".ActivityTwo"  android:label="Activity Two">
        <intent-filter>
                <action android:name="android.intent.action.MAIN" />
                <category android:name="android.intent.category.LAUNCHER" />
        </intent-filter>
</activity>
```

I've made a few changes. For one, I've replaced the generic appname label with a specific label for each Activity, which will be reflected in the title bar.

Also, I've copied the Intent filter from ActivityOne into ActivityTwo. And guess what? If you install this onto your device (running it is the simplest way) and pull up the Apps window, what do you see?

Two icons! One for Activity One, and one for Activity Two! So your user can start in either screen.

45

If you take this example as is, and play with it, you may notice some odd behavior when you hit the Back button. Each time you hit Back, you'll flip back to the previous screen.

This is because the default behavior for startActivity() leaves a stack of Activities, and when the user hits Back, he or she is taken back to the previous screen..

This is quite nice . . . you may have noticed this behavior with onBrowseClick earlier.

But we don't always want to do this. Fortunately, Intent has a number of flags with which we can modify how it works.

In this case, we're going to add the follow flags to our Intents:

```
intent.setFlags(Intent.FLAG_ACTIVITY_NEW_TASK|Intent.FLAG_ACTIVITY_CLEAR_TASK);
```

I've told it that I don't want to keep a track of my history. The "|" is Java for Boolean "or", just in case you were wondering.

Now, let us say we want to pass some information to the Activity we just started. Intents have a very flexible mechanism for this, called Extras. You can stuff as much extra data into an Intent as takes your fancy.

So I've made some changes to ActivityOne to pass a count of how many times it's switched backward and forward:

```java
public class ActivityOne extends Activity {
  public static final String COUNT = "com.apress.ba3tp.testIntents.count";
  int mCount = 0; // Track how many times we've been called, via the Intent.

  /** Called when the activity is first created. */
  @Override
  public void onCreate(Bundle savedInstanceState) {
    super.onCreate(savedInstanceState);
    setContentView(R.layout.activityone);
  }

  public void onSwap(View v) {
    Intent intent = new Intent(this, ActivityTwo.class);
    intent.setFlags(Intent.FLAG_ACTIVITY_NEW_TASK
        | Intent.FLAG_ACTIVITY_CLEAR_TASK);
    intent.putExtra(COUNT, mCount + 1);
    startActivity(intent);
  }

  @Override
  public void onStart() {
    super.onStart();
    Intent intent = getIntent(); // Get the intent that started this.
    mCount = intent.getIntExtra(COUNT, 0);
    Toast.makeText(this, "Called " + mCount + " times so far.", Toast.LENGTH_SHORT).show();
  }

}
```

There are a few things worth noting here. I've created a member called mCount, in which I keep track of the value passed to me by my Intent. I've created a constant key called COUNT, which contains a string defining the key (not absolutely needed but it helps avoid confusion), and when I call startActivity I'm sticking an extra value in using putExtra.

On the receiving end, I've added an onStart() event, which is called when an Activity is started, using getIntent() to retrieve the Intent that started this Activity, and queried it for the value defined by my constant, COUNT. getIntExtra() has a second parameter to provide a default value in case the one we're looking for is not set.

I've then added a Toast message to show us that something is happening..

■ **Java Note** Constants (static final fields) are by convention identified by being entirely in uppercase, and using underscore (_) to separate words. Java has a lot of conventions.

I've then duplicated that code into ActivityTwo, with the following slight difference:

```
mCount = intent.getIntExtra(ActivityOne.COUNT, 0);
```

Even though ActivityOne is in the same package (and application) as ActivityTwo, ActivityTwo still needs to supply the class name to access that field.

There are many ways to build an Intent. Just as a random example, here's one I used in ScriptingLayerForAndroid (SL4A) to open a local HTML file in a specific browser:

```java
public void clickHelp(View v) {
    Intent intent = new Intent();
    intent.setAction(Intent.ACTION_VIEW);
    intent.setDataAndType(Uri.parse("file:///sdcard/sl4a/doc/index.html"), "text/html");
    intent.setComponent(new ComponentName("com.android.browser",
"com.android.browser.BrowserActivity"));

    startActivity(intent);
}
```

In this case, I told it I wanted com.android.browser.BrowserActivity to open this file, not just some random other browser. Note that you need to pass the fully qualified names of both the package (com.android.browser) and the actual Activity (com.android.browser.BrowserActivity); you can't use ".BrowserActivity".

Intent Filters

When passing an implicit Intent, you can narrow down which Activities Android will choose by using Categories.

You can build up a list of Categories by using Intent.addCategory. When searching through a list of all the available Activities, only Activities that match *all* the Categories you've provided will be offered.

If Android still can't decide which Activity to use, a list will be popped up for the user to choose from. So, if there was more than one Text Editor on your Android, a call to the following will pop up a list of editors ready to work with your text, which is quite useful behavior.

```java
Intent intent = new Intent();
intent.setAction(Intent.ACTION_EDIT);
```

```
        intent.setDataAndType(Uri.parse("file:///sdcard/Downloads/README.txt "),↩
"text/plain");
```

Here's an example from another project I'm working on:

```
<activity android:name=".PythonMain" android:label="@string/app_name"
        android:configChanges="keyboardHidden|orientation">
    <intent-filter>
            <action android:name="android.intent.action.MAIN" />
            <category android:name="android.intent.category.LAUNCHER" />
    </intent-filter>
    <intent-filter>
            <action android:name="com.googlecode.android_scripting.↩
DISCOVER_INTERPRETERS" />
            <category android:name="android.intent.category.LAUNCHER" />
            <data android:mimeType="script/.py" />
    </intent-filter>
    <intent-filter>
            <action android:name="android.intent.action.VIEW" />
            <action android:name="android.intent.action.EDIT" />
            <category android:name="android.intent.category.DEFAULT" />
            <data android:mimeType="application/x-zip" />
    </intent-filter>
</activity>
```

This a section from the Python For Android AndroidManifest.xml file.

The first intent-filter will respond to the apps launcher, having action=*"android.intent.action.MAIN"* and category=*"android.intent.category.LAUNCHER"*, just like ActivityOne early. The next one is kind of fancy, in that it will respond to a query about what script interpreters are available. The MIME type restricts this to files tagged as script/.py (Python scripts)

The last will cause the PythonMain Activity to become active when Android attempts to edit or view an application/x-zip file. This will give the user the opportunity to allow the Python installer to load in a ZIP file, on the off-chance it's a Python module.

An important category, and one that caused me much heartache, was "android.intent.category.DEFAULT". This is *required* if you want your Activity to respond to an implicit startActivity request on arbitrary data.

Common Intents

There are many common Intents defined, too, things so basic or commonly used that you just need to declare the action, and your Android will take care of the rest—for example:

```
startActivity(new Intent(Intent.ACTION_DIAL, Uri.parse("tel:5559999")) ); // Dial a number
startActivity(new Intent(Intent.ACTION_ANSWER));    // Answer the phone
startActivity(new Intent(Intent.ACTION_ALL_APPS)); // List all apps.
```

Finally

How do we stop an Activity when we're done with it?

```
  public void onFinishClick(View v) {
    finish();
  }
```

Secretly Linux

Here's an interesting thing about Android. It's built on a Linux core. And most of the power of Linux is still there, ready to be tapped.

Don't believe me? Try this. Open a command-line window on your host, make sure that your Android is connected (or your emulator is running), and type:

```
adb shell
```

What you should see is the following:

```
root@android:/data #
```

And you can then use a bunch of standard Linux commands, like ls, ps, cp, rm.

Not all standard Linux commands are available by any means—it is a *cutdown* Linux, after all—but all the key stuff is there. This means that all the file handling routines will behave like Linux.

Here's a bit of semi-complex code (you can download the project BA3TPExec from Apress.com) shown as Listing 1-1:

Listing 1-1

```
public class ExecExample extends Activity {
  /** Called when the activity is first created. */
  @Override
  public void onCreate(Bundle savedInstanceState) {
    super.onCreate(savedInstanceState);
    setContentView(R.layout.main);
  }

  public void onExec(View v) {
    TextView tv = (TextView) findViewById(R.id.mytext);
    try {
      Process p = Runtime.getRuntime().exec("ls /mnt/sdcard");
      BufferedReader r = new BufferedReader(new InputStreamReader(
          p.getInputStream()));
      StringBuilder builder = new StringBuilder();
      StringBuilderPrinter sp = new StringBuilderPrinter(builder);
      String line;
      while ((line = r.readLine()) != null) {
        sp.println(line);
      }
      tv.setText(builder.toString());
      r.close();
    } catch (Exception e) {
      tv.setText(e.getMessage());
```

```
        }
    }
}
```

This, quite simply, executes "ls" (the Linux command to list files) and displays the result in our more or less standard TextView.

What you should get is something like Figure 2-8.

Figure 2-8. *A quick and dirty file lister*

So you can leverage quite a lot of Linux knowledge if you are so inclined.

MORE JAVA: STREAMS AND READERS

The foregoing chunk of code (Listing 1-1) may look scary at first, but it's not as complex as it looks.

The Runtime.exec runs a command as if from a command line. It returns a Process class, which you can use to control the process you've just kicked off.

From that, you can get access to an inputStream, which is hooked up to the stdout of the process.

Most Java file handling is done with some form of Stream, but Streams are for binary input and output, and work on bytes.

To handle Text, you really need a Reader. A Reader handles characters instead of bytes.

InputStreamReader acts as a link between Streams and Readers, and BufferedReader (among other things) gives us a readLine() method, to allow us to easily read in a line at a time.

StringBuilder is a convenience class to make building Strings more efficient, and StringBuilderPrinter will allow us to write to a StringBuilder using println() and other useful methods. FYI, the venerable System.out is a Printer.

Having set all of that up, I'm simply reading the output from ls a line at a time until it returns a null.

Then I have a nicely built String sitting in Builder, which I can just assign to the TextView to show it to the user. Simple, right? (Well, simpler than some of the other options.)

Knowing that Android is built over a Linux core helps make the way things fit together much clearer. For example, the basis of security and package control maps onto the Linux frame like so:

Each package is given its own user ID, and a number of predefined folders to store data and program files. This means that other applications can't directly access your application's files. It's also how the package manager deals with cleaning when being uninstalled. But knowing it's a Linux frame, you can do clever things with chmod to allow others to access your files, for example.

Summary

In this chapter, I've covered the basics of how Android programs are structured. I've shown the important link between the Android OS and tasty desserts, and walked you through building your first interactive Android application.

I've demonstrated some more on how to use the graphical layout editor, and introduced you to some fundamental widgets such as EditText and Button.

I've shown what happens when you have unhandled exceptions and how to make them *handled* exceptions.

I've introduced you to the concept of Intents, and started into some of the many things you can do with them.

I've shown you the importance of Toast, and what Streams are.

I've even lifted up the hood and peeked at the Linux engine on which Android is built.

Not a bad chapter's work, if I do say so myself.

CHAPTER 3

What Can You Do with an Android Tablet?

Your Android device is a remarkably powerful computer in its own right. This device can do things that even a few years ago would have been the province of high-end desktop computers. And a few years before that, the stuff of science fiction.

It can play movies, music, search the Internet, tell you where you are and where to go, recognize voice commands, translate signs, connect to an astonishing array of devices, and has more sensors than the CIA. It's almost ridiculous.

This is the sort of thing I used to read about. Wrist communicators and tricorders. The future is here, people, and it's in the form of a cute little green guy that looks like a garbage can.

Although I still want to know where my jetpack is.

Figure 3-1. Android tablets—good for what ails ya

More Sensors Than the CIA

Ages ago, when I had my little PalmPilot, there was an application floating around called "Tricorder." It just made your Palm PDA look like a Star Trek Tricorder, that device that Spock was always waving around. In the show, this was a prop that could sense and record a wide variety of phenomena, restricted only to the speed of plot.

The old Palm app looked pretty and made appropriate noises when you pressed buttons, but that was the size of it.

When I first laid my hands on my very own Android phone and was exploring the apps market, I found another Tricorder app, so I promptly downloaded it. It was pretty obviously a descendant of the original Palm app, but this actually made use of the astonishing array of sensors that my phone had. It could show the available wireless networks and their field strengths, be used as a compass, detect satellites in orbit, and even be used as a stud finder by detecting fluctuations in the magnetic field.

This frankly astonished me, and the more I thought about what this little phone could do, the more I realized that this was, in truth, the science-fictional Tricorder—and then some.

Let's have a look at what sorts of sensors Android supports.

- Accelerometer

- Gravity sensor

- Gyroscope

- Light levels

- Linear acceleration

- Magnetic field

- Orientation

- Pressure

- Proximity

- Rotation vector

- Temperature

And that doesn't even include the GPS, which has its own section.

Not all devices have every type of sensor, and to be fair, some of the listed sensor types are just different interpretations of the same basic data.

Almost all devices will have an orientation sensor. Many will have light-level sensors. And most, if not all, will support cameras and microphones, which a determined programmer can also do quite a bit with.

Let's have a quick play with sensors. Here's a quicky example program. (See BA3TPSensor1 in the downloads.) First, our screen layout (Listing 3-1).

Listing 3-1. Sample Screen Layout

```
<?xml version="1.0" encoding="utf-8"?>
<LinearLayout xmlns:android="http://schemas.android.com/apk/res/android"
        android:layout_width="fill_parent" android:layout_height="fill_parent"
        android:orientation="vertical">
```

```
<LinearLayout android:id="@+id/linearLayout1"
        android:layout_width="match_parent" android:layout_height="wrap_content"
        android:orientation="horizontal">
        <Button android:layout_width="wrap_content" android:id="@+id/button1"
                android:layout_height="wrap_content" android:text="List"
                android:onClick="onListClick"></Button>
        <Button android:text="Light" android:layout_width="wrap_content"
                android:layout_height="wrap_content" android:id="@+id/button2"
                android:onClick="onLightClick"></Button>
        <Button android:text="Mag" android:layout_width="wrap_content"
                android:layout_height="wrap_content" android:id="@+id/button3"
                android:onClick="onMagClick"></Button>
        <Button android:text="Orient" android:layout_width="wrap_content"
                android:layout_height="wrap_content" android:id="@+id/button4"
                android:onClick="onOrientClick"></Button>
        <Button android:text="Acc" android:layout_height="wrap_content"
                android:id="@+id/button5" android:layout_width="wrap_content"
                android:onClick="onAccClick"></Button>
        <Button android:text="Prox" android:layout_height="wrap_content"
                android:id="@+id/button6" android:layout_width="wrap_content"
                android:onClick="onProxClick"></Button>
</LinearLayout>
<TextView android:layout_width="fill_parent"
        android:layout_height="wrap_content" android:text="Display"
        android:id="@+id/eDisplay"></TextView>
</LinearLayout>
```

This should look a lot like Figure 3-2.

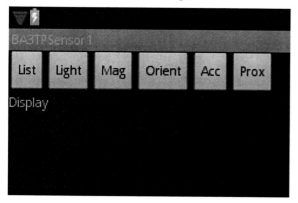

Figure 3-2. *Sensor testing*

Now, what I've done here is set up my default LinearLayout (which just lines up controls one after the other) oriented vertically. Then the first thing I've put into that is another LinearLayout, oriented horizontally. That way I can drop a bunch of buttons onto the second LinearLayout (which keeps them in a nice group at the top of the screen), and then I've put a TextView under that, into which I can display whatever text happens to strike my fancy as we proceed.

I'll be using this sort of layout a lot. It's not pretty, but it's nice and simple, and makes a handy testbed for this type of messing about.

Pretty much all access to the sensors is managed by the aptly named SensorManager class. See Listing 3-2.

Listing 3-2. Accessing the SensorManager

```java
public class SensorActivity extends Activity implements SensorEventListener {
  TextView mDisplay;
  SensorManager mSensorManager;
  Sensor mListening = null;

  /** Called when the activity is first created. */
  @Override
  public void onCreate(Bundle savedInstanceState) {
    super.onCreate(savedInstanceState);
    setContentView(R.layout.main);
    mDisplay = (TextView) findViewById(R.id.eDisplay);
    mSensorManager = (SensorManager) getSystemService(SENSOR_SERVICE);
  }
```

As you can see in Listing 3-2, the first thing I do after the basic boilerplate is grab a reference to the system SensorManager service. This is done using the getSystemService call with the appropriate flag. Note the cast to SensorManager, because getSystemService can return a variety of different manager types.

The first button, List, is in many ways the most interesting one. This will return a list of the available sensors. See Listing 3-3..

Listing 3-3. The onListClick Event

```java
  public void onListClick(View v) {
    List<Sensor> list = mSensorManager.getSensorList(Sensor.TYPE_ALL);
    StringBuilder b = new StringBuilder();
    for (Sensor sensor : list) {
      b.append(sensor.getName() +" (" +sensor.getType()+") "+sensor.getPower()+"mA\n");
    }
    mDisplay.setText(b);
  }
```

Listing 3-3 grabs a list of available sensors, builds them into a string, and displays the results on the screen.

StringBuilder is just a handy utility class to efficiently build a string.

JAVA NOTES: ESCAPE CODES

Note the "\n" at the end of the append. It stands for a linefeed. C, C++, and JavaScript programmers will know all about this. Just note that a "\" in a constant string always indicates an escape of some kind.

Common Java Escape Sequences

\n	New line
\t	Tab
\b	Backspace
\r	Carriage return
\f	Formfeed
\\	Backslash
\'	Single quotation mark
\"	Double quotation mark
\d	Octal
\xd	Hexadecimal
\ud	Unicode character

One side effect of this that can bite Windows programmers particularly is that a file like "C:\temp\test.txt" has to be encoded "c:\\temp\\test.txt". Not that this should affect us Android programmers . . .

Go ahead, try it. The results will vary quite dramatically, depending on what device you run this on. For example, my HTC Desire phone gives me the following list:

```
BMA150 3-axis Accelerometer (1) 3.0mA

AK8973 3-axis Magnetic field sensor (2) 6.7mA

AK8973 Orientation sensor (3) 9.7mA

CM3602 Proximity sensor (8) 0.5mA

CM3602 Light sensor (5) 0.5mA
```

This is kind of cool, I feel.

Checking the various fields, we've got a user-friendly name, the type of sensor, and how much power (in milliamps) the sensor will draw when active. There is more, but this gives us a bit of an idea. In contrast, the emulator returns a fairly boring:

```
Goldfish 3-axis Accelerometer (1) 3.0mA
```

Why the Android emulator called its accelerometer "Goldfish" is a mystery to me.

Now, how do we access these sensors? It would be nice if we could just query each sensor for its current value, but it's not quite that simple.

Because the sensors are hardware that has to be initialized and brought up to speed, the values that you're sensing are not always available at any given time. Android really discourages just sitting around waiting for things to wake up, too, because that gives poor user response.

So what we do is register a Listener with the sensor manager, and then respond to sensor events.

I found Listeners a daunting concept at first, but at heart they're pretty simple. A Listener is just an implementation of an interface. These can be registered with whatever wants to send an event, which then just calls the agreed-upon method.

You can create a separate class to be a Listener, or just implement the Listener in your current class, or even create an anonymous class. I'll touch on all these options in due time. For the moment, I'll just implement the listener interface in our current class, as in Listing 3-4.

Listing 3-4. Implementing a SensorEventListener

```
public class SensorActivity extends Activity implements SensorEventListener {
....
  // Listener events
  @Override
  public void onAccuracyChanged(Sensor sensor, int accuracy) {
    mDisplay.setText("Accuracy changed.");
  }

  @Override
  public void onSensorChanged(SensorEvent event) {
    String s = "Event: "+event.sensor.getName()+"\n";
    for(float v : event.values) {
      s+=v+"\n";
    }
    mDisplay.setText(s);
  }
}
```

As you can see in Listing 3-4, there are two events that our SensorEventListener has to implement. An onAccuracyChanged (for when the accuracy of the Sensor changes, for whatever reason) and onSensorChanged. The workhorse, and the one most people are likely to use, is onSensorChanged.

What you get when that event triggers is a SensorEvent. This can be queried for what sort of sensor it is, an exact timestamp, and a reference to the sensor itself.

This code just displays the contents of the values array. Which data is where depends on the type of sensor. For example, Light and Proximity events return a single value, whereas the accelerometer and magnetic sensors return 3.

The link http://developer.android.com/reference/android/hardware/SensorEvent.html will give you more information.

I've hooked up each of the sensors to a button, which will fire up the appropriate listener (see Listing 3-5).

Listing 3-5. The Code to Start Listening to Sensors

```java
public void doListen(int sensorType){
  if (mListening!=null) {
    stopListening();
    mDisplay.setText("stopped");
    return;
  }
  List<Sensor> sensors = mSensorManager.getSensorList(sensorType);
  if (sensors.size()==0) {
    mDisplay.setText("No appropriate Sensor available.");
    return;
  }
  stopListening(); // Make sure we've only go one listening at a time.
  mListening = sensors.get(0); // Lazily just grab first one.
  if (mSensorManager.registerListener(this, mListening, SensorManager.↵
SENSOR_DELAY_NORMAL)) {
      mDisplay.setText("Listening to "+mListening.getName());
  } else {
      mDisplay.setText("Listening failed.");
  }
}

public void stopListening() {
  if (mListening!=null) {
    mSensorManager.unregisterListener(this, mListening);
    mListening=null;
  }
}

@Override
public void onPause() {
    super.onPause();
    stopListening();
}
```

When called with a valid sensor type, the doListen will query SensorManager for a list of appropriate sensors (displaying an error if none are available), and then register a listener. One of the things you can specify is the delay. In this case, we've chosen SENSOR_DELAY_NORMAL. This will keep the rate of event updates down to something sensible. You can also define a delay in microseconds.

Note the several calls to stopListening. Once a listener has been registered, it's quite important to make sure you unregister it once you're finished with it, otherwise your sensor will remain active and sucking power.

If doListen is called a second time, it will stop listening to the current sensor. It will also stop if the activity pauses.

All that remains is to hook up the buttons (Listing 3-6).

Listing 3-6. Button Click Events

```java
public void onLightClick(View v) {
  doListen(Sensor.TYPE_LIGHT);
}

public void onMagClick(View v) {
  doListen(Sensor.TYPE_MAGNETIC_FIELD);
}

public void onOrientClick(View v) {
  doListen(Sensor.TYPE_ORIENTATION);
}

public void onAccClick(View v) {
  doListen(Sensor.TYPE_ACCELEROMETER);
}

public void onProxClick(View v) {
  doListen(Sensor.TYPE_PROXIMITY);
}
```

Go on. Have another play. Your actual results will probably vary depending on your device. However, you should see numbers being displayed on your screen. Table 3-1 lists some of the available types.

Table 3-1. Sensor Values

Sensor.TYPE_LIGHT	values[0]: Ambient light level in SI lux units
Sensor.TYPE_PROXIMITY	values[0]: Proximity sensor distance measured in centimeters—in theory; sometimes this just returns a 0 or 1, depending on implementation.
Sensor.TYPE_ORIENTATION	In degrees: values[0]: Azimuth, angle between the magnetic north direction and the y axis, around the z axis (0 to 359). 0=North, 90=East, 180=South, 270=West values[1]: Pitch, rotation around x axis (-180 to 180), with positive values when the z axis moves toward the y axis values[2]: Roll, rotation around y axis (-90 to 90), with positive values when the x axis moves toward the z axis
Sensor.TYPE_ACCELEROMETER	All values are in SI units (m/s^2) values[0]: Acceleration minus Gx on the x axis values[1]: Acceleration minus Gy on the y axis values[2]: Acceleration minus Gz on the z axis

Sensor.TYPE_MAGNETIC_FIELD	All values are in micro-Tesla (uT) and measure the ambient magnetic field in the x, y, and z axis.

One annoying thing if you're trying to see what happens when you tilt your tablet about the place is that the orientation may flip. This results in an onPause event, which (as we've set it up at present) will turn off the listener.

There are a number of solutions to this, but the easy way is to go into AndroidManifest.xml and add the change shown in Listing 3-7.

Listing 3-7. Forcing an Activity into Portrait Mode

```
<activity android:name=".SensorActivity"
          android:label="@string/app_name"
       android:screenOrientation="portrait">
```

This will force our activity to always stay in portrait mode.

The orientation sensor type is quite useful. Typically, it's a sort of pretend sensor that combines input from the accelerometer and magnetic field sensor to tell us which way up our device is, and where it's pointing.

Unfortunately, for a number of reasons, the orientation sensor has been deprecated, which is to say, Android no longer wants you to use it, and it may disappear in future releases.

Also, this example program is a very simplistic method of handling the event listener. We're listening to only one sensor at a time, for example. Quite often we'll want multiple sensors up and running. Case in point: The significantly more complex method of getting orientation information that Android now offers.

So I've created a second version of the program: BA3TPSensor2. This new program listens to two sensors, the accelerometer and magnetic fields, and uses the new getOrientationMatrix to build an orientation matrix that can then be passed to getOrientation.

These changes bear some explaining. See Listing 3-8.

Listing 3-8. The New Way of Getting Orientation

```
public void onSensorChanged(SensorEvent event) {
  if (event.sensor.getType()==Sensor.TYPE_ACCELEROMETER) {
    System.arraycopy(event.values, 0, mGrav, 0, 3); // Note copy, because this array will↵
be reused.
    showEvent(event,mAcclerometer);
  } else if (event.sensor.getType()==Sensor.TYPE_MAGNETIC_FIELD) {
    System.arraycopy(event.values, 0, mMag, 0, 3); // Note copy, because this array will↵
be reused.
    showEvent(event,mMagnetic);
  }
  if (SensorManager.getRotationMatrix(mMatrix, null, mGrav, mMag)) {
    if (mRemap==1 ) { // Camera - map X->X, Y->Z
      SensorManager.remapCoordinateSystem(mMatrix, SensorManager.AXIS_X,↵
SensorManager.AXIS_Z, mRemapped);
    }
    else if (mRemap==2) { // Compass, 90 degree rotation. Map X->Y, Y-> minus X
      SensorManager.remapCoordinateSystem(mMatrix, SensorManager.AXIS_Y,↵
```

```
SensorManager.AXIS_MINUS_X, mRemapped);
    }
    else System.arraycopy(mMatrix, 0, mRemapped, 0, 9); // Just copy
    SensorManager.getOrientation(mRemapped, mOrient);
    String s = "Orientation:\n"+
      "azimuth="+Math.round(Math.toDegrees(mOrient[0]))+"\n"+
      "pitch="+Math.round(Math.toDegrees(mOrient[1]))+"\n"+
      "roll="+Math.round(Math.toDegrees(mOrient[2]));
    mOrientation.setText(s);
  }
}
```

Now, as far as I'm concerned, the documentation in the SDK may as well have been written in Swahili. Why give up a perfectly straightforward orientation event for this extremely complex chunk of code? That's a good question, and I don't have the answer, actually. However, there are a couple of possible explanations that spring to mind.

If you look, you'll see that we collect readings from both the accelerometer and magnetic field sensors as they come, and combine them into a single rotation matrix. This allows finer control over when the calculations are made.

If you're asking what a rotation matrix is, and why we should care, then you aren't alone. The short answer is that it is used in 3D graphics handling, and the matrix can be fed directly into the OpenGL 3D routines that Android supports.

The longer answer should be touched on in Chapter 9.

getOrientation can be called to translate everything into azimuth, pitch, and roll (in radians). The final step is to convert these back to degrees using the standard Math function, Math.toDegrees().

I've added one fillip to this, in the shape of a few calls to remapCoordinateSystem. The documentation for this is also written in Swahili, but it's actually quite useful.

Prior to converting back to an orientation, it's sometimes desirable to change some assumptions about which way is up. For orientation, the x axis is horizontal and points to the right, the y axis is vertical and points up, and the z axis points toward the outside of the front face of the screen. But if we're using the phone as, for example, a compass or a camera, it may be useful to swap some of these axes around. And this is what remapCoordinateSystem does.

So SensorManager.remapCoordinateSystem(mMatrix, SensorManager.AXIS_X, SensorManager.AXIS_Z, mRemapped) takes the original matrix and maps the x axis to the x axis, and the y axis to the z axis. The result is stored in mRemapped. This then allows us to assume that the user is holding our device like a camera, and behave accordingly.

LOOKING FORWARD

Sometimes it's good to know that people are looking toward the future. In the SensorManager class, there is a constant for earth gravity, $9.8 m/s^2$.

Some forward-thinking individual has included constants for all the planets (including Pluto), the Moon, the Sun, the Death Star, and The Island.

So if your device ever ends up in any of those places, then you're covered.

Lights, Camera, Action

Almost every Android device will support a camera (many have more than one), and there is ample support for recording photos and videos.

If you look at BA3TPCamera, you'll see a few different ways of using the camera.

First, and by far the simplest, is Listing 3-9.

Listing 3-9. Using an Intent to Access the Camera

```
public void onButtonClick(View v) {
  Intent intent = new Intent(MediaStore.ACTION_IMAGE_CAPTURE);
  try {
    intent.putExtra(MediaStore.EXTRA_OUTPUT,↩
Uri.parse("file:///sdcard/Download/ba3tpCamera.jpg"));
    startActivity(intent);
  } catch (Exception e) {
    display(e);
  }
}
```

Dead easy. Build an Intent, call it. Job done.

▓ **Note** In Listing 3-9, I refer to /sdard/Download. This is the usual location for downloaded data, and as such a fairly safe place to play in. On some devices, this will be /sdcard/download (note case). Since by convention the SD-card device is formatted as FAT32, and FAT32 is case-insensitive for file names, this should not matter. Oh, and the /sdcard is the default external storage device on an Android, typically a micro-SD card. You will sometimes see this referred to as /mnt/sdcard—don't worry, one is a shortcut to the other.

MediaStore will do an awful lot of the work for you. For example, let's try a very simple video capture (Listing 3-10).

Listing 3-10. Using MediaStore to Capture Video

```
public void onVideoClick(View v) {
  Intent intent = new Intent(MediaStore.ACTION_VIDEO_CAPTURE);
  try {
    intent.putExtra(MediaStore.EXTRA_DURATION_LIMIT,10); // Limit to 10 seconds
    startActivityForResult(intent,99);
  } catch (Exception e) {
    display(e);
  }
}

public void onPlayClick(View v) {
  if (mVideo==null) display("Nothing recorded.");
```

```
    else {
       Intent intent = new Intent(Intent.ACTION_VIEW);
       intent.setData(mVideo);
       startActivity(intent);
    }
}

@Override
public void onActivityResult(int requestCode, int resultCode, Intent data) {
   if (requestCode==99) {
      display(data.getData());
      mVideo = data.getData();
   }
}
```

This shows us a new behavior: startActivityForResult. This is a very neat way of various apps talking to each other.

startActivityForResult can be tagged with an identifier (the requestCode). When the called Activity finishes, it calls onActivityResult.

An Intent is returned, usually containing some useful data. In the case of MediaStore.ACTION_VIDEO_CAPTURE, this returns the location of the stored file in the data element. I'm leveraging off this to store the position of the saved video in mVideo, which I can then play using Intent.ACTION_VIEW.

▪ **Note** MediaStore.ACTION_VIDEO_CAPTURE supposedly supports MediaStore.EXTRA_OUTPUT and MediaStore.EXTRA_DURATION_LIMIT. However, the first time I tried this on a real device, it totally ignored the duration limit, and failed to save the file where I expected. So I suspect this is for future expansion, and should not be relied upon.

These are the quick and easy approaches. There are other ways of managing video and image capture, which offer much finer control, but they're a lot more involved. I'll address these in later chapters.

Browsing for Fun and Profit

As might be expected, Android devices come with a powerful browser—actually, several, depending on model and manufacturer. There are a number of ways of browsing the Web—the simplest is with Intents again (Listing 3-11).

Listing 3-11. Browsing with Intent

```
Intent intent = new Intent(Intent.ACTION_VIEW,Uri.parse("http://www.google.com"));
startActivity(intent);
```

Pretty simple. But let's say we want more fine control. Android offers a handy control called WebView (Listing 3-12).

Listing 3-12. Using a WebView Control

```
public void onWebViewClick(View v) {
  WebView webview = new WebView(this);
  setContentView(webview);
  webview.loadUrl("http://www.google.com");
}
```

Again, pretty simple. Create a WebView, set the screen to display that WebView, and then load a URL.

In this mode, it really doesn't offer that much advantage over our first approach with the Intent. But WebView offers quite a bit of control, should you want it. I've put an example together in BA3TPBrowser. Have a look at Listing 3-13.

Listing 3-13. Different Ways to Load a WebView

```
WebView getWebView() {
    if (mWebView==null) mWebView=new WebView(this);
    return mWebView;
}

public void onWebViewClick(View v) {
  mWebView = getWebView();
  setContentView(mWebView);
  mWebView.loadUrl("http://www.google.com");
}

public void onHtmlClick(View v) {
  mWebView = getWebView();
  setContentView(mWebView);
  mWebView.loadData("<html><head><title>Test</title></head><body>Hi there!</body>", ↵
"text/html", "utf-8");
}

@Override
public void onBackPressed() {
  if (mWebView!=null) {
    setContentView(R.layout.main);
    mWebView=null;
  }
  else super.onBackPressed();
}
```

There are a couple of things worth noting here. In Listing 3-12, there is no provision for ever changing back to your first screen. onBackPressed intercepts the back button, which lets me switch the view back to main if needed.

Oh, and if you look in AndroidManifest.xml, you'll see I've included a permission:

```
<uses-permission android:name="android.permission.INTERNET"></uses-permission>
```

Without this line, Android will refuse permission to your WebView to access the Internet, so your web pages won't go very far.

Because I'll be calling it multiple times, I've set up a getWebView() method, which will create mWebView if needed.

onHtmlClick demonstrates loading html data directly, as a string, using WebView.loadData. Handy as that may be, encoding HTML pages by hand and embedding them in code is not the easiest way to go about this sort of thing.

So I'll take a slight detour and talk about assets.

Managing Your Assets

Assets can be any file, of any type. You simply place them in the assets folder of your project, and they are included in your application package (APK) when you compile your program. These files (which have been compressed along with everything else in your APK file) can then be accessed as files from within your code.

You access these files using the AssetManager class, and you get hold of your AssetManager object by calling the Activity's getAssets() method—like Listing 3-14.

Listing 3-14. Loading an Asset File

```
boolean loadFromAsset(String assetName) {
  AssetManager am = getAssets();
  try {
    InputStream is = am.open("test.html");
    try {
      BufferedReader ir = new BufferedReader(new InputStreamReader(is));
      StringBuilder b = new StringBuilder();
      String s;
      while ((s = ir.readLine()) != null) {
        b.append(s + "\n");
      }
      getWebView();
      mWebView.loadData(b.toString(), "text/html", "utf-8");
    } finally {
      is.close();
    }
    return true;
  } catch (Exception e) {
    display(e);
    return false;
  }
}

public void onAssetClick(View v) {
  if (loadFromAsset("test.html")) {
    setContentView(mWebView);
  }
}
```

I'm using the BufferedReader and StringBuilder classes we discussed last chapter, and reading my source file a line at a time. This is not guaranteed to be the fastest way of doing things, but I wanted to keep it simple. Once loaded into a string, it's an easy task to load it into our WebView using load data.

Now, let's have a look at test.html (Listing 3-15).

Listing 3-15. A Sample Web Page, with JavaScript

```html
<html>
  <head>
    <title>This is a test page</title>
    <script language="javascript">
      function testme(msg) {
        document.getElementById("myId").innerHTML=msg;
      }
    </script>
  </head>
  <body>
    <h1>Test of Asset Loading</h1>
    <p>This should have been loaded from an asset file.</p>
    <p><button type="button" onClick="androidTest.showToast('Toast
Message');">Toast</button></p>
    <p>Set value by id=<b><span id="myId">Data goes here</span></b></p>
    <p><a href="http://www.google.com">Google</a></p>
  </body>
</html>
```

Note the button and the Setvalue line, and chunks of JavaScript. As it stands, these don't do an awful lot.

Getting Fancy

But WebView is a pretty versatile beasty. I'm going to just quickly demonstrate a few tricks, as shown in Listing 3-16.

Listing 3-16. A Few Tricks with WebView

```java
  public void onFancyClick(View v) {
    getWebView(); // Make sure mWebView is initialised.
    mWebView.getSettings().setJavaScriptEnabled(true); // Allow javascript to run
    mWebView.addJavascriptInterface(new AndroidTest(this), "androidTest");
    mWebView.setWebViewClient(new MyClient());
    if (loadFromAsset("test.html")) {
      setContentView(mWebView);
    }
  }


  // This is an example class that can be accessed from within javascript on our web page.
  class AndroidTest {
    final public Context mContext;
```

```
    AndroidTest(Context context) {
      mContext=context;
    }

    public void showToast(String message) {
      Toast.makeText(mContext, message, Toast.LENGTH_SHORT).show();
      mWebView.loadUrl("javascript:testme('"+message+"')"); // Just here to show other ways↵
to access page.
    }
  }

  // And this is an example class that can be used to change behavior of your webview
  class MyClient extends WebViewClient {

    @Override
    public void onPageFinished(WebView view, String url) {
      Log.v("ba3tp","Page loaded."); //Writing your own entry into LogCat
      // This is how you can run javascript on your page.
      view.loadUrl("javascript:document.getElementById('myId').innerHTML='Loaded.';");
      super.onPageFinished(view, url);
    }

    @Override
    public boolean shouldOverrideUrlLoading(WebView view, String url) {
      return true; // This will force the webview to load all urls internally rather↵
than flicking them to the browser.
    }

  }
```

If you look at Listing 3-16, you'll see I've been pretty busy. I've added a "Fancy" button, to show some of the fancier things you can do with WebView.

The first thing we do is tell our WebView component to allow JavaScript.

```
mWebView.getSettings().setJavaScriptEnabled(true); // Allow javascript to run
```

There are quite a few settings you can play with in getSettings(). Then, I set up my own WebViewClient to override some of the default behavior.

```
mWebView.setWebViewClient(new MyClient());
```

One of the neatest things WebView does is allow you to give the JavaScript on your page access to a Java object in your application:

```
mWebView.addJavascriptInterface(new AndroidTest(this), "androidTest");
```

Then we just load our web page as before. Except this time, stuff happens.

You'll note that I've declared a few new classes. In this case, I've declared them as internal classes to the MainActivity, but that's as much about wanting to keep things compact as anything else. Classes could be declared in their own files, or you could declare an anonymous class.

AndroidTest declares a single method, showToast. This (self-evidently) shows a Toast message. Note that in the constructor, I've passed the parent's Context. This is because Toast needs a Context to run, and AndroidTest does not have one of its own.

By adding an instance of this class in addJavaScriptInterface, the JavaScript on my page can then call androidTest.showToast() and a toast message pops up. "androidTest" is the name that JavaScript will refer to it as. I could have called it anything.

In Listing 3-15, the onClick event on the button does just that—it calls androidTest.showToast().

Now, a WebViewClient is just a bunch of overridable methods.

I've made my own class, MyClient, and overridden two: onPageLoaded and shouldOverrideUrlLoading.

By default, WebView will follow Url links by passing them to the normal browser. You can override this on a case-by-case basis by overriding shouldOverrideUrlLoading. In this case, I've told it I want to keep everything in house, so to speak.

onPageLoaded is called when the current page has finished loading. The only reason I've added it is that I wanted to demonstrate a method of controlling the loaded page.

```
view.loadUrl("javascript:document.getElementById('myId').innerHTML='Loaded.';");
```

The "javascript:" tag can be used to execute JavaScript. In this case, I'm locating the span tagged with "myId", and setting it to "Loaded".

In another example (and purely to show off), I've added similar code into showToast.

Tip To save much typing, Eclipse offers a bunch of useful code building functions. In the case of MyClient, I declared the MyClient class, and right-clicked the new class ➤ Source ➤ Override/Implement Methods. Then I selected the methods I wanted to override and let Eclipse do the rest.

WebView sadly does not offer direct access to the page's DOM (Document Object Model). However, you can do quite a lot with the javascript tag.

My Little Black Book—Managing Contacts

Android is built around portable devices, and being a communication center. Unsurprisingly, it has a lot of built-in support for managing your address book.

Let's look at BA3TPContacts.

Accessing Contacts

The basic query, which gives us a simple list of contact names, can be seen in Listing 3-17.

Listing 3-17. Retrieving a List of Contacts.

```
public void onButtonClick(View v) {
    try {
      ContentResolver cr = getContentResolver();
      Cursor cur = cr.query(ContactsContract.Contacts.CONTENT_URI, null, null,
```

```
        null, null);
      display("Contacts");
      if (cur.getCount() > 0) {
        while (cur.moveToNext()) {
          String id = cur.getString(cur
              .getColumnIndex(ContactsContract.Contacts._ID));
          String name = cur.getString(cur
              .getColumnIndex(ContactsContract.Contacts.DISPLAY_NAME));
          addln(id + " : " + name);
        }
      }
      cur.close();
      addln("Done");
    } catch (Exception e) {
      display(e);
    }
  }
```

This should show a list of people in your contacts database. In fact, what it will probably show first is the following:

```
04-14 22:35:21.961: ERROR/DatabaseUtils(211): java.lang.SecurityException: Permission
Denial: reading com.android.providers.contacts.HtcContactsProvider2 uri
content://com.android.contacts/contacts from pid=21405, uid=10131 requires
android.permission.READ_CONTACTS
```

The import piece of information here is that we need to add android.permission.READ_CONTACTS to our uses-permission list in AndroidManifest.xml.

```
<uses-permission android:name="android.permission.READ_CONTACTS"></uses-permission>
```

Examining the key bits of the code, you'll see the first thing we do is grab a ContentResolver. This handles pretty much anything to do with Android content. This is a powerful class, and content can come from a wide variety of sources. You can even write your own content provider. But for the moment we'll be using it just for contacts.

```
ContentResolver cr = getContentResolver();
```

Then, I'm going to perform a very simple query.

```
Cursor cur = cr.query(ContactsContract.Contacts.CONTENT_URI, null, null, null, null);
```

I'm just asking for a list of all the contacts the phone has. There are a bunch of predefined "Contracts" you can use. See Table 3-2 for a short list.

Table 3-2. *Various Types of Contact Information*

ContactsContract.Data	Any kind of personal data
ContactsContract.RawContacts	A set of data describing a person and associated with a single account
ContactsContract.Contacts	An aggregate of one or more RawContacts presumably describing the same person
ContactsContract.Groups	Contains information about raw contact groups such as Gmail contact groups
ContactsContract.StatusUpdates	Contains social status updates including IM availability
ContactsContract.AggregationExceptions	Used for manual aggregation and disaggregation of raw contacts
ContactsContract.Settings	Contains visibility and sync settings for accounts and groups
ContactsContract.SyncState	Used for quick caller-ID lookup

A cursor is a way of handling query results, and its use should be familiar to anyone who has done any sort of SQL. In fact, the query() call is extremely SQL-like, as you'll see once I start explaining what all the other parameters do.

For the moment, I'm just checking to see that the query returned any rows, and then looping through those rows with moveToNext(). Listing 3-18 is the core of the piece.

Listing 3-18. *Extracting Fields from a Query*

```
String id = cur.getString(cur
    .getColumnIndex(ContactsContract.Contacts._ID));
String name = cur.getString(cur
    .getColumnIndex(ContactsContract.Contacts.DISPLAY_NAME));
addln(id + " : " + name);
```

The cursor contains a bunch of fields, or columns. You can retrieve the data in those fields in a number of ways. What I'm doing is looking up the column number of the _ID field and the DISPLAY_NAME field, both of which are predefined. I'm then getting that data as a String via the getString() method.

addln is a handy helper utility that adds a line to the current display.

One thing that became immediately clear when I ran this program on my Android was that I had way too many contacts to fit on my screen. As a quick fix, I dropped a ScrollView onto my form, and moved the display TextView onto that—which solved the problem, but pointed out the need for something a bit nicer.

A Quick Side Trip into Lists

I'm going to give a quick side trip into the displaying of lists. One of the standard controls available to Android is the ListView. It's powerful and reasonably neat, but it's not immediately clear how to use it.

Your basic ListView is just a placeholder on the screen. To do anything useful, it has to be linked up to a ListAdapter, which tells it what to display and how to display it.

I've created two new layouts (Listing 3-19 and 3-20).

Listing 3-19. A Basic ListView

```
mylistview.xml:
<?xml version="1.0" encoding="utf-8"?>
<ListView
  xmlns:android="http://schemas.android.com/apk/res/android"
  android:layout_width="match_parent"
  android:layout_height="match_parent" android:id="@+id/listview1">
</ListView>
```

Listing 3-20. What Goes in the ListView

```
mytextview.xml:
<?xml version="1.0" encoding="utf-8"?>
<TextView
  xmlns:android="http://schemas.android.com/apk/res/android"
  android:layout_width="match_parent"
  android:layout_height="match_parent" android:text="Sample Text" android:textColor="#0f0"↵
 android:textStyle="italic">
</TextView>
```

mylistview is a layout that consists purely of a ListView. I could put other stuff around it, but I want to keep it simple.

mytextview is a layout that consists purely of a TextView. This is a layout that will go inside each cell of the list. Again, it's pretty simple. You could build quite an elaborate layout if you liked, but for the moment, a plain TextView will do. I did play around a bit with the colors and the font, just because I could.

I'm going to be using ArrayAdapter, probably the easiest of the ListAdapters to use. You pass it a list and a TextView layout, and it will do the rest.

Listing 3-21 shows the code that displays everything in a list.

Listing 3-21. Populating the ListView with Contacts

```
public void onListClick(View v) {
  List<String> mylist = new ArrayList<String>();
  try {
    ContentResolver cr = getContentResolver();
    String[] fields = {Contacts._ID,Contacts.DISPLAY_NAME};
    // This time I'm telling it which fields to display, and in what order.
    Cursor cur = cr.query(Contacts.CONTENT_URI,fields, null, null, Contacts.DISPLAY_NAME);
    if (cur.getCount() > 0) {
      while (cur.moveToNext()) {
        mylist.add(getCurString(cur,Contacts._ID)+" :↵
```

```
                     "+getCurString(cur,Contacts.DISPLAY_NAME));
        }
      }
      cur.close();
      showList(mylist);
    } catch (Exception e) {
      display(e);
    }
  }

  String getCurString(Cursor cur,String name) {
    return cur.getString(cur.getColumnIndex(name));
  }

  @Override
  public void onBackPressed() {
    if (mBack) {
      setContentView(R.layout.main);
      mBack=false;
      mDisplay=(TextView) findViewById(R.id.eDisplay);
    }
    else {
      super.onBackPressed();
    }
  }

  public void showList(List<String> mylist) {
    setContentView(R.layout.mylistview);
    ArrayAdapter<String> a = new ArrayAdapter<String>(this,R.layout.mytextview,mylist);
    ListView v = (ListView) findViewById(R.id.listview1);
    v.setAdapter(a);
    mBack=true;
  }
```

Looking at showList, I'm setting the content view to be my ListView. It's important to do that first, because until then, the ListView object doesn't actually exist. There are other ways of doing this, but we're still sticking with the KISS[1] principle here.

I then build an ArrayAdapter. This will link a previously generated list and show the result in a TextView layout (ArrayAdapter will work only with TextViews).

We then assign our new adapter to our ListView using setAdapter(), and we're home and hosed.

mBack is a Boolean member I've declared, because I want to be able to go back to my main screen. I've intercepted the back button in onBackPressed, and I switch the view back to the main screen if I think it's warranted. Note too that I'm resetting mDisplay in the onBackPressed method. In moving to a new view and back again, Android has created a brand new object. If I don't find it again, my display functions will stop working.

This is not the neatest way of handling this issue, but it will do for the moment.

onListClick bears a look, too. As well as changing the code to build a list rather than display straight to the screen, I've taken the opportunity to streamline the query a bit.

---

[1] Keep It Simple, Stupid.

query is, as mentioned before, very SQL-like. As well as being able to define the source of the data, `Contacts.CONTENT_URI`, we can also give it a list of what fields we want to display, selection criteria on what rows to select, and we can even tell it in what order to return the rows.

Instead of returning all the columns available, I've asked it to return only `DISPLAY_NAME` and ID, since that's all we're using. You should notice that `List` is a lot quicker than our original query. I've also told it to return the rows sorted by the display name.

`getCurString` is a little utility method that will return a column by name as a string.

Different Things to Access

As implied earlier, there are quite a few different ways of accessing information from a Contacts query. Let's try some more examples. See Listing 3-22.

Listing 3-22. Some Different Queries You Can Make

```
// Show only those that have phones
  public void onHasPhoneClick(View v) {
    ContentResolver cr = getContentResolver();
    String[] fields = {Contacts._ID,Contacts.DISPLAY_NAME};
    Cursor cur = cr.query(Contacts.CONTENT_URI,fields,↵
Contacts.HAS_PHONE_NUMBER+"=1",null,Contacts.DISPLAY_NAME);
    showQuery(cur);
  }

  // Show names and primary phone numbers
  public void onPhoneClick(View v) {
    ContentResolver cr = getContentResolver();
    String[] fields = {Phone.DISPLAY_NAME, Phone.NUMBER};
    Cursor cur = cr.query(Phone.CONTENT_URI, fields,↵
Phone.IS_PRIMARY+">0",null,Phone.DISPLAY_NAME);
    showQuery(cur);
  }
```

Listing 3-22 demonstrates a few other methods of accessing Contacts. `onHasPhoneClick` will list only Contacts who have a phone number.

```
cr.query(Contacts.CONTENT_URI,fields,Contacts.HAS_PHONE_NUMBER+"=1",null,↵
Contacts.DISPLAY_NAME);
```

The third argument is our selection criteria. In this case, it will return only rows where the `HAS_PHONE_NUMBER` field equals 1.

The mysterious fourth argument allows you to supply a list of parameters to feed into your select statement, should you ever desire. The fifth argument defines the sort order.

And, since simply knowing who has a phone number is not terribly useful, this is how to show a list of phone numbers:

```
    Cursor cur = cr.query(Phone.CONTENT_URI, fields, Phone.IS_PRIMARY+">0",↵
null,Phone.DISPLAY_NAME);
```

Note that I'm using Phone, not Contacts, and filtering to show only that contact's primary phone number.

We'll get back to more advanced uses of the Content Resolver in its own chapter, Chapter 7.

Share My Stuff (Sending and Receiving, Well, Everything)

Sometimes you want to send files or other data about the place. Sometimes to a different app to play with, sometimes you just want to post some text to yourself without having to type it out all over again.

Sometimes—as a completely random example—you're writing a book on programming in Android and you want to be able to send the samples from your Android to your desktop computer.

Fortunately, Android makes this easy. If you go all the way back to the beginning of this chapter, in BA3TPSensor1 (from the downloads), and go look at the code, you'll see I've snuck in some bonus useful behavior, a la Listing 3-23.

Listing 3-23. Sharing Stuff

```
public void doShare() {
  Intent intent = new Intent(Intent.ACTION_SEND);
  intent.putExtra(Intent.EXTRA_TEXT, mDisplay.getText());
  intent.putExtra(Intent.EXTRA_SUBJECT, "Sensor Dump");
  intent.setType("text/plain");
  startActivity(Intent.createChooser(intent, "Send Sensor info to:"));
}
```

Once more we circle back around to the Intent, and once more we can see it doing something useful.

In this case, I'm using the ACTION_SEND action. I tell it that what I am sending is "text/plain," sticking the value of my display textView in EXTRA_TEXT, and adding a subject line in EXTRA_SUBJECT.

And then I call Intent.createChooser, which pops up a nice little list of apps that can do something with this information. On my phone, this list contains my e-mail program, a text editor I've loaded, Facebook, Bluetooth, and SMS messages, to name only a few.

This createChooser method returns an explicit Intent, and startActivity will take it from there.

Bonus Stuff—Menu Options

While we're here, I'll show you how to add an options menu. I decided to use menus since I was running out of space for buttons.

This is the menu that will show up if you hit the Menu key on a normal Android device. It will also show in the ActionBar on an Android 3.0 (or above) device. They're easy to implement. See Listing 3-24.

Listing 3-24. Building an Options Menu

```
private static enum MenuId {
    SHARE,MAIL;
    public int getId() {
      return ordinal() + Menu.FIRST;
    }
  }
@Override
  public boolean onCreateOptionsMenu(Menu menu) {
```

```
    menu.add(Menu.NONE, MenuId.SHARE.getId(), Menu.NONE, "Share").setIcon(
        android.R.drawable.ic_menu_share);
    menu.add(Menu.NONE, MenuId.MAIL.getId(), Menu.NONE, "Mail").setIcon(
        android.R.drawable.ic_menu_send);
    return super.onCreateOptionsMenu(menu);
  }

  @Override
  public boolean onOptionsItemSelected(MenuItem item) {
    int itemId = item.getItemId();
    if (itemId==MenuId.SHARE.getId()) {
      doShare();
    } else if (itemId==MenuId.MAIL.getId()) {
      doMail();
    }

    return super.onOptionsItemSelected(item);
  }
```

First things first: enum. This structure is not absolutely necessary. You can identify your menu items with just numbers, as long as they are >= Menu.FIRST. enum is a Java structure that allows you to easily define unique values.

Being Java, you can also define a method that will convert these back to a number. MenuId uniquely defines two values, SHARE and MAIL. onCreateOptionsMenu allows you to add your own menu items into the options menu.

```
    menu.add(Menu.NONE, MenuId.SHARE.getId(), Menu.NONE,↵
  "Share").setIcon(android.R.drawable.ic_menu_share);
```

This is adding the SHARE menu item, giving it a title of "Share". We are also taking the opportunity to set a standard icon. This is optional, but pretty.

Then later, onOptionsItemSelected catches that a menu item has been selected, and processes it accordingly.

If you want your options menu to be more dynamic, you can also add a onPrepareOptionsMenu event, which is called immediately prior to the menu being shown each time the menu button is hit, but we don't need that now.

Sending E-mail

While we're here, and sharing our text about, it would be nice to be able to send an e-mail. See Listing 3-25.

Listing 3-25. Sending an E-mail, with Intent

```
  public void doMail() {
    Intent intent = new Intent(Intent.ACTION_SENDTO);
    intent.putExtra(Intent.EXTRA_TEXT, mDisplay.getText());
    intent.putExtra(Intent.EXTRA_SUBJECT, "Sensor Email");
    intent.setData(Uri.parse("mailto:sales@apress.com"));
    try {
      startActivity(intent);
```

```
  } catch (Exception e) {
    mDisplay.setText(e.toString());
  }
}
```

A slight variant on the theme, doMail uses ACTION_SENDTO to give finer control than ACTION_SEND. In this case, I'm explicitly sending my text to an e-mail program. I'm also *not* wrapping the startActivity in a chooser.

The chooser will still appear if you have more than one e-mail program, but you can tell Android to remember which program to use and then you won't be asked again.

Sound and Fury (Managing Media Files)

Not surprisingly, Android has strong support for playing media files of many different types. In BA3TPMedia1, I've put together a very simple media player. Have a look at Listing 3-26.

Listing 3-26. Playing a Media File

```
public void onButtonClick(View v) {
  try {
    File media = new File("/sdcard/MP3/canon1.mp3");
    Intent intent=new Intent(Intent.ACTION_VIEW);
    intent.setDataAndType(Uri.fromFile(media),"audio/mpeg");
    startActivity(intent);
  } catch (Exception e) {
    display(e);
  }
}
```

Now, as written, this will work only if you happen to have an MP3 file installed at /sdcard/MP3/canon1.mp3. You may wish to change it to something you do have. Once again, we're using Intents.

There is a simple and powerful class called MediaPlayer that gives you a great deal of control over your media files, but since I have a whole chapter devoted to that (Chapter 5), I think I'll cover that there.

JAVA NOTES

The File class is used all over the place in Java. File is used to specify file names in a system-independent fashion. It copes with whether your OS is using "\" or "/" to separate file names, and has methods to get information on a file such as its existence, size, and last modified date.

It also has methods to manage directories, including making them and removing them, and can be used to rename or delete a file.

The one file-related thing it won't do is read or write to a file. Having said that, most things that do manipulate file contents (i.e., FileInputStream) will take a File as a constructor argument.

Summary

We've covered a lot of ground in this chapter. You should now have a reasonable grasp of some of the many things your Android can do, and how to manipulate them. If you're still reeling from this data dump, don't panic. I'll be covering most of these sections in more depth when we get to the specific example projects.

If this chapter shows us anything, it's that we can do an awful lot with Intents, even before we get to use the classes that will give us fine control.

In passing, I've attempted to show some of the many ways to construct and manipulate an Android app. What I really haven't done yet is get into some of the more specific tablet APIs, mostly because I've been focusing on basic Android behavior. I will get to them very soon now, I promise.

CHAPTER 4

Beyond Java: Programming in Python and Friends

While Java is undoubtedly the major programming language for Android devices, it is a long way from the only method available.

Figure 4-1. Some people are naturally multi-lingual.

Scripting Layer for Android (SL4A) is an open source project that allows programmers to write applications not only for Android devices, but also *on* Android devices.

SL4A is a common framework that permits programming in any of a host of scripting languages: Python, JavaScript, Beanshell, LUA, TCL, PHP, Ruby, and Perl are all supported, with options for porting more.

All of these languages use a common API, so for the most part it is a matter of picking your favorite language and going for it.

The thing that first attracted me to SL4A is the fact that you can actually develop on the phone itself. It has a simple text editor, and allows you to manage, edit, and run your scripts either with a terminal display or without. It also supports a simple Linux shell, and you can get into the command line environment of all the interpreters.

Without doubt the most popular of the supported scripting languages is Python, so I'll concentrate on that.

Why Use Another Language?

But the Android SDK is mainly programmed in Java. Why would we use anything else?

Well, Java at this stage requires a host computer to do all your compiling and editing, for a start. Java itself can be a bit daunting to learn, and there tends to be a moderate amount of setup for each program you wish to write.

Or you might just like Python (or PHP or JavaScript or Ruby or whatever), or you may wish to take advantage of some of the many third-party libraries written in these languages.

■ **Note** I'm not going to attempt to teach you Python, just how to use it on an Android. If you want to learn Python, check out python.org, or get one of Apress's fine books on the subject.[1]

Getting Started

Go to the SL4A web site at http://code.google.com/p/android-scripting/, and download the latest version of SL4A. Conveniently, there is a barcode on the front page that you can scan in, and it will start downloading the APK. Remember to allow Unknown Sources in your application settings. Once it has downloaded, install it and run it.

At this point, you've downloaded the framework, but no actual interpreter. Menu ➤ View ➤ Interpreters, Menu ➤ View ➤ Add will get you a list of interpreters to add. I'm going to do all of my examples in Python, so go with that.

Once you've downloaded and installed your Python for Android app, there is still one more step to do, which is to download all the supporting files. This is quite simple, though: just hit the Install button.

Once the three libraries are downloaded, you should be good to go. Open up SL4A, and you should now see a selection of scripts to run.

Script Management

One of the nice things SL4A does for you is include a number of sample scripts to get you started (see Figure 4-2).

---

[1] Such as *Beginning Python: From Novice to Professional*, by Magnus Lie Hetland (Apress, 2008)

Figure 4-2. List of sample programs that come with SL4A and Python

Let's start with the simplest, the ubiquitous hello_world script. Tap the script, and a menu will pop up (Figure 4-3).

Figure 4-3. The SL4A menu

Pick the one that looks like a terminal screen, and you should see it print the words "Hello world" on the screen, and also pop up a little "Hello, Android!" toast box.

Let's have a look at our first script. Tap hello_world.py, and pick the little pencil icon to open up the editor. You should see something like Listing 4-1.

Listing 4-1. Hello World! in Python

```python
import android
droid = android.Android()
droid.makeToast('Hello, Android!')
print 'Hello world!'
```

As you can see, this is pretty short and sweet—much less typing than getting even a simple Java Activity up and running. And this script is about three more lines than it has to be. We could have stopped at print "Hello World"!

Whichever language you choose, an SL4A script will start with the equivalent of import android and droid=android.Android(). This loads in the library for accessing the Android-specific functions, and initializes the same. As a convenience, when you create a new script, these lines will be automatically added for you, so there is even less typing.

By convention, the initialized Android object is called droid. You can call it what you like, but it's probably a good idea to keep things consistent.

It's worth noting that you have full access to all the normal file and HTTP handling you would normally have with Python. The methods in droid are specifically for taking advantage of Android functionality.

Help! I Need Somebody

. . . was a very fine song by the Beatles. More to the point, one of the nice things SL4A has is a fair to middling help system.

In your editor, you can access the API browser (Menu ➤ Api Browser). This gives a comprehensive list of every Droid API function you can access. You can tap an item to bring up the parameters and some more detail. If you long-press the item, you'll be offered the choice of Insert, Prompt, and Help.

Help will bring up more detailed help, often with an overview of how to use this group of functions, and sometimes example code. Insert will put the function into your code (saving much typing). Prompt will allow you to fill in all the parameters, and then put the function into code.

Python Help

If you are familiar with the Python help system, you can go into the Python Shell (Menu ➤ View ➤ Interpreters ➤ Python) and use that. Or you can get a bit fancy—and this is a fine and dandy excuse for our first brand new Python script.

In the scripts list, Menu ➤ Add ➤ Python.

In the top box, type **helpserv.py**.

In the bottom box, you'll see that the import and droid lines have already been added. These aren't actually needed, as we'll be using plain Python capabilities, but they do no harm. The full code is in Listing 4-2.

Listing 4-2. *Starting the Python Help Server*

```
import pydoc
pydoc.serve(4321)
```

Menu ➤ Save and Exit.

Now find helpserv.py in the scripts list, tap it, and hit the cogwheel to run your script in background. Hit the HOME button, fire up your browser, and enter http://localhost:4321. If all is going well, you should now be hooked into the Python HTML help screen.

Two lines of code! Awesome!

4321 is the port that the pydoc server is listening on; you can pick any unused port that takes your fancy. Once you're done playing, go back to the home screen. You should see the little SL4A icon in the notification screen. If you bring that up, it will show a list of the scripts running in background, including your helpserv.py. Tap it to bring it to the foreground, and then hitting the BACK button should offer to kill it for you.

What's a Facade?

You may notice that the help screens are organized into Facades. Each Facade is actually a module in SL4A that handles related API functions. Part of the reason for this arrangement is that SL4A will run on a wide variety of phones as well as tablets. Varying versions of Android support different capabilities (such as Bluetooth), or sometimes radically changed interfaces between two different versions (such as Text-To-Speech). SL4A will look at the environment it is running in, and load the appropriate set of Facades.

Honeycomb being the latest and greatest, you'll have access to all the available Facades. At the time of writing, there is no particular support for Honeycomb-specific capabilities, but SL4A is being actively developed, so I'm quite confident there will be by the time you are reading this book.

Intents (Again)

As might be expected, SL4A has good support for Intents, with both AndroidFacade and CommonIntentsFacade. Listing 4-3 shows a remarkably simple yet breathtakingly useful script.

Listing 4-3. Scan the Barcode of a Book and Find It on Google

```
import android
droid = android.Android()
code=droid.scanBarcode()
isbn= int(code.result['extras']['SCAN_RESULT'])
url="http://books.google.com?q=%d" % isbn
droid.startActivity('android.intent.action.VIEW', url)
```

This will scan the barcode of a book (using scanBarcode, which is part of CommonIntentsFacade), store the result in ISBN, construct a URL for Google Books with the ISBN, and then bring up details of that book (using startActivity).

AndroidFacade contains a bunch of general-purpose methods, including most of the routines for accessing Intents.

Something worth noting is that in calling startActivity to view the URL, we aren't using Intent.ACTION_VIEW, as we would in Java. This is because ACTION_VIEW is a constant (final static). startActivity needs to know the *value* of this constant, which we can find out by looking up http://developer.android.com/reference/android/content/Intent.html#ACTION_VIEW. From this, we can find out the value of ACTION_VIEW is, in fact, android.intent.action.VIEW.

It is a common mistake to try to call droid.startActivity('Intent.ACTION_VIEW',url). Be warned.

Sometimes you may need to know what the value of a constant is without going and looking it up on the net. Sometimes because it is not readily apparent from the documentation what the value actually is, sometimes because it may change between versions of Android.

There is a handy function to find out what constants are available, as shown in Listing 4-4.

Listing 4-4. Retrieve a List of Available Intent Constants

```
import android
droid = android.Android()
myconst = droid.getConstants("android.content.Intent").result
for c in myconst:
        print c,"=",myconst[c]
```

Listing 4-4 demonstrates getConstants. This will query a Java class and return a map of all the static final fields defined. Please note the indenting on the print line. Indenting is actually part of the Python language, and is used instead of begin/end or braces {} to indicate blocks.

▓ **Note** The actual name of the Python class that allows you to store and access objects via a key is a `dict` (short for dictionary). As everywhere else in this book we refer to these as `map`s, I'll continue to do so (unless the difference is important). Besides, `dict` makes me snigger.

Note that you need to use the fully qualified name of the class, in this case `Intent`. More usefully, you could get the value of `ACTION_VIEW` like so:

```
view=myconst["ACTION_VIEW"]
```

While we're on that subject, it is sometimes desirable to know exactly which version of Android you are running on. Listing 4-5 demonstrates this.

Listing 4-5. Find Out Which Version of Android We Are Running

```
import android

droid = android.Android()
version=droid.getConstants("android.os.Build$VERSION").result
print version["SDK_INT"]
```

This gets a map of constants from `android.os.Build.VERSION` and looks up `SDK_INT`.

The "$" notation is used for version because it is an *internal* class. You can get more detail by looking at this link: `http://developer.android.com/reference/android/os/Build.VERSION.html`. The fact that the documentation refers to `Build.VERSION` rather than just `VERSION` is a giveaway that this is a class defined inside `Build`, and thus uses the "$" notation.

Different Ways of Using the Intent Methods

As shown in Chapter 2, you can do quite a lot with `Intent`s, but they can be complicated little things. Listing 4-6 shows the full list of arguments for `startActivity`.

Listing 4-6. All the Arguments for `startActivity`

```
action (String)
uri (String) (optional)
type (String) MIME type/subtype of the URI (optional)
extras (JSONObject) a Map of extras to add to the Intent (optional)
wait (Boolean) block until the user exits the started activity (optional)
packagename (String) name of package. If used, requires classname to be useful (optional)
classname (String) name of class. If used, requires packagename to be useful (optional)
packagename and classname, if provided, are used in a 'setComponent' call.
```

This is a bit of a handful. Most of the arguments are optional. Much of the time you need to specify only the action and the URL, but things can start getting complex quickly. Also, there's no way to specify categories, for example.

As a possibly more convenient option, you can choose to build an `Intent` out of a Python map. There's a list of the `Intent` methods in Table 4-1.

Table 4-1. Intent-Related Functions in the SL4A API

Method	Description
getIntent	Get the Intent this Activity was called with
makeIntent	Build an Intent for later use
sendBroadcast	Send a Broadcast
sendBroadcastIntent	Send a Broadcast using a previously built Intent
startActivity	Start an Activity
startActivityIntent	Start an Activity using a previously built Intent
startActivityForResult	Start an Activity and return the result
startActivityForResultIntent	Start an Activity and return the result using a previously built Intent

makeIntent is a convenience method that will build an Intent for you (see Listing 4-7).

Listing 4-7. Parameters for makeIntent

action (String)
uri (String) (optional)
type (String) MIME type/subtype of the URI (optional)
extras (JSONObject) a Map of extras to add to the Intent (optional)
categories (JSONArray) a List of categories to add to the Intent (optional)
packagename (String) name of package. If used, requires classname to be useful (optional)
classname (String) name of class. If used, requires packagename to be useful (optional)
flags (Integer) Intent flags (optional)

This will return a Python map object, which you can manipulate as you like, and then call one of the Intent methods, as show in Listing 4-8.

Listing 4-8. Return a List of Recently Made Calls

```
import android
droid = android.Android()
myconst = droid.getConstants("android.content.Intent").result
action = myconst["ACTION_VIEW"]
uri = "content://android.provider.Contacts.People.CONTENT_URI"
itype = "vnd.android.cursor.dir/calls"
intent = droid.makeIntent(action,uri,itype).result
print intent
droid.startActivityIntent(intent)
```

Listing 4-8 demonstrates a simple script to display a list of recently made calls (assuming your tablet has a phone capability).

makeIntent (and for that matter, getIntent) will return something that looks like Listing 4-9 when printed.

Listing 4-9. What an Intent Map Looks Like in Python

```
{u'type': u'vnd.android.cursor.dir/calls',
u'extras': None,
u'flags': 268435456,
u'action': u'android.intent.action.VIEW',
 u'data': u'content://android.provider.Contacts.People.CONTENT_URI',
u'categories': None}
```

There is nothing to stop you modifying this object in Python, or indeed, building it from scratch.

■ **Note** You may realize that the notation that Python uses to display these objects is very similar to JavaScript or JSON. This may prove useful at some point.

For example, you could get an identical result with the code in Listing 4-10.

Listing 4-10. Building an Intent from Scratch

```
intent=dict()
intent['action']='android.intent.action.VIEW'
intent['data']='content://android.provider.Contacts.People.CONTENT_URI'
intent['type']='vnd.android.cursor.dir/calls'
intent['flags']=0x10000000
```

A note about the flags field: Starting an Intent this way requires Intent.FLAG_ACTIVITY_NEW_TASK to be set, which is defined as 0x10000000 (decimal 268435456). makeIntent will set it automatically for you.

User Interaction

As might also be expected, SL4A provides a fair selection of methods to communicate with the user. Most of these can be found in UIFacade. Simplest to use are things like dialogGetInput and dialogGetPassword, as shown in Listing 4-11.

Listing 4-11. Using a Simple Dialog

```
import android

droid = android.Android()
name= droid.dialogGetInput("Sample Input","Your Name").result
print name
```

Thus, Listing 4-11 will produce something like Figure 4-4.

Figure 4-4. What the dialog in Listing 4-11 should look like

You can also produce a variety of customized dialog boxes. See Listing 4-12 for a quick example.

Listing 4-12. More Complex Use of a Dialog

```
import android
droid=android.Android()
droid.dialogCreateAlert("I like swords.","Do you like swords?")
droid.dialogSetPositiveButtonText("Yes")
droid.dialogSetNegativeButtonText("No")
droid.dialogShow()
response=droid.dialogGetResponse().result
droid.dialogDismiss()
if response.has_key("which"):
  result=response["which"]
  if result=="positive":
    print "Yay! I like swords too!"
  elif result=="negative":
    print "Oh. How sad."
elif response.has_key("canceled"):
  print "You can't even make up your mind?"
else:
  print "Unknown response=",response

print "Done"
```

It's a pretty silly bit of code, but it does nicely demonstrate the basics of building your own dialog box.

First, we call `dialogCreateAlert`, to create an alert style dialog box. Then we give it a positive button (labelled "Yes") and a negative button (labelled "No").

Then we show it, and finally we wait for the result with `dialogGetResponse`. This last is important, because otherwise Python will carry on cheerfully in the background.

Sometimes you want to be able to carry on in the background. If that's the case, you can listen for a "dialog" event instead. See the "Events" topic later in this chapter for more detail.

Table 4-2 shows a list of the available dialog types.

Table 4-2. Available Dialog Types

Method	Description
dialogCreateAlert	Create alert dialog
dialogCreateDatePicker	Create date picker dialog
dialogCreateHorizontalProgress	Create horizontal progress dialog
dialogCreateInput	Create text input dialog
dialogCreatePassword	Create password input dialog
dialogCreateSeekBar	Create seek bar dialog
dialogCreateSpinnerProgress	Create spinner progress dialog
dialogCreateTimePicker	Create time picker dialog

Some of these types, particularly the progress types, you never actually need to get a result from. You can get rid of these by calling dialogDismiss, as in Listing 4-13.

Listing 4-13. Display a Progress Bar

```
import android,time
droid=android.Android()
droid.dialogCreateHorizontalProgress("My Progress","Snoozing",10)
droid.dialogShow()
for i in range(10):
  droid.dialogSetCurrentProgress(i)
  time.sleep(1)
droid.dialogDismiss()
```

It should produce something like Figure 4-5.

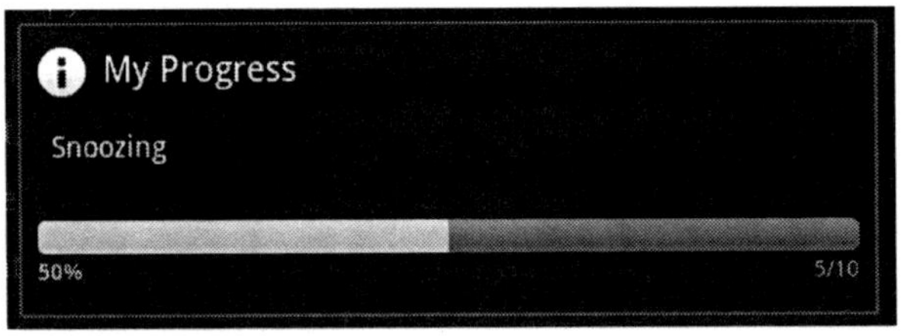

Figure 4-5. What Listing 4-13 should look like

This can be useful if you are performing a time-consuming task.

Events

SL4A handles asynchronous activity by means of an event queue. Most of the routines for handling these events are in EventFacade, as shown in Table 4-3.

Table 4-3. Event Handling Routines

Method	Description
eventClearBuffer	Clears all events from the event buffer
eventPoll	Returns and removes the oldest n events (i.e., location or sensor update, etc.) from the event buffer
eventPost	Posts an event to the event queue
eventWait	Blocks until an event occurs
eventWaitFor	Blocks until an event with the supplied name occurs

Various methods in SL4A will trigger events, or your scripting language can communicate internally using eventPost. Each event has a unique name, such as "dialog," and some data, which will be a map of the event.

An important difference between eventWait (which waits for any event, with an optional timeout) and eventWaitFor (which waits for a specific event, also with an optional timeout) is that eventWait will remove the next event from the queue, whereas eventWaitFor won't.

An example of why you might want to use events is in Listing 4-14.

Listing 4-14. Example of Using Events

```
# Test of Seekbar events.
import android
droid=android.Android()
droid.dialogCreateSeekBar(50,100,"I like swords.","How much you like swords?")
droid.dialogSetPositiveButtonText("Yes")
droid.dialogSetNegativeButtonText("No")
droid.dialogShow()
looping=True
while looping: # Wait for events for up to 10 seconds.from the menu.
  response=droid.eventWait(10000).result
  if response==None: # No events to process. exit.
    break
  if response["name"]=="dialog":
    looping=False # Fall out of loop unless told otherwise.
    data=response["data"]
    if data.has_key("which"):
      which=data["which"]
      if which=="seekbar":
        print "Progress=",data["progress"]," User input=",data["fromuser"]
        looping=True  # Keep Looping
```

```
# Have fallen out of loop. Close the dialog

droid.dialogDismiss()
if response==None:
  print "Timed out."
else:
  rdialog=response["data"] # dialog response is stored in data.
  if  rdialog.has_key("which"):
    result=rdialog["which"]
    if result=="positive":
      print "Yay! I like swords too!"
    elif result=="negative":
      print "Oh. How sad."
  elif rdialog.has_key("canceled"):
    print "You can't even make up your mind?"
  print "You like swords this much: ",rdialog["progress"]

print "Done"
```

It should produce something like Figure 4-6.

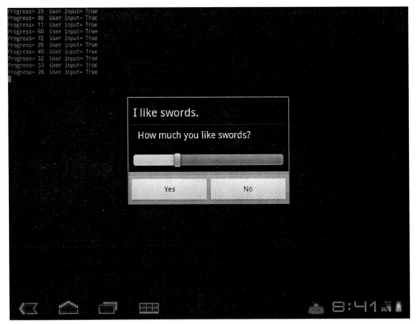

Figure 4-6. What Listing 4-14 should look like

The key here is droid.eventWait(10000). This will wait for an event—any event—for ten seconds. (The wait time is in milliseconds, and defaults to forever.) We then examine the event, looking specifically for "dialog" events. If it's from "seekbar," then we'll display the results and keep looping. Any other dialog event will cause it to drop out.

This is an extremely trivial example, but you could use the same basic structure to implement a volume control for playing a media file, as a random example . . .

Media Files

MediaPlayerFacade and MediaRecorderFacade provide facilities to play and record media files. Listing 4-15 shows a more complex script that demonstrates mediaPlayer, use of UI components, and some pure Python code to implement a simple media player application.

Listing 4-15. Simple MP3 Player Implemented in Python

```python
import android,sys,os
droid=android.Android()

def showdialog():
  volume=droid.getMediaVolume().result
  droid.dialogCreateSeekBar(volume,maxvolume,"Media Play","Volume")
  if droid.mediaIsPlaying("mp3").result:
    caption="Pause"
  else:
    caption="Play"
  droid.dialogSetPositiveButtonText(caption)
  droid.dialogSetNegativeButtonText("Rewind");
  droid.dialogShow()

def eventloop():
  while True:
    event=droid.eventWait().result
    print event
    data=event["data"]
    if event["name"]=="dialog":
      if data.has_key("canceled"):
        break
      which=data["which"]
      if which=="seekbar":
        droid.setMediaVolume(data["progress"])
      elif which=="positive":
        if droid.mediaIsPlaying("mp3").result:
          droid.mediaPlayPause("mp3")
        else:
          droid.mediaPlayStart("mp3")
        showdialog()
      elif which=="negative":
        droid.mediaPlaySeek(0,"mp3")
        showdialog()


def showerror(msg): # Display an error message
  droid.dialogCreateAlert("Error",msg)
  droid.dialogShow()
  droid.dialogGetResponse()
```

```python
def findmp3(): # Search sdcard for an mp3 file.
  mylist=[]
  names=[]
  for root,dirs,files in os.walk("/sdcard"):
    for name in files:
      fname,fext = os.path.splitext(name)
      if fext.lower()==".mp3":
          mylist.append(os.path.join(root,name))
          names.append(fname)
  droid.dialogCreateAlert("MP3 File")
  droid.dialogSetItems(names)
  droid.dialogShow()
  result=droid.dialogGetResponse().result
  droid.eventClearBuffer() # Get rid of unwanted events
  print result
  if not result.has_key("canceled"):
    return mylist[result['item']]
  else:
    return None

maxvolume=droid.getMaxMediaVolume().result
mp3=findmp3()
if mp3==None:
  showerror("No media file chosen")
  sys.exit(0)
if not droid.mediaPlay("file://"+mp3,"mp3",False).result:
  showerror("Can't open mp3 file.")
  sys.exit(0)
showdialog()
eventloop()
droid.mediaPlayClose("mp3")
droid.dialogDismiss()
```

Breaking it down, findmp3 will search your SDCard for any MP3 files, put them into a list, and then display the names in a pop-up list.

When the user picks an item from the list, droid.mediaPlay attempts to open the file. Note that mediaPlay requires a URL, so in theory it should be possible to load a file directly from the Web. The second parameter is a tag, in this case mp3, which I can use to identify which open media file I wish to work with. The last parameter is telling mediaPlay not to start playing immediately.

Then showdialog() builds a simple seekBar dialog, which will look a bit like Figure 4-7.

Figure 4-7. Implementing a simple control dialog

The dialog box has its maximum value set to the return from getMaxMediaVolume, and its current value set to getMediaVolume.

The script then goes into eventLoop, which listens for events coming from the dialog box. When the seek bar gets moved, it adjusts the volume. Play and Pause will switch depending on whether the media file is playing (mediaIsPlaying), and Rewind will go back to the beginning.

Hitting the Back button will throw a dialog event with "canceled" (yes, one "l"—depending on where you are from, this will either be grating or perfectly normal. I did check).

Table 4-4 shows the various methods for playing or recording stuff.

Table 4-4. Media-Related API Functions

Method	Description
mediaIsPlaying	Checks if media file is playing
mediaPlay	Opens a media
mediaPlayClose	Closes media file
mediaPlayInfo	Information on current media
mediaPlayList	Lists currently loaded media
mediaPlayPause	Pauses playing media file
mediaPlaySeek	Seeks to position
mediaPlaySetLooping	Sets looping
mediaPlayStart	Starts playing media file
recorderCaptureVideo	Records video (and optionally audio) from the camera and saves it to the given location
recorderStartMicrophone	Records audio from the microphone and saves it to the given location

Method	Description
recorderStartVideo	Records video from the camera and saves it to the given location; allows specifying video size and format
recorderStop	Stops a previously started recording
startInteractiveVideoRecording	Starts the video capture application to record a video and saves it to the specified path

As you can see, there's quite good support for playing and recording various types of audio and video files, although at present, the mediaPlay functions will play only the audio track of a video file. Still, SL4A is continuously evolving, so there's a good chance video will be supported by the time this book comes out.

Controlling Your Phone

There are a significant number of options to check and control various device settings. Table 4-5 shows a list of these methods.

Table 4-5. Methods to Control Phone Settings

Method	Description
checkAirplaneMode	Checks the airplane mode setting
checkBluetoothState	Checks if Bluetooth is on
checkRingerSilentMode	Checks the ringer silent mode setting
checkScreenOn	Checks if the screen is on or off (requires API level 7)
checkWifiState	Checks Wi-Fi state
getMaxMediaVolume	Returns the maximum media volume
getMaxRingerVolume	Returns the maximum ringer volume
getMediaVolume	Returns the current media volume
getRingerVolume	Returns the current ringer volume
getScreenBrightness	Returns the screen backlight brightness
getScreenTimeout	Returns the current screen timeout in seconds

Method	Description
getVibrateMode	Checks vibration setting
setMediaVolume	Sets the media volume
setRingerVolume	Sets the ringer volume
setScreenBrightness	Sets the screen backlight brightness
setScreenTimeout	Sets the screen timeout to this number of seconds
toggleAirplaneMode	Toggles airplane mode on and off
toggleBluetoothState	Toggles Bluetooth on and off
toggleRingerSilentMode	Toggles ringer silent mode on and off
toggleVibrateMode	Toggles vibrate mode on and off
toggleWifiState	Wi-Fi on and off

You may notice there is no convenient function to control mobile broadband. Android does not (as yet) have a standard API for this, so neither does SL4A. However, you can at least get the right menu up by calling droid.startActivity('android.settings.WIRELESS_SETTINGS').

Where Am I?

LocationFacade offers some nice functionality for working out where you are, assuming your device has either a 3G interface or GPS, preferably both. Table 4-6 shows your basic methods.

Table 4-6. Location API Functions

Method	Description
geocode	Returns a list of addresses for the given latitude and longitude
getLastKnownLocation	Returns the last known location of the device
readLocation	Returns the current location as indicated by all available providers
startLocating	Starts collecting location data
stopLocating	Stops collecting location data

These do require a little explanation. In order to find out where you are, you need to startLocating. But then you have to wait until your device has worked out where it is. You can just pause for a bit, as in Listing 4-16.

Listing 4-16. Basic Use of the Location Functions

```
droid.startLocating()
time.sleep(15)
loc = droid.readLocation().result
droid.stopLocating()
```

This is crude, but will probably work. Listing 4-17 shows a rather more comprehensive example.

Listing 4-17. A Better Example

```
import android

droid = android.Android()

mylocation={} # Store last location shown.

def showmessage(msg):
   droid.dialogCreateAlert("Location",msg)
   droid.dialogSetPositiveButtonText("Geocode")
   droid.dialogShow()

def showlocation(data):
   global mylocation
   if data.has_key('gps'): # Use the more accurate gps if available
     location=data['gps']
   elif data.has_key('network'):
     location=data['network']
   else:
     showmessage('No location data')
     return
   mylocation=location
   showmessage("Location: %(provider)s\nLatitude=%(latitude)0.5f,Longitude=%(longitude)0.5f" \
       % location)

def getgeocode():
   global mylocation
   print mylocation
   showmessage('Getting geocode')
   result=droid.geocode(mylocation['latitude'],mylocation['longitude']).result
   s="Geocode"
   if len(result)<1:
     s=s+"\nUnknown"
   else:
     result=result[0]
     for k in result:
       s=s+"\n"+k+"="+str(result[k])
   showmessage(s)
```

```
def eventloop():
  while True:
    event=droid.eventWait().result
    name=event['name']
    data=event['data']
    if name=='location':
      showlocation(data)
    elif name=='dialog':
      if data.has_key('canceled'):
        break
      if data.has_key('which'):
        if data['which']=='positive':
          getgeocode()

droid.startLocating()
# It will take a little while to actually get a fresh location
# so start off using last known.
showlocation(droid.getLastKnownLocation().result)
eventloop()
droid.stopLocating()
droid.dialogDismiss()
```

Now, a couple of things are worth noting in this code. SL4A typically returns two chunks of location data, one from "network", and one from "gps" (always assuming your device has such capabilities). "network" is calculated from the position of the cell towers, and is not terribly accurate but is quite quick. "gps" uses the GPS satellites to acquire quite a precise position, but takes a while, and is relatively power-hungry.

readLocation will be empty until the first "location" event is received.

getLastKnownLocation is data from the last time your device worked out where it was, so it is a handy fallback when your device hasn't quite woken up yet.

showlocation looks first for the more accurate "gps" fix, and then falls back to network.

geocode is quite a nice addition. It queries Google to get the address from a given latitude and longitude. It will return an array of street addresses, typically in order of decreasing accuracy or detail. The default number of these addresses is 1. Note that I'm extracting the first element [0] to display the address when the user presses the Geocode button.

Note also that geocode requires a network connection to talk to Google.

Battery

BatteryManagerFacade can tell you quite a lot about the state of your battery. Table 4-7 lists the basic commands.

Table 4-7. Battery Management API Functions

Method	Description
batteryCheckPresent	Returns the most recently received battery presence data
batteryGetHealth	Returns the most recently received battery health data
batteryGetLevel	Returns the most recently received battery level (percentage)
batteryGetPlugType	Returns the most recently received plug type data
batteryGetStatus	Returns the most recently received battery status data
batteryGetTechnology	Returns the most recently received battery technology data
batteryGetTemperature	Returns the most recently received battery temperature
batteryGetVoltage	Returns the most recently received battery voltage
batteryStartMonitoring	Starts tracking battery state . . . throws "battery" events
batteryStopMonitoring	Stops tracking battery state
readBatteryData	Returns the most recently recorded battery data

A couple of small gotchas: Most of these values are not available until SDK 5 or better. It's not a problem with Honeycomb, but worth remembering if you're using your code in other devices. Also, no data is available until you have, first of all, enabled battery monitoring and received your first "battery" event. Listing 4-18 demonstrates most of these functions.

Listing 4-18. Basic Use of Battery Monitoring

```
droid = android.Android()
droid.batteryStartMonitoring()
health={1:"Unknown",2:"Good",3:"Overheat",4:"Dead",5:"Over voltage",6:"Failure"}
plug={-1:"unknown",0:"unplugged",1:"AC charger",2:"USB port"}
status={1:"unknown",2:"charging",3:"discharging",4:"not charging",5:"full"}
droid.eventWaitFor("battery")
droid.eventClearBuffer() # eventWaitFor leaves event in queue.
print "Voltage: ",droid.batteryGetVoltage().result,"mV"
print "Present: ",droid.batteryCheckPresent().result
print "Health: ",health[droid.batteryGetHealth().result]
print "Level: ",droid.batteryGetLevel().result,"%"
print "Plug Type: ",plug[droid.batteryGetPlugType().result]
print "Status: ",status[droid.batteryGetStatus().result]
print "Technology: ",droid.batteryGetTechnology().result
```

```
print u"Temperature: %0.1f C" % (droid.batteryGetTemperature().result/10.0)
droid.batteryStopMonitoring()
```

This should produce an output something like the following:

```
Voltage:   4172 mV

Present:   True

Health:   Good

Level:   99 %

Plug Type:   USB port

Status:   charging

Technology:   Li-ion

Temperature: 30.1 C
```

The first event after batteryStartMonitoring arrives pretty quickly. In most cases, you'd be hard pressed to see a delay, but nonetheless, you do need to wait for that event to arrive.

Fresh "battery" events will arrive if the battery manager decides there's something you need to know. This is not normally that often, but you could easily write a script to monitor your battery levels, and do something if they drop or rise too far.

Keeping the Device Awake

Like most mobile devices, battery life is a major concern for Android, and the OS will work quite hard to keep from using power when it doesn't need too.

When your Android goes to sleep, any script will go to sleep as well. Fortunately, there is a way around this.

WakeLockFacade will help you tell your Android if it can go to sleep yet, or if it has to stay awake. Table 4-8 lists the WakeLock commands.

Table 4-8. The Various WakeLock Functions.

Method	Description
wakeLockAcquireBright	Acquires a bright wake lock (CPU on, screen bright)
wakeLockAcquireDim	Acquires a dim wake lock (CPU on, screen dim)
wakeLockAcquireFull	Acquires a full wake lock (CPU on, screen bright, keyboard bright)

Method	Description
wakeLockAcquirePartial	Acquires a partial wake lock (CPU on)
wakeLockRelease	Releases the wake lock

You call a wakeLockAcquire method to keep your Android functioning at a certain level. For example, if you wanted something to run in background, but don't need the screen illuminated, you'd use wakeLockAcquirePartial. If you really needed to keep the screen bright, you'd use wakeLockAcquireBright. When you're done, it's important to call wakeLockRelease. As a general rule, it's a good idea to use the lowest level of wakefulness you need, so as not to use power unnecessarily.

Editing Tips

Tablets have much nicer keyboards than their smaller brothers, but even so, for serious development it's nice to have a real keyboard.

The simplest approach is just to use an editor on your desktop computer and send the script to your Android when done. The command for this is as follows:

```
adb push myscript.py /sdcard/SL4A/scripts
```

The key here is to put the script in the right place, which is /sdcard/SL4A/scripts. You can get cleverer than that, though. It's possible to do most of your development on your desktop, and control your phone remotely, using the SL4A remote control feature.

First, make sure you've got Python installed on your desktop.

Then, make sure you've got android.py installed somewhere that Python can find it.

In SL4A, start a server with Menu ➤ View ➤ Interpreters, Menu ➤ Start Server ➤ Private.

Now, look in the notification bar and you should see an SL4A notification, saying something along the lines of the following:

SL4A Service	Tap to view running scripts
Number of runnings scripts 1	

Tap this to find out what port the server is running on. For example, you might see the following:

Server	00:00
127.0.0.1:44837	PID-1

The figure we want here is the 44837, which is the port the server is listening on.

Now, back on your desktop, enter the following commands (Windows):

```
set AP_HOST=localhost

set AP_PORT=9999

adb forward tcp:9999 tcp:44837

python myscript.py
```

This will run your script on your desktop computer.

> ▒ **Note** For Linux (and Mac) computers, use "export" instead of "set".

A couple of things to realize here is that the script is running on your desktop, but any droid methods will be controlling your Android device.

Dialog boxes will appear on your Android; print will display at your desktop. Any native Python commands, such as opening a file, will still be accessing your desktop computer's files, not your Android's.

So the script in Listing 4-18 will work fine, and give you the current battery state of your Android, but the script in Listing 4-15 won't, because it won't be able to find any MP3 files . . . unless you cunningly make your desktop file structure exactly mirror your Android file structure, which is possible, if you're keen—I suppose.

A third way to run a script remote is to use Android built-in shell command, am. am is short for Activity Manager, and can be used to start Activities from the command line. Since SL4A is an Activity, and has a defined method for starting scripts, you can tell it to run a script from the command line.

Let us say you had a script called battery2.py. You could work on it from your desktop, then copy it and run it with the batch/shell file in Listing 4-19.

Listing 4-19. Running a Script Remotely from Your Desktop

```
adb push battery2.py /sdcard/SL4A/scripts
adb shell am start
  -a com.googlecode.android_scripting.action.LAUNCH_FOREGROUND_SCRIPT
  -n com.googlecode.android_scripting/.activity.ScriptingLayerServiceLauncher
  -e com.googlecode.android_scripting.extra.SCRIPT_PATH /sdcard/SL4A/scripts/battery2.py
```

And yes, that last command is all one line—kind of long-winded, which is why you put it in a batch file or shell script.

This uses the handy-dandy Android utility adb to copy the script you are working on to your Android, and then launch it as a foreground activity.

> ▨ **Note** If you have problems running `adb`, it may be that it is not in the path. Make sure you have `platform-tools` downloaded from the Android SDK, and that `adb` is in your path. It would normally be in `<android-sdk-location>/platform-tools`.

Contacts and Phone Numbers

`ContactsFacade` exposes some handy routines for accessing your contacts, as shown in Table 4-9.

Table 4-9. Contacts-Related API Functions

Method	Description
contactsGet	Returns a List of all contacts
contactsGetAttributes	Returns a List of all possible attributes for contacts
contactsGetById	Returns contacts by ID
contactsGetCount	Returns the number of contacts
contactsGetIds	Returns a List of all contact IDs
pickContact	Displays a list of contacts to pick from
pickPhone	Displays a list of phone numbers to pick from
queryAttributes	Content Resolver Query Attributes
queryContent	Content Resolver Query

Listing 4-20 shows a quick script to select a contact from your contact list, then show all the info you have on that person.

Listing 4-20. Select a Contact

```
import android
droid = android.Android()
contact=droid.pickContact().result
if contact==None:
  print "Nothing selected."
else:
  print contact["data"]
  details=droid.queryContent(contact["data"]).result
  for row in details:
    for k in row:
      print k,"=",row[k]
```

There are some interesting things about the way this works. pickContact will return some details on someone in your contact list. However, since the interface to Content changed somewhere between Android 1.6 and 2.0, what it returns is pretty brief.

Fortunately, one of the things it returns is "data," which will be in the form content://contacts/people/3031, which (if you can remember all the way back to the last chapter) can be fed directly into a queryContent to get a lot more info.

In fact, queryContent maps directly to a call to ContentResolver.query, so you can retrieve an awful lot of useful information from it. Again, see previous chapter for more detail.

SQL

Android natively ships with SQLite3, a lightweight SQL library. In fact, Android uses SQLite for a lot of internal storage. Much Android Content is actually stored in SQLite databases. Conveniently, the version of Python that comes with SL4A includes a SQLite3 library. Listing 4-21 shows an example script.

Listing 4-21. Using SQL in Python

```
import android,sqlite3

droid = android.Android()
def checktables():
  global con
  # Check to see if table exists
  if sqlvalue("select count(*) from sqlite_master where name='zzz'")==0:
    c=con.cursor()
    c.execute('create table zzz (id integer,info text)')
    c.execute("insert into zzz values (1,'Fred Smith')")
    c.execute("insert into zzz values (2,'John Smith')")
    c.close()
    con.commit()

def sqlvalue(query): # return a single value from a query
  global con
  row=con.execute(query).fetchone()
  if row==None:
    return None
  return row[0]

def dumpquery(query):
  global con
  for row in con.execute(query):
    print row

print "Connecting"
con = sqlite3.connect("/sdcard/test.db")
print "Checking tables"
checktables()
print "Dump table"
dumpquery("select * from zzz")
print "Done"
```

■ **Note** SQLite3 should automatically create the file /sdcard/test.db. If it doesn't, it may be a permissions problem. /sdcard is usually formatted as a FAT32, which doesn't really have permissions. However, some Motorola Xoom tablets may not, and have restricted access. You may need to find a folder that will allow write access. /sdcard/Download or possibly /sdcard/download should be safe options.

More Stuff

There are interfaces for monitoring and managing Wi-Fi, Bluetooth, sensors, and signal strength, most of which work similarly to those already demonstrated. There is a simple but effective text-to-speech function, a façade for managing Shared Preferences, and even some clever methods to turn your device into a web cam.

In short, most of the things you can think of to do on an Android, you can do with SL4A.

What's more, as I've stated previously, SL4A is continuously evolving, so it's worth keeping an eye on.

It is, admittedly, a little light on actual screen handling functions, but I fully expect that to have changed by the time you read this.

Even without these features, it is a very useful tool, if only for prototyping and getting the hang of what your Android can do.

Summary

What this chapter should have shown is that there is more than one way to skin a cat.

The Android OS is a versatile environment, being built as it is on top of a fully featured Linux kernel. Therefore, over time, you can expect to see more and more alternative language options. I already know of one trial project to implement a full Java compiler and IDE directly on Android.

Python is a compact and powerful scripting language, allowing you to do a lot with not a lot of typing. This can be a great time saver! You'll note that most of the sample scripts have been included in their entirety, whereas I've been including only key parts of my Java examples. This should say something about Python's compactness.

More to the point, it's a prime language for just playing, and is famous for having a low entry barrier to beginning programmers. This is not to say that it does everything that you can do with Java. Not yet, anyway. And Java has arguably superior compile time error checking. I say arguably, because people will . . .

But it is a worthwhile addition to your toolkit.

CHAPTER 5

Project 1: Media Player

A picture is worth a thousand words. In computer terms, an example is worth a bunch more than documentation alone.

Okay, it's not so snappy, but you get what I mean. I'm going to start by building a simple but hopefully useful media player application. In the process, I'm also going to demonstrate some Honeycomb-specific functionality. In fact, that's where I'm going to start.

Figure 5-1. Not quite what I had in mind . . .

Fragments

Before we start in on building a media player, let's have a look at two of the most obvious differences between an application on Honeycomb and on previous versions of Android: ActionBars and Fragments.

The full source code for my example Fragment demo is in BA3TPFragment.

What's a Fragment?

A Fragment is a new user interface feature, and for most intents and purposes can be considered a sort of mini Activity. Each Activity can have one or more Fragments on display at any given time, and each Fragment can be reused by other Activities. Each Fragment has its own life cycle, which closely resembles the life cycle of the Activity. You can also define different layouts for different orientations, which is always useful.

Examining the Example

BA3TPFragment is a very minimalist example, but it covers quite a lot of bases in the simplest way possible. Listing 5-1 shows the basic layout, which is saved in fragholder.xml.

Listing 5-1. *A Simple Fragment Layout*

```
<?xml version="1.0" encoding="utf-8"?>
<LinearLayout xmlns:android="http://schemas.android.com/apk/res/android"
        android:layout_width="match_parent" android:layout_height="match_parent"
        android:orientation="horizontal">
    <fragment class="com.apress.ba3tp.fragment.TitleFragment"
                android:id="@+id/frag_title"
                android:layout_height="match_parent"
                android:layout_width="0px"
                android:layout_weight="1"
                />

        <fragment class="com.apress.ba3tp.fragment.ContentFragment"
                android:id="@+id/frag_content"
                android:layout_height="match_parent"
                android:layout_width="0px"
                android:layout_weight="1"
                />
</LinearLayout>
```

What you see is two Fragments in a LinearLayout.

class is the fully qualified name of the class that's going to handle this Fragment.

android:id can be used to identify this Fragment at runtime.

android:layout_height is set to just be as large as possible.

android:layout_width is set to 0 pixels, which in effect allows the width to be controlled by android:layout_weight.

So our separate Fragments, each with its own backing class, are displayed side by side. Because the layout_weights are the same for each Fragment, you get two equal panes, side by side.

■ **Note** Another thing I struggled with for a while is the concept of "weights" in Java-related layouts. Simply put, in a layout with multiple children, the weight of each child indicates how much of the available space it will use. So, two children each of weight 1 will take up 50% each. If one has a weight of 3 and the other a weight of 1, the first will take 75% of the space and the second 25%. Adding a third child with weight 2 will give you 3:1:2, or 50%, 16%, and 34% (rounding somewhat—actually, 1/2, 1/6, 1/3).

Now, as an added enhancement, I've added another copy of fragholder in res/layout-port. This version is almost identical, except that when your tablet is tilted into portrait mode, your application will use that instead. The portrait version of fragholder.xml is shown in Listing 5-2.

Listing 5-2. The Simple Fragment Layout in Portrait Mode

```xml
<?xml version="1.0" encoding="utf-8"?>
<LinearLayout xmlns:android="http://schemas.android.com/apk/res/android"
        android:layout_width="match_parent" android:layout_height="match_parent"↵
  android:orientation="vertical">
        <fragment class="com.apress.ba3tp.fragment.TitleFragment"
                android:id="@+id/frag_title"
                android:layout_height="0px"
                android:layout_width="match_parent"
                android:layout_weight="1"
                />

        <fragment class="com.apress.ba3tp.fragment.ContentFragment"
                android:id="@+id/frag_content"
                android:layout_height="0px"
                android:layout_width="match_parent"
                android:layout_weight="1"
                />
</LinearLayout>
```

As you can see, it's almost identical, with the exception that it is laid out vertically. The way this works is that layout-port will be checked when your device is in portrait mode, before checking in layout. You can also define layout-land for landscape mode instead. This works in much the same way that you have drawable folders for high-, medium-, and low-density displays. In fact, there is a massive array of different configuration options you can provide. I'll cover these if and when they seem appropriate.

Into these Fragments, I'm placing the main and other layouts. Now, these layouts were not carefully considered. I just randomly threw widgets on two forms as a demo, but it does allow me to demonstrate a number of features.

Okay, this is what our application will look like (Figure 5-2).

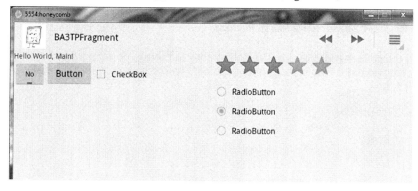

Figure 5-2. What our Simple Fragment Layout looks like

This is two Fragments, one with some buttons on it, one with some stars and stuff. Just to show what happens, Figure 5-3 shows exactly the same application in portrait mode.

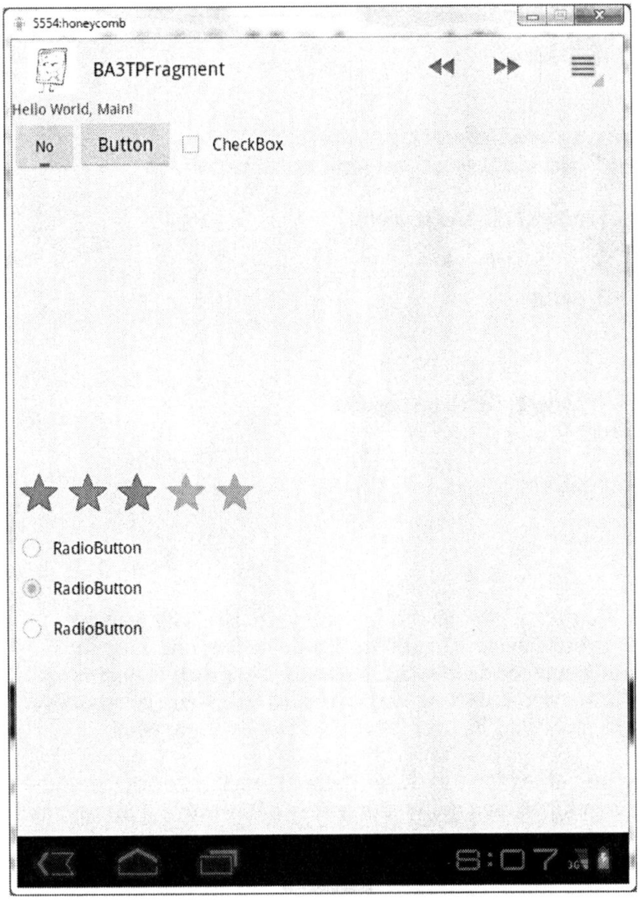

Figure 5-3. What our Simple Fragment Layout looks like in Portrait

Right, let's have a look at the code that drives this. I've deliberately left things pretty minimalist. I've defined two Fragments, TitleFragment and ContentFragment. ContentFragment is the simplest possible Fragment, as shown in Listing 5-3.

Listing 5-3. Simplest Possible Fragment Code

```
package com.apress.ba3tp.fragment;

import android.app.Fragment;
import android.os.Bundle;
import android.view.LayoutInflater;
import android.view.View;
```

```
import android.view.ViewGroup;

public class ContentFragment extends Fragment {

  @Override
  public View onCreateView(LayoutInflater inflater, ViewGroup container,
          Bundle savedInstanceState) {
    return = inflater.inflate(R.layout.other, null);
  }
}
```

That is your absolute minimum Fragment, and the important thing that's happening here is that onCreateView is loading (or in this case, inflating) the "other" layout, and returning it as a view.

Note that LayoutInflater is a class that interprets the layout.xml and turns it into an actual initialized object, and we will almost certainly come back to this object. container refers to the containing view, or in this case, a LinearLayout in which the Fragment lives. We don't need to know that this time, but it can be useful.

If we look at the onCreate method in Main.java (Listing 5-4), it's pretty straightforward.

Listing 5-4. The onCreate for the Main Activity

```
@Override
public void onCreate(Bundle savedInstanceState) {
  super.onCreate(savedInstanceState);
  setContentView(R.layout.fragholder);
}
```

So all it's doing is setting the content view, and the rest is managed by Android or the Fragments themselves. All of this would be enough to demonstrate Fragments, but I thought I'd have a bit of a look at the other major UI element that Honeycomb introduces.

The ActionBar

Let's have a look at Main.java's onCreateOptions method (Listing 5-5).

Listing 5-5. Creating an Options Menu

```
@Override
public boolean onCreateOptionsMenu(Menu menu) {
  menu.add(Menu.NONE, MenuId.SHARE.getId(), Menu.NONE, "Share")
      .setIcon(android.R.drawable.ic_menu_share);
  menu.add(Menu.NONE, MenuId.MAIL.getId(), Menu.NONE, "Mail")
  .setIcon(android.R.drawable.ic_menu_send);
  menu.add(Menu.NONE, MenuId.BACK.getId(), Menu.NONE, "Back")
  .setIcon(android.R.drawable.ic_media_rew)
  .setShowAsAction(MenuItem.SHOW_AS_ACTION_IF_ROOM);
  menu.add(Menu.NONE, MenuId.FORWARD.getId(), Menu.NONE, "Fwd")
  .setIcon(android.R.drawable.ic_media_ff)
  .setShowAsAction(MenuItem.SHOW_AS_ACTION_IF_ROOM);
  return super.onCreateOptionsMenu(menu);
}
```

Note the calls to setShowAsAction. This (called with the constant SHOW_AS_ACTION_IF_ROOM) tells the ActionBar to display these menu items directly. Other menu items are accessible through the menu button (see Figure 5-4).

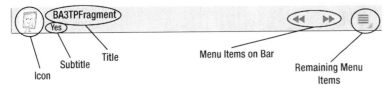

Figure 5-4. *Anatomy of an* ActionBar

The Icon is the application Icon (in this case, something bodgy hand-drawn by yours truly). You have a title and a subtitle, settable at runtime.

The fast-forward and rewind icons are the menu items I told Android to display on the ActionBar. The remaining menu items are accessed through the menu button.

Now let's look at the buttons we've defined. The first button I picked was a ToggleButton, which is for all intents and purposes a prettier CheckBox. I added an onClick event, the way we have everywhere else, only to discover an unexpected behavior: the onClick had to be defined in the Activity, not in the Fragment. This is a trap for young players, but easily dealt with by, you know, putting the onClick method in the main Activity.

This is all well and good, but at least part of the reason for using Fragments is that you can make them reuseable. So I've used two different approaches to programmatically set up onClickListeners for the remaining two buttons (see Listing 5-6).

Listing 5-6. *Alternative Ways of Responding to Click Events*

```
public class TitleFragment extends Fragment {
    private View mContentView;
    private Button mButton;
    @Override
    public View onCreateView(LayoutInflater inflater, ViewGroup container,
            Bundle savedInstanceState) {
        mContentView = inflater.inflate(R.layout.main, null);
        mButton=(Button) mContentView.findViewById(R.id.button1);
        mButton.setOnClickListener(new OnClickListener() {

            @Override
            public void onClick(View v) {
                getActivity().getActionBar().setTitle("Button");
            }
        });
        View.OnClickListener btnlisten = new ButtonListener();
        mContentView.findViewById(R.id.checkBox1).setOnClickListener(btnlisten);
        return mContentView;
    }

    private class ButtonListener implements View.OnClickListener {

        @Override
```

```java
    public void onClick(View v) {
      ActionBar ab = getActivity().getActionBar();
      if (v.getId() == R.id.checkBox1) {
        CheckBox chk = (CheckBox) v;
        ab.setTitle("Checkbox");
        if (chk.isChecked()) {
          ab.setSubtitle("Checked");
        } else {
          ab.setSubtitle("Not checked today.");
        }
      }
    }
  }
}
```

Listing 5-6 shows the onCreateView for TitleFragment. Note we're using the findViewById method of the freshly inflated mContentView to locate the buttons.

For the first button, I'm defining an anonymous class to handle the click. For the next button, I have defined a separate OnClickListener class, which I could (if I was more organized) share between multiple buttons.

The button events demonstrate a couple of trivial but useful functions. I'm using them to set various features on the ActionBar. I can find the ActionBar easily enough by calling the Activity's getActionBar method. And I can find the Fragment's owning Activity by calling getActivity.

ANONYMOUS CLASSES

Java allows what are known as "anonymous classes," where you define a one-off, nameless class.

JavaScript programmers will also be familiar with this. You can see the syntax in mButton.setOnClickListener in Listing 5-6.

While handy, I feel this feature can be overused. As a rule, I'd use only anonymous classes where it improves readability, and when you never intend to reuse that functionality.

FragmentManager

Obviously, once we've defined our layout with Fragments, it would be handy to be able to manipulate them. This is handled through FragmentManager, which is retrieved by calling getFragmentManager. This can be used to add or modify other Fragments to your layout. For the moment, though, I'm just going to use it to find the Fragment containing the RatingBar I want to modify. See Listing 5-7.

Listing 5-7. Managing the RatingBar

```java
private RatingBar getRating() {
  Fragment f = getFragmentManager().findFragmentById(R.id.frag_content);
  return (RatingBar) f.getView().findViewById(R.id.ratingBar1);
}

private void doForward() {
```

```
    RatingBar r = getRating();
    r.setProgress(Math.min(r.getMax(), r.getProgress()+1));
}

private void doBack() {
  RatingBar r = getRating();
  r.setProgress(Math.max(0, r.getProgress()-1));
}
```

Media Player Application

And now, after that detour, we proceed on with our example media player application. This is an application I threw together to demonstrate a number of features. It searches your tablet for any media files and displays them in a list. It will also query any file and show you all the metadata Android has for that file, and even play and stop audio and video files. This is not intended as the perfect media player application. I would expect you to already have quite respectable sound and video player software installed. Nor is it perfect . . . it could be much prettier and offer finer controls. On the other hand, I have a book to write. Otherwise I'd be cheerfully tweaking this application still. To paraphrase Leonardo da Vinci, programs are never finished, only abandoned. Feel free to play with and improve. That's what it's there for, after all.

The media player project is BA3TPMediaPlayer. We're going to cover a bunch of subjects here.

- Fragments and ActivityBars

- Icons and Logos

- ListViews

- ListAdapters

- Content providers and cursors

- Dialog boxes

- Surface holders (for displaying the videos)

- SeekBars and, incidentally, Threads

- The versatile MediaPlayer class

There are three classes in this project:

- MainActivity

- ListFragment

- ContentFragment

This is mostly self-explanatory. The screen looks something like Figure 5-5.

Figure 5-5. The media player in action

As we discussed earlier this chapter, I've organized this Activity to display a list of available media files in one pane (or Fragment), and all the details of what I'm playing in the other.

I'm going to start with ListFragment, as shown in Listing 5-8.

Listing 5-8. Implementing a ListFragment

```java
public class ListFragment extends android.app.ListFragment {

  @Override
  public void onListItemClick(ListView l, View v, int position, long id) {
    Cursor c = mAdapter.getCursor();
    c.moveToPosition(position);
    ((MainActivity) getActivity()).setSelectedMedia(c);
  }

  @Override
  public void onStart() {
    super.onStart();
    String[] columns = { MediaStore.MediaColumns.TITLE,MediaStore.MediaColumns.DISPLAY_NAME};
    int[] to = { android.R.id.text1,android.R.id.text2 };
    mAdapter=new SimpleCursorAdapter(getActivity(),
        android.R.layout.two_line_list_item, getCursor(), columns, to, 0);
    setListAdapter(mAdapter);
  }

}
```

Fortunately, Android has provided us with a handy, ready-to-use `ListFragment` class. I've descended my own `ListFragment` class from the standard `android.app.ListFragment`. This `ListFragment` contains a single `ListView`, and some utility methods.

Now, a `ListView` does nothing by itself. It needs a `ListAdapter`, which is an interface that tells the `ListView` what data to display, and how. Again, you can build your own, but I'm going to be lazy and use one of the classes that Android has conveniently made available.

Displaying a List from a Cursor

This time, I'm using a `SimpleCursorAdapter`. The constructor for this seems a little daunting at first, but is actually elegantly simple. It requires the following:

- A `Context`

- A layout resource ID—this layout is used for each item in the list.

- A cursor (as returned from a `ContentResolver.query`, or an `Activity` managedQuery)

- A "from" `String Array`, containing a list of the fields from the `Cursor` to display in the list

- A "to" Array of `TextView` IDs that map to the "from" columns names

- Some flags

For the layout, I've chosen a standard Android layout designed for just this purpose, `android.R.layout.two_line_list_item`. This is literally just two `TextViews`, one on top of the other, called (imaginatively) `text1` and `text2`.

Examine the actual construction of the `SimpleCursorAdapter` (in Listing 5-9).

Listing 5-9. Constructing a SimpleCursorAdapter

```
String[] columns = { MediaStore.MediaColumns.TITLE,MediaStore.MediaColumns.DISPLAY_NAME};
int[] to = { android.R.id.text1,android.R.id.text2 };
mAdapter=new SimpleCursorAdapter(getActivity(),
    android.R.layout.two_line_list_item,
  getCursor(),
  columns,
  to, 0);
setListAdapter(mAdapter);
```

Looking at the columns array, I've used two predefined field names, `MediaStore.MediaColumns.TITLE` and `MediaStore.MediaColumns.DISPLAY_NAME`. These are common to all the `MediaStore` queries, whether video or audio.

These will be mapped in turn to `android.R.id.text1` and to `android.R.id.text2`. You could easily define your own layout, but we'll keep things simple for the moment.

`getActivity()` returns the master `Activity` this `Fragment` lives in (in this case, `MainActivity`), which we will use for the `Context` (a `Fragment` is not, in itself, a `Context`).

I'll get to getCursor in a moment.

There are a number of flags that can be set to control the precise behavior of the `SimpleCursorAdapter`, but just using the default behavior will do for the moment.

Querying Media Files

Listing 5-10 shows the getCursor method.

Listing 5-10. A Query of Available Media Files

```
private Uri mMediaSource = MediaStore.Audio.Media.EXTERNAL_CONTENT_URI;

public Cursor getCursor() {
  Activity a = getActivity();
  return a.managedQuery(mMediaSource,
      null, null, null, MediaStore.Audio.Media.TITLE);
}
```

We've previously discussed querying content providers via ContentResolver. However, you can get the same result from Activity.managedQuery. The difference between managedQuery and query is that the Activity automatically deals with unloading and requerying itself when the Activity stops and restarts. Since that's what we want to happen here, that's what I'm using.

Now, mMediaSource can be set to several different settings. I'm going to let it default to MediaStore.Audio.Media.EXTERNAL_CONTENT_URI. This will access all the media files on your SDCard, which is where you'd expect to find most of your music files.

And I'm sorting by TITLE. One of the ways we could enhance this application is to offer different sort options (which I'll leave as an exercise for the reader).

Responding to Clicks

Displaying this list is all very well, but what if we want to actually do something with it? Looking at Listing 5-8, you can see I've overridden onListItemClick. One of the parameters passed is position.

I'm getting the current cursor from mAdapter.getCursor(), and using the position parameter to set the cursor where I want it by calling moveToPosition. I'm then passing that cursor, now pointing to the row I've selected, to MainActivity. This will then store the selected media item, display all the metadata we have, and be ready to play it when the user hits the right menu item.

Some More on the ActionBar

Figure 5-6. The media player ActionBar

Moving on to the MainActivity, which is where we do most of the actual work, I'll just draw your attention to my somewhat dodgy hand-drawn logo.

Keen-eyed observers will note that this image is not square. This is because the ActionBar allows you to display a Logo, which can be just about any sort of image, instead of an Icon. This Logo has to be defined in the AndroidManifest.xml (android:logo) and will be resized as needed, although designing it to a similar height to your Icon is probably a good idea.

For no particular reason (apart from demonstrating this fact), I've included a menu item (Icon/Logo) to toggle between the two (see Listing 5-11).

Listing 5-11. The Main Activity onCreate

```
@Override
public void onCreate(Bundle savedInstanceState) {
    super.onCreate(savedInstanceState);
    setContentView(R.layout.main);
    FragmentManager fm = getFragmentManager();
    mList = (ListFragment) fm.findFragmentById(R.id.frag_list);
    mContent = (ContentFragment) fm.findFragmentById(R.id.frag_content);
    getActionBar().setDisplayUseLogoEnabled(true);
}
```

The key method here is setDisplayUseLogoEnabled.

Menu

Listing 5-12. The Options Menu

```
@Override
public boolean onCreateOptionsMenu(Menu menu) {
    menu.add(Menu.NONE, MenuId.PLAY.getId(), Menu.NONE, "Play")
        .setIcon(android.R.drawable.ic_media_play)
        .setShowAsAction(MenuItem.SHOW_AS_ACTION_IF_ROOM);
    menu.add(Menu.NONE, MenuId.STOP.getId(), Menu.NONE, "Stop")
        .setIcon(android.R.drawable.ic_media_pause)
        .setShowAsAction(MenuItem.SHOW_AS_ACTION_IF_ROOM);
    menu.add(Menu.NONE, MenuId.MEDIATYPE.getId(), Menu.NONE, "Source")
    .setIcon(android.R.drawable.ic_menu_preferences)
    .setShowAsAction(MenuItem.SHOW_AS_ACTION_IF_ROOM);
    menu.add(Menu.NONE, MenuId.LOGO.getId(), Menu.NONE, "Logo/Icon")
    .setIcon(android.R.drawable.ic_menu_crop)
    .setShowAsAction(MenuItem.SHOW_AS_ACTION_IF_ROOM);
    return super.onCreateOptionsMenu(menu);
}
```

This is how I set up the menu. I've gone mad with power and put all of them on ActionBar (with SHOW_AS_ACTION_IF_ROOM).

Getting a Media URI

Listing 5-13. Interrogating a Media URI

```
public void setSelectedMedia(Cursor c) {
    mCurrentMedia = Uri.withAppendedPath(mList.getMediaSource(), getString(c,Media._ID));
    String title = getString(c, Media.TITLE);
    mTitle = title;
    String info = "Artist " + getString(c, Media.ARTIST) + "\nAlbum "
```

```
          + getString(c, Media.ALBUM) + "\nLength " + getLong(c, Media.DURATION)
          / 1000 + " seconds";
    mContent.getTitle().setText(title);
    mContent.getInfo().setText(info);
    mContent.getDump().setText(mCurrentMedia+"\n"+dumpCursor(c));
}

private String getString(Cursor c, String fieldname) {
    int column = c.getColumnIndex(fieldname);
    return (column >= 0) ? c.getString(column) : "";
}
```

Listing 5-13 shows the chunk of code that processes the item the user has selected, and then displays what information we have on it. You can see where setSelectedMedia is being called by looking back to onListItemClick in Listing 5-8. This is being passed a previous generated Cursor, which fortunately contains all the info the MediaStore provider has collected on our media files. getString (and getLong) are just some helper methods to return a cursor field by name, rather than number.

Now, the most important bit of all this is how to actually tell the MediaPlayer class what file to play. We need a Uri, and it's not immediately obvious how to derive this from the data that we've got. Fortunately, all we need is to append the _ID field to the actual Uri we are using to make the original query. Uri.withAppendedPath is a useful method to add a path to an existing Uri. What we end up with is a Uri that looks like content://media/external/audio/media/859. This can be fed into MediaPlayer later.

This is not the only possible path to our media file. The _data field actually contains the full path to the media file. Why not just use "file://"+ path? Well, actually, that will work. And we could have gone hunting for our external disk for any file ending in mp3.

But not all of the things MediaPlayer can cope with are directly accessible by file name. By passing it a "content://" Uri, MediaPlayer knows to call ContentResolver to get a data stream, and this makes our MediaPlayer capable of handling more options.

The rest of Listing 5-13 simply updates the ContentFragment with all the info it has on our media file.

Playing Media

The core of this whole application is the MediaPlayer class. This is a remarkably simple class, and easy to use. It can be as simple to use as Listing 5-14.

Listing 5-14.

```
mPlayer = MediaPlayer.create(this, selectedUri);
if (mPlayer == null)
  toast("Unable to open.\n" + getSelectedMedia());
else {
  mPlayer.start();
}
```

Or, here it is expressed as a single line without error-checking:

```
mPlayer = MediaPlayer.create(this, selectedUri).start();
```

And this will work fine. It will even work on video files, but as it stands, will play only the audio track. BA3TPMediaPlayer will, in fact, play video, but first a small digression.

Different Media Sources

We've been concentrating on music, but there are other forms of media available. I've concentrated on these four:

MediaStore.Audio.Media.*EXTERNAL_CONTENT_URI*

MediaStore.Audio.Media.*INTERNAL_CONTENT_URI*

MediaStore.Video.Media.*EXTERNAL_CONTENT_URI*

MediaStore.Video.Media.*INTERNAL_CONTENT_URI*

Internal audio files contain all the built-in ringtones, alarms, and sound effects. External video contains any video files on your SDCard, and I'm not sure what you'd find for internal video, but it lets you snoop about on your Android device.

Dialog Boxes

How do we select these different media files? I've elected to use a dialog box to get these options from the user (see Figure 5-7).

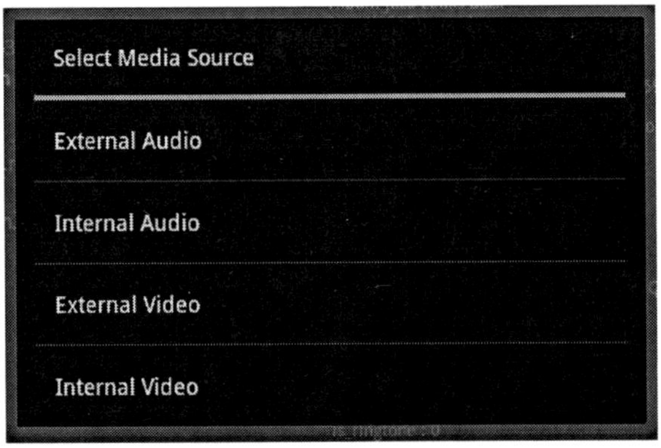

Figure 5-7. A dialog box

There are a couple of ways to build and display these boxes, but I'll stick with the one Android recommends (see Listing 5-15).

Listing 5-15. Creating a Dialog Box

```
@Override
protected Dialog onCreateDialog(int id) {
  switch (id) {
  case 1:
    AlertDialog.Builder builder = new AlertDialog.Builder(this);
```

```
        builder.setTitle("Select Media Source");
        String[] options = { "External Audio", "Internal Audio","External Video",↵
"Internal Video" };
        builder.setItems(options, new OnClickListener() {

            @Override
            public void onClick(DialogInterface dialog, int which) {
                if (which==0) mList.setMediaSource(MediaStore.Audio.Media.EXTERNAL_CONTENT_URI);
                else if (which==1) mList.setMediaSource↵
(MediaStore.Audio.Media.INTERNAL_CONTENT_URI);
                else if (which==2) mList.setMediaSource↵
(MediaStore.Video.Media.EXTERNAL_CONTENT_URI);
                else if (which==3) mList.setMediaSource↵
(MediaStore.Video.Media.INTERNAL_CONTENT_URI);
            }
        });
        mDialog = builder.create();
        return mDialog;
    }
    return null;
}
```

Listing 5-15 shows the code I'm using to create the dialog box (in this case, an AlertDialog) in Figure 5-7.

I've overridden onCreateDialog. This is called by the Activity when you wish to display a dialog. This is called with an integer ID, and generally speaking is called only once for each ID. There is another event you can override, onPrepareDialog, which is called each time the dialog is displayed. This allows you to modify the dialog each time.

Dialogs created in the onCreateDialog callback are *managed* dialogs, meaning the Activity will keep track of them and release resources as needed. You can just create dialogs on the fly, too.

The easiest way to create an AlertDialog is to use an AlertDialog.Builder. I'm setting a list of options, giving it a title, and then creating it with builder.Create.

Of special interest is the setItems, because it requires a listener to be linked to it. I'm implementing this listener as an anonymous function. When an item is chosen, the which parameter is passed with the index of the selected item.

This dialog is displayed with showDialog. In this case, I've defined only one dialog in onCreatedDialog, which I've given the ID of 1. If I had more than one, I would have been inclined to set up static final fields, or possibly an enum. Here, I'm confident that I'm going to remember "1".

Now, a trap for young players—or players familiar with other environments, anyway—is that showDialog is always "modeless." This is to say that if you show a dialog, the code will keep running. For example, see Listing 5-16.

Listing 5-16. How Dialogs Behave

```
    showDialog(1);
    toast("Dialog");
```

The dialog will pop up, and then a toast message will immediately appear. In Visual Basic, Delphi et al., the next line would not be executed until the user had made his or her selection. It is, in fact, possible to make a dialog box that you can wait on, but it requires a degree of fiddling around with threads and message passing, and is beyond the scope of this example. When the user selects an item from the list, our dialog will respond to that by going and setting a different media source for our list.

Changing a List Cursor

Listing 5-17. Changing the Media Source

```
public void setMediaSource(Uri mMediaSource) {
    this.mMediaSource = mMediaSource;
    Cursor c = getCursor();
    mAdapter.swapCursor(c).close();
}
```

When we set a new media source, we need to tell the SimpleCursorAdapter to use a new cursor. Listing 5-17 shows how this is done. In this case, we are simply setting a new media source and getting a fresh cursor. Then I call swapCursor to set the new cursor into the ListAdapter that is managing our ListFragment. The neat thing here is that swapCursor returns the old cursor. We could save this for later, but in this case I've no use for it. I don't want it hanging about sucking up resources, so I immediately call close(), and then it's gone.

Advanced Media Playing

Listing 5-18. Playing a Media File with More Options

```
private void playMedia() {
    clearMedia();
    if (getSelectedMedia().toString().contains("/video/")) {
        showVideo(true);
        mPlayer = MediaPlayer.create(this, getSelectedMedia(),↵
mContent.getSurface().getHolder());
    } else {
        showVideo(false);
        mPlayer = MediaPlayer.create(this, getSelectedMedia());
    }
    if (mPlayer == null)
        toast("Unable to open.\n" + getSelectedMedia());
    else {
        mPlayer.start();
        getActionBar().setSubtitle(mTitle);
        startProgressThread();
    }
}

private void showVideo(boolean onOff) {
    mContent.getSurface().setVisibility(onOff ? View.VISIBLE : View.GONE);
    mContent.getDump().setVisibility(onOff ? View.GONE : View.VISIBLE);
}
```

As shown in Listing 5-14, the MediaPlayer class can be used very simply. However, I want to be able to show videos. I also want to display a progress bar, and allow the user to seek backward and forward.

It's not actually very hard to display a video with a MediaPlayer. It just needs an area of screen to play on. This is called a SurfaceHolder.

Listing 5-18 shows the actual code I use to start playing the selected media. content.xml has a SurfaceView component. I've set this initially to be invisible (setVisibility(View.GONE)). When I detect that what I'm playing is a video (by the simple but not necessarily reliable method of seeing if the Uri contains "/video/"), I hide the Dump control (which is just a TextView that I dump the contents of the cursor row into) to make room, and make the SurfaceView visible. Then I create the MediaPlayer with an additional parameter, the SurfaceHolder embedded in the SurfaceView.

And that is basically that. Well, not quite. I'm making no effort to make sure the screen ratio is set correctly. Thus, I found that in portrait mode the video tended to be somewhat truncated. I'm going to leave making that prettier as another exercise to the reader. Lazy, moi? Never!

Displaying Our Progress

Listing 5-19. Showing the Progress of the Playing Media

```
private void startProgressThread() {

    Runnable _progressUpdater = new Runnable() {
      @Override
      public void run() {
        SeekBar progressBar = getSeekBar();
        while (mPlayer != null && mPlayer.isPlaying()) {
          try {
            int current = 0;
            int total = mPlayer.getDuration();
            progressBar.setMax(total);
            progressBar.setIndeterminate(false);

            while (mPlayer != null && current < total) {
              Thread.sleep(1000); // Update once per second
              current = mPlayer.getCurrentPosition();
              // Removing this line, the track plays normally.
              progressBar.setProgress(current);
            }
          } catch (Exception e) {
            break;
          }
        }
      }
    };
    Thread thread = new Thread(_progressUpdater);
    thread.start();
}
```

I also wanted to display the progress of our media file as it played. The chunk of code in Listing 5-19 handles this. It sets up a separate Java thread to run in the background. This finds the SeekBar on ContentFragment and sets its maximum length to the duration of the media. (getDuration returns the length of the media file in milliseconds.) Then, every second, it will look at the current position of our file, and update the SeekBar accordingly.

This monitoring thread is set up to exit as soon as mPlayer stops playing, or if it is set to null, or if the thread gets any exceptions.

Controlling Our Progress

What makes a SeekBar different from a ProgressBar is that a SeekBar has a thumb that allows the user to adjust it (see Listing 5-20).

Listing 5-20. *Using the SeekBar to Control the Media File*

```
@Override
  public void onProgressChanged(SeekBar seekBar, int progress, boolean fromUser) {
    if (fromUser) {
      MediaPlayer mp = ((MainActivity) getActivity()).mPlayer;
      if (mp!=null) {
        mp.seekTo(progress);
      }
    }
  }
```

Listing 5-20 shows the onProgressChanged event, which is called every time that SeekBar is moved. It's important to realize that this will be triggered every time the position changes. This definitely includes calls to setProgress. Fortunately, we can tell when it's been moved by the user by looking at the fromUser parameter, and respond only to those events.

The MediaPlayer can seek to a specific position (in milliseconds) by using the seekTo method.

Summary

And there we have it—a workable, if not pretty, media player application. On the way, we've touched on quite a few of the ins and outs of Fragments and Lists, had a bit of a play with ActionBars, and got our hands dirty with threads and various user interface options.

This is also the first project that we've seriously started designing to actually do something useful, rather than purely as a demonstration of specific Android features.

Hopefully, BA3TPMediaPlayer should give you a solid basis to build your own applications— probably prettier and with more features.

Now, onto the next project . . .

CHAPTER 6

Explorer

An Android File Explorer

Probably because of its origin as a phone-based OS, or possibly just because of sheer cussedness, Android does not come with a file explorer by default. This is not to say they don't exist . . . there are a number of quite acceptable apps on the market that work fine. For that matter, quite a few applications include a simple file browser as a matter of course. However, I thought building a file browser from scratch might be a useful exercise . . . and indeed it was.

Figure 6-1. Exploring: Sometimes, what you find is not what you expect . . .

Anatomy of a File Explorer

Consistent with my highly imaginative naming conventions, this project is called BA3TPExplorer (see Figure 6-2).

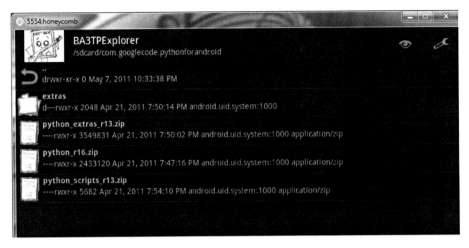

Figure 6-2. *Explorer in action*

ListActivity for Fun and Profit

In our previous project, BA3TPMediaPlayer, we used a `ListView` contained in a `Fragment`, conveniently prepackaged in a `ListFragment`. I considered using a similar approach for this project, but in the end decided that `Fragments` would not massively improve the functionality of this application, so I've built this on a `ListActivity`. This, as you might imagine, is an `Activity` containing a single `ListView`.

As such, the important layout is not the layout of the screen per se. Instead, the key layout here is `filelist.xml`. `Filelist.xml` is shown in Listing 6-1.

Listing 6-1. *Layout of the* `ListView`

```xml
<?xml version="1.0" encoding="utf-8"?>
<LinearLayout xmlns:android="http://schemas.android.com/apk/res/android"
        android:layout_width="match_parent" android:layout_height="wrap_content"
        android:orientation="horizontal">
        <ImageView android:id="@+id/image1" android:layout_width=↵
"@android:dimen/app_icon_size"
                android:layout_height="@android:dimen/app_icon_size"↵
 android:src="@android:drawable/ic_menu_help"></ImageView>
        <LinearLayout android:id="@+id/linearLayout1"
                android:orientation="vertical" android:layout_height="wrap_content"
                android:layout_width="match_parent">
                <TextView android:text="TextView" android:layout_height="wrap_content"
                        android:layout_width="wrap_content" android:textStyle="bold"
                        android:id="@+id/tvFileName"></TextView>
                <TextView android:text="TextView" android:layout_height="wrap_content"
                        android:layout_width="wrap_content"↵
 android:id="@+id/tvAdditional"></TextView>
        </LinearLayout>
</LinearLayout>
```

Once again I've gone with that old reliable, LinearLayout, as my basic layout. So far I've done quite well by it . . . a nice, simple, well-defined layout manager. It looks a lot like Figure 6-3.

Figure 6-3. *What the* ListView *layout looks like*

The actual layout is pretty simple: two TextViews, one in bold for the file name, and the other in plain text for details on the file.

There are a couple of things to note about this layout. It's worth understanding two standard settings for layout_width and layout_height:

- match_parent = expand to match the full dimension of the parent of this control

- wrap_content = expand to be large enough to contain the children of this control

Thus, linearLayout1, which is horizontally oriented, will expand out to the full available width of the screen, and have sufficient height to contain both the image and the TextViews.

The excitingly named image1 will be used to display icons based on which Activity will manage this particular file, or some defaults if it can't work that out.

What I found on experimentation was that because the images could be different sizes, things didn't line up neatly, so I decided to force the image to be a standard icon size. This is cunningly pulled from a standard Android resource, @android:dimen/app_icon_size.

A Note on Resources

I've skipped fairly lightly over resources to this point. Resources are generally identified by a unique integer, which Android uses to manage all sorts of handy items. Local resources are stored in various places in the project's res folder, and adt automatically maintains a Java class known as R, which can be accessed at runtime. There are also quite a few standard global resources available in android.R. These resources are divided roughly into the sections shown in Table 6-1.

Table 6-1. *Types of Resources, and Where to Find Them*

Class	Description
anim	Animations
animator	Also animations
array	Stored arrays of various types
attr	Attributes that can be used or defined by various styles
bool	Boolean values

Class	Description
color	Predefined colors
dimen	Useful dimensions, which can be tailored things like screen resolution and orientation
drawable	Images that can be drawn on a screen, typically used for various icons
fraction	Fractions—first defined in SDK 11
id	IDs
integer	Integer values
interpolator	Various acceleration curves used for pretty animations and transitions
layout	Layouts
menu	Menus
raw	Raw data
string	Stored strings, useful for implementing internationalization
style	Predefined styles and themes

These can be referred to in code as android.R.dimen.app_icon_size, or in the XML as
@android:dimen/app_icon_size. Local resources don't need the android prefix. Resources in other
packages can also be accessed in a similar fashion.

ID needs a special note. You'll see this notation quite often: android:id="@+id/tvFileName". The "+"
tells adt to allocate a new ID with the given name. Otherwise, it behaves as for all the other resources.

The thing to remember about these resource identifiers is that these are just tags. Android will take
these integer IDs, and unpack the actual resources from various places about its person.

Many Android constructors will take resource IDs as arguments, which will typically wrap a call to
the resource manager—for example, getResources().getDrawable(android.R.ic_menu_help).

Build Your Own List Adapter

As previously noted, ListActivity already contains its own screen layout (a single ListView). But a
ListView does nothing without an Adapter to tell it what to display.

In our MediaPlayer project, I used a standard Adapter (SimpleCursorAdapter) to do all the work for
me. In this case, I *could* have used its cousin (SimpleAdapter) and just passed it an array of strings. But
that would have been boring, and not as pretty. So in this case, I've built my own, FileListAdapter.
Listing 6-2 shows the raw bones of the adapter code.

Listing 6-2. The Raw Bones of a ListAdapter

```java
public class FileListAdapter extends {

  protected final Context mContext;
  protected final LayoutInflater mInflater;
  protected List<File> mFiles;
  private PackageManager mPackageManager;

  public FileListAdapter(Context context) {
    mContext = context;
    mInflater = (LayoutInflater) mContext
        .getSystemService(Context.LAYOUT_INFLATER_SERVICE);
    mPackageManager = mContext.getPackageManager();
  }

  @Override
  public int getCount() {
    return getFileList().size();
  }

  @Override
  public Object getItem(int position) {
    return getFileList().get(position);
  }

  @Override
  public long getItemId(int position) {
    return position;
  }

  public List<File> getFileList() {
    return mFiles;
  }

  public View getView(int position, View convertView, ViewGroup parent) {
    LinearLayout container;
    File file = getFileList().get(position);

    if (convertView == null) {
      container = (LinearLayout) mInflater.inflate(R.layout.filelist, null);
    } else {
      container = (LinearLayout) convertView;
    }
// More code goes here
    return container;
}
```

There's some interesting stuff going on here. BaseAdapter is the class you are most likely going to want to build your ListAdapter from. It's an abstract class that requires you to tell it how to determine the length of the list, how to retrieve an item from the list, and how to display that value.

There is another function you need to supply, getItemId, which can be used to uniquely identify an item at a position. In this case, the position itself is all we need to find the item we want, so that's all we'll return.

A ListAdapter is not, in itself, a Context, and we'll want a Context for various actions around the place. Thus, the constructor is passed a Context for later use. We also want the PackageManager to get bits and pieces of information about each file, so we'll pull that from the Context now so we don't have to keep looking it up.

Inflation

The last thing the constructor does is grab a reference to the context's Inflation service. A layout.xml is a handy way of defining a view, but until it is inflated, it's just an XML file. The inflation service takes a layout ID, pulls it from the resources as previously mentioned, and translates that into a living, breathing Java object. This happens automagically when you setContentView in an Activity, but here we have to call it explicitly.

If you look at getView, you can see it calling the inflater to create a container View. The View may have already been created, in which case it is just cast to an appropriate type so that the fields in the View can be set.

Populating the List

Listing 6-3. *Populating a List of Files*

```
public void setFileList(List<File> list) {
  mFiles = list;
  notifyDataSetChanged();
}

public void setFileList(File file) throws Exception {
  File[] list = file.listFiles();
  if (list==null) {
    throw new Exception("Access denied.");
  }
  ArrayList<File> files = new ArrayList<File>(list.length);
  for (File f : list) {
    if (mShowHidden || !f.isHidden()) {
      files.add(f);
    }
  }
  Collections.sort(files,this);
  if (file.getParentFile()!=null) files.add(0,new File(".."));
  setFileList(files);
}
```

Listing 6-3 is the code that actually populates the list. If you look, I've got two different versions of setFileList. (Remember overloading?) The first version of setFileList does two simple things. It sets our internal field (mFiles) and then calls notifyDataSetChanged(). This lets the containing ListView know that something has changed, and it should redraw itself.

The second version does a lot more work. The parameter file is assumed to point to a folder. We then take advantage of the standard method listFiles(), which returns a list of files in the given folder. listFiles() will sometimes return a null, when it is unable to determine a file list. This is normally due to a lack of permissions, so I take the opportunity here to throw an exception. The calling method is then responsible for deciding what to do next.

▨ **Note** The error handling in Explorer—what to do if something goes wrong—is a prime example of the 80/20 rule. Getting the basic structure together was quick and easy. Handling all the various things that could cause problems took up most of the rest of my programming time.

---

listFiles() returns an array, whereas I've decided I actually want a List for its flexibility, so the next thing I do is a quick loop to copy the contents of the array into an ArrayList. I make a nod to efficiency by presetting the length of my list to the length of the Array, since we know it. (Although I then will typically add an entry to point to the parent, which means I should have set it to length + 1, but there's a limit to how much I care about efficiency . . .)

And then I sort the list, with Collections.sort(files,this). Keen-eyed readers may be wondering what "this" is doing there. Just stay calm—I'll get to the details of the sorting in a bit.

Finally, I add a File entry containing "..", to point to the parent folder and as an aid to navigation—but only if file.getParent()!=null, because if it's null then we've got to the root of our file system.

A FASTER ARRAY TO LIST CONVERSION

After some trial and error, I've decided that a for..each loop is the simplest way to copy the contents of an array into a list.

But there is another way, probably faster, and with fewer lines of code.

There is a handy Java class called java.util.Arrays, which contains a number of useful methods. The for loop in Listing 6-3 could have been implemented as follows.

```
List<File> list = Arrays.asList(files);
```

So why not do this all the time? It looks simple enough.

Well, it is simple, but what it returns is a direct wrap of the array. Changes to the list will be reflected in the underlying array. More to the point, it's a fixed-length list. You can't add or delete from this list, which rather takes away the point of having a List in the first place.

There is another option you may wish to experiment with, the List.addAll() method:

```
public List<File> fromArray2(File[] files) {
    List<File> list = new ArrayList<File>();
    list.addAll(Arrays.asList(files));
```

```
        return list;

    }
```

It doesn't save a lot of code, but you may find it more convenient for your coding style.

Finding Out About Your File

Android is built on a Linux kernel, so I wanted to present something similar to the standard Linux "ls -l" display format. I *could* have just grabbed the output from an "ls -l", but I got stubborn, so I spent a lot of time (read: too much) working out how to get as much info on my files as I could.

Listing 6-4. Building a List Item with All the Trimmings

```
// Build the individual list item.
public View getView(int position, View convertView, ViewGroup parent) {
  LinearLayout container;
  File file = getFileList().get(position);
  String mime = getMimeFromFile(file);

  if (convertView == null) {
    container = (LinearLayout) mInflater.inflate(R.layout.filelist, null);
  } else {
    container = (LinearLayout) convertView;
  }

  ImageView icon = (ImageView) container.findViewById(R.id.image1);
  int resourceId = 0;
  if (file.toString().equals("..")) {
    resourceId = android.R.drawable.ic_menu_revert;
  } else if (file.isDirectory()) {
    resourceId = R.drawable.folder;
  } else {
    Drawable d = getFileIcon(file);
    if (d != null) {
      icon.setImageDrawable(d);
      resourceId = -1;
    }
  }
  if (resourceId == 0)
    resourceId = R.drawable.file;
  if (resourceId >= 0) {
    icon.setImageResource(resourceId);
  }
  TextView text = (TextView) container.findViewById(R.id.tvFileName);
  TextView extra = (TextView) container.findViewById(R.id.tvAdditional);
  text.setText(file.getName());
  String perms;
  String line = "";
  if (mShowPermissions) {
    try {
```

```
        perms = permString(FileUtils.getPermissions(file));
      } catch (Exception e) {
        perms = "????";
      }
      line += " " + perms;

    }
    line += " " + file.length()+" " + mDateFormat.format(new Date(file.lastModified())));
    if (mShowOwner) {
      String owner = "";
      try {
        FileStatus fs = FileUtils.getFileStatus(file);
        if (fs.uid != 0) {
          owner = mPackageManager.getNameForUid(fs.uid);
        }
      } catch (Exception e) {
        owner = "?";
      }
      line += " " + owner;
    }
    if (mime != null)
      line += " " + mime;
    extra.setText(line.trim());
    return container;
  }
```

Listing 6-4 shows the full code of our adapter's getView method. There's quite a bit going on here. We've already discussed the role of the inflater, so I'm going to move onto the rest of it. The very first thing I do is attempt to determine what sort of icon I should display for the list.

First, I check to see if this is a ".." (which, as you should recall, is a pointer to the parent folder), which I set to android.R.drawable.ic_menu_revert, which is a nice-looking bent arrow.

■ **Note for perfectionists** I'm not exactly using this resource as intended: I just picked a standard resource that looked nice. But be aware that new Android releases or different manufacturers may decide to use a different image, so it's possible that at some time in the future we may end up with something unsuitable. It's a risk I'm willing to take, but you have been warned.

Then I check to see if this is a folder (file.isDirectory()) and if so, I tell it to use the folder resource. This is a resource I've created and stored locally, so I know exactly what I'm getting.

Next, I attempt to work out which Activity will deal with this sort of file, by calling getFileIcon. The chunk of code to determine the Icon I want is shown in Listing 6-5.

Listing 6-5. Finding an Appropriate Icon for a Given File

```
private String getMimeFromFile(File file) {
  return MimeTypeMap.getSingleton()
```

```
                        .getMimeTypeFromExtension(FileUtils.getExtension(file));
    }

    private Drawable getIntentIcon(Intent intent) {
      Drawable result = null;
      try {
        result=mPackageManager.getActivityIcon(intent);
      } catch (Exception e) {
        result=null;
      }
      return result;
    }

    public Intent getViewIntentForFile(File file) {
      Intent intent = new Intent(Intent.ACTION_VIEW);
      String mime = getMimeFromFile(file);
      intent.setDataAndType(Uri.fromFile(file), mime);
      return intent;
    }

    private Drawable getFileIcon(File file) {
      Drawable result = null;
      Intent intent = new Intent(Intent.ACTION_VIEW,Uri.fromFile(file));
      result=getIntentIcon(intent);
      if (result==null) {
        String mime = getMimeFromFile(file);
        if (mime!=null) {
          intent.setDataAndType(Uri.fromFile(file), mime);
          result=getIntentIcon(intent);
          if (result==null) {
            intent.setType(mime);
            result=getIntentIcon(intent);
          }
        }
      }
      return result;
    }
```

I actually have a couple of goes to make my best guess about which Activity I want to use.

The PackageManager has a neat function that'll return a Drawable from an Intent: getActivityIcon(). The difficult part is working out what Intent to use. We have to use implicit Intents, and not every application handles files the same way. Sometimes they look for a file extension, sometimes for a MIME type, sometimes even for what folders the file is stored in.

If the PackageManager can't resolve an Activity from an Intent, it'll throw an Exception: not very useful. So I've wrapped getActivityIcon in a method that'll catch the Exception and let me try again with some different settings. I try the following:

1.   The file by itself

2.   The file and the MIME type

3.   The MIME type by itself

I could proceed to different actions, but you reach a point of diminishing returns pretty quickly, and that seemed to give me a reasonable hit rate.

Learning to Mime

Android maintains a list of MIME types (i.e., text/plain, text/html, image/jpeg, that sort of thing). A lot of applications look for a MIME type to decide if they want to handle a file, and this appears to be behavior that Android is encouraging.

The class that maintains this list is MimeTypeMap, and you get an instance of it by calling MimeTypeMap.getSingleton(). (The getSingleton() notation tells you that MimeTypeMap maintains a single instance of itself, so in theory there will only ever be one. Is this important to know? Could be.) And this class has a convenient function to look up the appropriate MIME type for an extension: getMimeTypeFromExtension.

Oddly enough, there does not seem to be a standard function to extract a file extension in Java, so I wrote my own. This I tucked into FileUtils, which contains some useful general-purpose utilities that I intend to reuse later.

Dating Your File

The length and last update for a file are easily obtained, via File.length() and File.lastModified(). lastModified deserves a little attention. It returns a long integer in the Unix epoch, which is the number of milliseconds since Jan. 1, 1970. This is a widely used timestamp, but it's not immediately human-readable.

Java offers a number of classes and methods for turning dates into something human-readable. In this case, I've used DateFormat and Date to do my dirty work:

```
public DateFormat mDateFormat = DateFormat.getDateTimeInstance();
```

DateFormat.getDateTimeInstance() returns a DateFormat object that will take a standard Date object and display it in a date and time format appropriate to your locale. So the following converts the File.lastModified() into something vaguely human-readable.

```
mDateFormat.format(new Date(file.lastModified()));
```

This works because one of the constructors for Date takes a long argument, which (conveniently) expects a Unix epoch timestamp.

Going Native

This is the point where we leave the reservation. I want to show the file permissions in a Linux fashion, and I want to know who owns the file. These can both be important if you're trying to work out why an installation isn't working as intended.

If you remember, Android manages its package security model by allocating an owner ID to each separate application package. Thus, knowing which app owns which folder can be quite useful information. Ditto, file permissions.

But there's no function in the Android SDK to get this info. Guess we're stuck. Except . . . there *are* some classes that Android uses internally that will return all this information, and with a little jiggery-pokery you can access these.

This makes use of a remarkably useful Java feature called Reflection, which allows Java to find out about itself at runtime. So, knowing these classes exist, we can pull a sneaky and access them anyway (see Listing 6-6).

■ **Note** I'm not exactly recommending this sort of sneaky behavior, because Android makes no promises that these internal classes will always be available in future versions. That's what the *internal* bit is about. Still, this was the only way I could get what I needed, and you never know when these sorts of techniques will come in handy.

Listing 6-6. Find File Permissions Using Reflection

```
public static int getPermissions(File path) throws Exception {
    Class<?> fileUtils = Class.forName("android.os.FileUtils");
    int[] result = new int[1];
    Method getPermissions = fileUtils.getMethod("getPermissions", String.class, int[].class);
    getPermissions.invoke(null, path.getAbsolutePath(), result);
    return result[0];
}
```

There are several techniques being demonstrated here. What we want is a static method from android.os.FileUtils called getPermissions. I found out about this by poking in the actual Android source, which is (mostly) readily found on the Web, or indeed can be downloaded from Google. So I already know I'm looking for a method like this:

```
static int getPermissions(String file, int[] outPermissions)
```

The first step is to manually load the class, using the Class.forName method. This will dynamically load a class, but we don't at this stage know *which* class it will actually return. Thus the Class<?> notation, to let Java know that we *don't* know what the class will be at compile time.

Because I already know the exact method I'm looking for, I can use getMethod on the fileUtils class we've just loaded. I'm passing the name and the classes of the arguments I'm expecting, so with any luck I'll get back a method I can then invoke.

The first argument for invoke is supposed to be the object we're invoking the method for, but since this is a static method, I just pass null. And, in case you haven't come across it before, an array of length 1 is a convenient way of returning a variable back to a calling procedure. This is why the result is an int[1], rather than an int.

Of course, there's a lot that could go wrong, from the class or method not being available, to the actual file not existing. I've decided to let the calling method deal with that, so I've just noted that this method throws an exception.

Okay, so far so good, FileUtils.getPermissions can be called to get an int that contains the permissions for our file. Displaying it is another matter. Fortunately, knowing a little about Linux internals (and a little hunting about on the Web), I put together the following method (Listing 6-7).

Listing 6-7. Translating the Permissions Flags

```
// Linux stat constants
public static final int S_IFMT = 0170000; /* type of file */
public static final int S_IFLNK = 0120000; /* symbolic link */
public static final int S_IFREG = 0100000; /* regular */
public static final int S_IFBLK = 0060000; /* block special */
```

```java
public static final int S_IFDIR = 0040000; /* directory */
public static final int S_IFCHR = 0020000; /* character special */
public static final int S_IFIFO = 0010000; /* this is a FIFO */
public static final int S_ISUID = 0004000; /* set user id on execution */
public static final int S_ISGID = 0002000; /* set group id on execution */

private FileUtils() {
  // Utility class.
}

private static String permRwx(int perm) {
  String result;
  result = ((perm & 04) != 0 ? "r" : "-") + ((perm & 02) != 0 ? "w" : "-")
      + ((perm & 1) != 0 ? "x" : "-");
  return result;
}

private static String permFileType(int perm) {
  String result = "?";
  switch (perm & S_IFMT) {
  case S_IFLNK:
    result = "s";
    break; /* symbolic link */
  case S_IFREG:
    result = "-";
    break; /* regular */
  case S_IFBLK:
    result = "b";
    break; /* block special */
  case S_IFDIR:
    result = "d";
    break; /* directory */
  case S_IFCHR:
    result = "c";
    break; /* character special */
  case S_IFIFO:
    result = "p";
    break; /* this is a FIFO */
  }
  return result;
}

public static String permString(int perms) {
  String result;
  result = permFileType(perms) + permRwx(perms >> 6) + permRwx(perms >> 3)
      + permRwx(perms);
  return result;
}
```

I'm not going to claim that the code is obvious, but it should be pretty easy to puzzle out.

All the constants are octal numbers—the leading 0 is the giveaway here. You don't use octal very much these days, but back in the day it was the bee's knees. More accurately, it mapped to the 12- and 24-bit words a lot of processors were using back then. You know, back in the early Jurassic.

The type of file is defined in the top 4 bits, and the bottom 9 bits (in groups of 3, neatly lining up with octal digits) define the read, write, and execute bits for owner, group, and other, respectively. I haven't bothered at this stage with the setUserId and setGroupId bits, but it would not be a major task to add.

This leaves us with trying to find owner and group. There is a standard Linux function called stat, which returns a bunch of info on a given file. We can use a similar technique to ask for permissions, as shown in Listing 6-8.

Listing 6-8. Obtaining a File's Stats

```java
public static FileStatus getFileStatus(File path) throws Exception {
    FileStatus result = new FileStatus();
    Class<?> fileUtils = Class.forName("android.os.FileUtils");
    Class<?> fileStatus = Class.forName("android.os.FileUtils$FileStatus");
    Method getOsFileStatus = fileUtils.getMethod("getFileStatus", String.class, fileStatus);
    Object fs = fileStatus.newInstance();
    if ((Boolean) getOsFileStatus.invoke(null, path.getAbsolutePath(), fs)) {
        result.atime = fileStatus.getField("atime").getLong(fs);
        result.blksize = fileStatus.getField("blksize").getInt(fs);
        result.blocks = fileStatus.getField("blocks").getLong(fs);
        result.ctime = fileStatus.getField("ctime").getLong(fs);
        result.dev = fileStatus.getField("dev").getInt(fs);
        result.gid = fileStatus.getField("gid").getInt(fs);
        result.ino = fileStatus.getField("ino").getInt(fs);
        result.mode = fileStatus.getField("mode").getInt(fs);
        result.mtime = fileStatus.getField("mtime").getLong(fs);
        result.nlink = fileStatus.getField("nlink").getInt(fs);
        result.rdev = fileStatus.getField("rdev").getInt(fs);
        result.size = fileStatus.getField("size").getLong(fs);
        result.uid = fileStatus.getField("uid").getInt(fs);
    }
    return result;
}

public static class FileStatus {
    public long atime;
    public int blksize;
    public long blocks;
    public long ctime;
    public int dev;
    public int gid;
    public int ino;
    public int mode;
    public long mtime;
    public int nlink;
    public int rdev;
    public long size;
```

```
    public int uid;

}
```

This starts out pretty similarly to getPermissions, but we immediately run into an issue: getFileStatus puts the data into an android.os.FileUtils.FileStatus class ... which we don't have access to at compile time, so the first thing we need to do is use Reflection to get an instance of this class to pass to the get status. Note the dollar notation in the Class.forName call: android.os.FileUtils$FileStatus. This is because FileStatus is an internal class. Why this is so is beyond me.

Having got the FileStatus object, I use Reflection to access each field in turn and populate my own version of FileStatus, which *is* available at compile time.

Anyway, having gone through all those hoops, I now know quite a bit about this file, including the owner. I then make a call to PackageManager, and it will tell me what application (if any) owns this file.

```
owner = mPackageManager.getNameForUid(fs.uid);
```

All ready for display.

State Your Preference

Clearly, sometimes you want your program to do different things depending on user preference. I've already touched on Shared Preference files. Now I'm going to show a simple but elegant method of setting and maintaining these preferences (see Listing 6-9).

Listing 6-9. Defining a PreferenceScreen

```
res/xml/preference.xml:
<?xml version="1.0" encoding="utf-8"?>
<PreferenceScreen xmlns:android="http://schemas.android.com/apk/res/android">
        <CheckBoxPreference android:key="showhidden"
                android:title="Show Hidden" android:summary="Display Hidden Files">
        </CheckBoxPreference>
        <ListPreference android:entries="@array/sortOrder"
                android:key="sortorder" android:title="Sort Order"
                android:entryValues="@array/sortOrder">
        </ListPreference>
        <CheckBoxPreference android:key="groupfolders"
                android:title="Group Folders" android:summary="Sort folders seperately↵
 from files">
        </CheckBoxPreference>
        <CheckBoxPreference android:title="Show Owner"
                android:key="showowner">
        </CheckBoxPreference>
        <CheckBoxPreference android:title="Show Permissions"
                android:key="showperms">
        </CheckBoxPreference>
</PreferenceScreen>
```

Listing 6-9 shows a simple PreferenceScreen layout, which I have called preference.xml. Without a great deal of work, Android will take that layout and build a fairly comprehensive Preference Maintenance screen, which should look a lot like Figure 6-4.

Figure 6-4. What the Preference layout in Listing 6-9 should look like

Most of these values are Boolean true/false values, so I declare these as CheckBoxes. There are a bunch of attributes that you can set to control look and behavior, but the key ones here are as follows:

- android:key: The internal key used to store this value

- android:title: The displayed title

- android:summary: Some more detail on this preference

The sort order is a bit more complex, as I offer three options (see Figure 6-5).

Sort Order	
Name	◎
Size	◉
Date	◎
Cancel	

Figure 6-5. The Sort Order options in the Preference screen

Because there are several options, I've elected to use a ListPreference class. This needs, among other things, a list of strings to display, and a list of values to store:

- android:entries="@array/sortOrder"

- android:entryValues="@array/sortOrder"

In this case, I've cheated a little and decided that what is displayed should be the same as what is stored, so I've set them to the same things. But where does this array actually come from (see Listing 6-10)?

Listing 6-10. Defining Array Resources

```
res/values/arrays.xml
<?xml version="1.0" encoding="utf-8"?>
<resources>
    <string-array name="sortOrder">
        <item>Name</item>
        <item>Size</item>
        <item>Date</item>
    </string-array>
</resources>
```

If you look back to the section on resources, you'll see that one of the types of resources you can store is arrays, and Listing 6-10 is an example.

Right, now how do we actually make this preference.xml do something? Well, there is a handy class called PreferenceActivity, and Listing 6-11 shows the entire code required to do what we need.

Listing 6-11. All the Code You Need to Display a Preference Screen

```
Preferences.java:
package com.apress.ba3tp.explorer;

import android.os.Bundle;
import android.preference.PreferenceActivity;

public class Preferences extends PreferenceActivity {
  @Override
  protected void onCreate(Bundle savedInstanceState) {
    super.onCreate(savedInstanceState);
    // Load the preferences from an XML resource
    addPreferencesFromResource(R.xml.preference);
  }
}
```

That is pretty much all that's needed, just to tell it where to find its preference definition: in this case, "preference".

A couple of extra bits are actually required to enable this Activity. The following line needs to be added to AndroidManifest.xml:

```
<activity android:name=".Preferences"  android:theme="@android:style/Theme.NoTitleBar" />
```

This is to tell Android that Preferences is a valid activity. This can then be called with the following:

```
startActivity(new Intent(this, Preferences.class));
```

And that's how you do it, boys and girls.

Reading Your Preferences

The next step is to actually refer to these preferences in code. Listing 6-12 shows how.

Listing 6-12. Reading Your Preferences

```java
@Override
protected void onCreate(Bundle savedInstanceState) {
    super.onCreate(savedInstanceState);
    mPreferences = PreferenceManager.getDefaultSharedPreferences(this);
    mPreferences.registerOnSharedPreferenceChangeListener(this);
    // More stuff goes here.
    loadPreferences();
}
private void loadPreferences() {
    mAdapter.mShowHidden = mPreferences.getBoolean("showhidden", false);
    mAdapter.mGroupFolders = mPreferences.getBoolean("groupfolders", true);
    mAdapter.mShowOwner = mPreferences.getBoolean("showowner", false);
    mAdapter.mShowPermissions = mPreferences.getBoolean("showperms", false);
    Resources res = getResources();
    String[] sorts = res.getStringArray(R.array.sortOrder);
    List<String> list = Arrays.asList(sorts);
    String sortby = mPreferences.getString("sortorder", "Name");
    mAdapter.mSortBy = list.indexOf(sortby);
}
@Override
public void onSharedPreferenceChanged(SharedPreferences sharedPreferences,
        String key) {
    loadPreferences();
    doRefresh(); // Reload screen.
}
```

We get a reference to the preference manager by calling
PreferenceManager.getDefaultSharedPreferences(this), which is fairly obvious. Where we get a bit
clever is to put in a listener to tell us when anything changes:
mPreferences.registerOnSharedPreferenceChangeListener(this).

For this to work, we need our class to implement
android.content.SharedPreferences.OnSharedPreferenceChangeListener. This is where
onSharedPreferenceChanged comes in. When something makes a change to our preference file, this
reloads the preferences and redraws the screen appropriately.

One of the advantages of using the Listener approach is that we'll pick up changes when *anything*
changes the preference file, not just when the user selects the right menu item. In this particular
application, that is unlikely to happen, but when we start building more complex applications it could
come in very handy.

If you look at the code to load the sort type, you'll see I've gotten a little fancy. I load the previously
defined sortOrder array from my resources, and turn it into a list so I can use indexOf to find the position
in the list of the selected sort order. There's no special reason I did it this way, apart from as an example
of some previously discussed techniques. In retrospect, I could have defined an Integer array for the
android:entryValues in my preferences file, but it works okay as it is.

And if it ain't broke, don't fix it.

Sorting Techniques

I thought it might be worth drawing your attention to how the sorting is implemented. I've chosen three sort orders: Name, Size, and Date, which I pass to the `ListAdapter` as an integer value 0,1 and 2 respectively.

So, how do you sort a list? Easily, as it turns out. See Listing 6-13.

Listing 6-13. Sorting a List

```
Collections.sort(files,this);

private String fileSort(File file) {
  String key;
  if (mSortBy==1) key= String.format("%11d",file.length());
  else if (mSortBy==2) key=String.format("%11d", file.lastModified());
  else key=file.getName().toLowerCase();
  if (mGroupFolders) key=(file.isDirectory() ? "1" : "2")+key;
  return key;
}

@Override
public int compare(File file1, File file2) {
  return fileSort(file1).compareTo(fileSort(file2));
}
```

`Collections.sort` can be called with or without a `Comparator`. Called without, it will use the "natural" order of these objects, pretty much based on the `toString()` value. By calling `Collections.sort` with a `Comparator`, we gain quite a degree of fine control over the sort order.

Again, I've taken the easy way out and made the current class implement `java.util.Comparator<File>` with the `compare` method. I just do a string compare on return from `fileSort`, which massages the file based on the current sort settings, and rerturns a string to sort on.

Note that for the numeric compare I'm making use of `String.format` to turn the numbers into a fixed width string . . . sorting numbers that are left-aligned into strings gets you unexpected results, like 1,10,11,2,3 . . .

I've made the slightly lazy assumption that a file will be no more than 11 digits long. Since this gets us up to 100 terabytes, I think we're safe enough for the time being. (I just know I'll have to eat those words when I get to the fifth edition of this book . . .)

Date is stored as a 32-bit integer, so again, we're safe until 2038.

I prefix a "1" if this file is a directory, and a "2" if it's a plain file. This is a quick and easy way to force folders to be sorted separately if requested.

And lastly, forcing the name to lowercase makes the name sorting more "natural." Otherwise the lowercase letters will be sorted after the uppercase letters.

The Actual Activity

Whew. Finally, we get the actual `Activity` itself. Really, the bulk of the work in this application is carried out by `FileListAdapter`, but without a framework to drive it, nothing much is going to happen. I'm also taking the opportunity to show a few variations on menus, and a little bit about using standard controls (see Figure 6-6).

Figure 6-6. *The* ActionBar *for BA3TPExplorer*

The basic behavior of Explorer is a list of files. Clicking a folder will take you into that folder, and clicking the special parent folder (shown in Figure 6-7) will take you back up (hitting the back button will also work).

In Figure 6-6, you can see the simple menu structure, with an Open option, preferences, and a submenu with more options.

Figure 6-7. *The parent folder*

Listing 6-14 shows how we build the Options menu in MainActivity, which is what appears in the ActionBar.

Listing 6-14. *Building the Options Menu*

```
@Override
public boolean onCreateOptionsMenu(Menu menu) {

    menu.add(Menu.NONE, MenuId.OPEN.getId(), Menu.NONE, "Open")
        .setIcon(android.R.drawable.ic_menu_view)
        .setShowAsAction(MenuItem.SHOW_AS_ACTION_IF_ROOM|MenuItem.SHOW_AS_ACTION_WITH_TEXT);
    menu.add(Menu.NONE, MenuId.PREFERENCES.getId(), Menu.NONE, "Preferences")
        .setIcon(android.R.drawable.ic_menu_preferences)
        .setShowAsAction(MenuItem.SHOW_AS_ACTION_IF_ROOM);
    SubMenu m = menu.addSubMenu("New");
    m.add(Menu.NONE,MenuId.NEWFILE.getId(),Menu.NONE,"File").
      setIcon(R.drawable.file);
    m.add(Menu.NONE,MenuId.NEWFOLDER.getId(), Menu.NONE,"Folder").
      setIcon(R.drawable.folder);
    return super.onCreateOptionsMenu(menu);
}
```

Some of this we've seen before, but I've thrown in a few new options, one of which is a submenu, because I wanted the ability to manually enter a new folder or a new file.

Also, the "eye" icon I found for "Open" didn't immediately tell me what this option did. By adding SHOW_AS_ACTION_WITH_TEXT, it displays the text as well.

Reacting to a List Selection

ListActivity provides a fair degree of support for the ListView it's displaying. So to react to a ListItemClick, just override onListItemClick (see figure 6-15).

Listing 6-15. Responding to a `ListItemClick`

```
@Override
  protected void onListItemClick(ListView l, View v, int position, long id) {
    File f = mAdapter.getFileList().get(position);
    mCurrentFile = null;
    if (f.toString().equals("..")) {
      setCurrentDir(mCurrentDir.getParentFile());
    } else if (f.isDirectory()) {
      setCurrentDir(f);
    } else {
      mCurrentFile = f;
    }
    super.onListItemClick(l, v, position, id);
  }
```

So in Listing 6-15, I simply grab the file from the `FileListAdapter` (`mAdapter`). If it's a folder, I make that folder the current folder and display the contents. Otherwise, I record that file for later use.

I don't know if the super statement is actually needed, but I tend to leave these things in unless there's a clear reason not to.

Creation at Last

Slightly belatedly, let's have a look at the `MainActivity OnCreate`, in Listing 6-16.

Listing 6-16. The Activity OnCreate Code

```
  @Override
  protected void onCreate(Bundle savedInstanceState) {
    super.onCreate(savedInstanceState);
    mAdapter = new FileListAdapter(this);
    mPreferences = PreferenceManager.getDefaultSharedPreferences(this);
    mPreferences.registerOnSharedPreferenceChangeListener(this);

    String startDir = "/sdcard";
    if (savedInstanceState != null
        && savedInstanceState.containsKey("startDir")) {
      startDir = savedInstanceState.getString("startDir");
    }
    setCurrentDir(new File(startDir));
    getListView().setAdapter(mAdapter);
    loadPreferences();
    registerForContextMenu(getListView()); // Allow context menu to appear
    mEditText = new EditText(this);
  }
```

I'm defaulting the start folder to `/sdcard`, which is a pretty safe bet, but I'm also saving the current folder in case the `Activity` gets interrupted.

I create the `FileListAdapter`, load the previously saved preferences, and then use `getListView` to tell the `ListView` to use that adapter to display everything.

A Different Menu

If you press and hold a file, you'll find the menu in Figure 6-8.

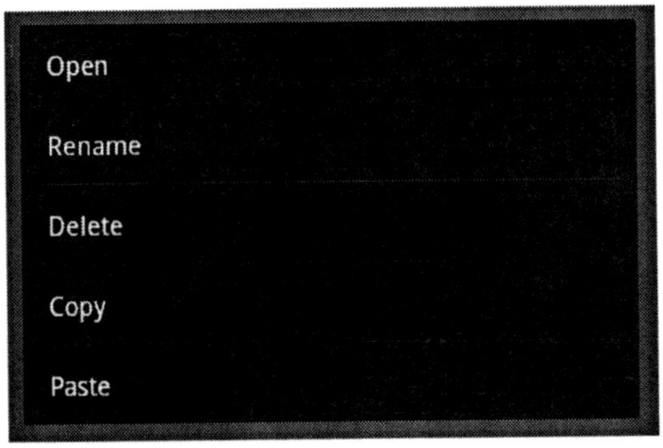

Figure 6-8. A Context menu

This is what is known as a Context menu, and it is a menu that can be associated with a particular view, much like the right-click pop-up menus in Windows.

The first thing you need to do for a Context menu is let the `Activity` know you want to display one. You do this with `registerForContextMenu(getListView())`. Next, you need an `onCreateContextMenu` method, as in Listing 6-17.

Listing 6-17. onCreate Context Menu method

```
@Override
public void onCreateContextMenu(ContextMenu menu, View v,
    ContextMenuInfo menuInfo) {
  super.onCreateContextMenu(menu, v, menuInfo);
  menu.add(Menu.NONE, MenuId.OPEN.getId(), Menu.NONE, "Open");
  menu.add(Menu.NONE, MenuId.RENAME.getId(), Menu.NONE, "Rename");
  menu.add(Menu.NONE,MenuId.DELETE.getId(), Menu.NONE, "Delete");
  menu.add(Menu.NONE,MenuId.COPY.getId(), Menu.NONE,"Copy");
  if (mClipboard!=null) {
    menu.add(Menu.NONE,MenuId.PASTE.getId(), Menu.NONE, "Paste");
  }
}
```

Context menus don't support icons or other pretties, although you can set a header icon on the menu if you like.

Unlike onCreateOptionsMenu, which is called only once, onCreateContextMenu is called each time the menu is displayed. I make use of this to only display the "Paste" menu option when there is something in my clipboard.

Reacting to a Context Menu

You handle Context menu requests a lot like Option menu requests. Listing 6-18 shows my onContextItemSelected code.

Listing 6-18. Responding to a Context Menu

```java
@Override
public boolean onContextItemSelected(MenuItem item) {
  int id = item.getItemId();
  AdapterView.AdapterContextMenuInfo info;
  try {
    info = (AdapterView.AdapterContextMenuInfo) item.getMenuInfo();
  } catch (ClassCastException e) {
    return false;
  }
  File file = (File) mAdapter.getItem(info.position);
  if (id == MenuId.RENAME.getId()) {
    mCurrentFile = file;
    showDialog(DialogId.RENAME.getId());
  } else if (id == MenuId.OPEN.getId()) {
    doOpen(file);
  } else if (id == MenuId.DELETE.getId()) {
    doDelete(file);
  } else if (id == MenuId.COPY.getId()) {
    mClipboard=file;
    toast("Copied to clipboard");
  } else if (id == MenuId.PASTE.getId()) {
    doPaste(file);
  }
  return true;
}
```

The important bit here is the getMenuInfo() call. This returns the "context" part of a Context menu. The actual class returned will vary, but by casting it to the AdapterContextMenuInfo we can get the currently selected position, and from there the currently selected file.

Dialogs

One of the funnies about Android is the lack of a modal dialog. In other words, you can't just call a dialog for user input and wait for a response. There are techniques that allow you to do this, but it does require moderately complex fiddling with threads and message passing, so I'll get to that later.

For the moment, I've chosen a couple of different techniques. Listing 6-19 shows a couple of different ways of using onCreateDialog.

Listing 6-19. A Selection of Dialogs

```java
@Override
protected Dialog onCreateDialog(int id, Bundle args) {
  if (id == DialogId.ASKTYPE.getId()) {
    AlertDialog.Builder b = new AlertDialog.Builder(this);
    String[] list = { "Text", "HTML" };
    b.setItems(list, new OnClickListener() {

      @Override
```

```java
      public void onClick(DialogInterface dialog, int which) {
        Intent intent = new Intent(Intent.ACTION_VIEW);
        if (which == 0)
          intent.setDataAndType(Uri.fromFile(mCurrentFile), "text/plain");
        else if (which == 1)
          intent.setDataAndType(Uri.fromFile(mCurrentFile), "text/html");
        try {
          startActivity(intent);
        } catch (Exception e) {
          toast(e);
        }
      }
    });
    return b.create();
  } else if (id == DialogId.RENAME.getId()) {
    AlertDialog.Builder b = new AlertDialog.Builder(this);
    b.setTitle("Rename");
    b.setView(mEditText);
    b.setPositiveButton("Ok", new OnClickListener() {

      @Override
      public void onClick(DialogInterface dialog, int which) {
        String newname = mEditText.getText().toString();
        File newfile = new File(mCurrentFile.getParentFile(),newname);
        if (mCurrentFile.renameTo(newfile)) {
          setCurrentDir(mCurrentDir); // Reload screen.
        } else {
          toast("Rename to " + newfile + " failed.");
        }
      }
    });
    return b.create();
  }
  return super.onCreateDialog(id, args);
}

@Override
protected void onPrepareDialog(int id, Dialog dialog) {
  if (id == DialogId.RENAME.getId()) {
    mEditText.setText(mCurrentFile.getName());
  }
  super.onPrepareDialog(id, dialog);
}
```

This covers two dialogs. One, ASKTYPE, simply asks whether to display a file as text or HTML, for situations where it can't work things out for itself. It achieves this by adding a List to the Alert dialog, and creating an anonymous Listener class to respond when something is selected. If the user chooses instead to hit Back, then default behavior will take over. In other words, the dialog will go away and nothing else will happen. RENAME is more complex, and requires a new file name to be entered into an edit box.

If you look back at Listing 6-16, I've created a global field, mEditText. This is popped into the new AlertDialog I'm building using the setView function. But onCreateDialog is called only once per dialog ID. I want to pre-populate the mEditText value with the current file name.

This is where the onPrepareDialog override comes in. It allows you to make adjustments to your Dialog before it is actually displayed.

■ **Note** A View can have only one parent. This means that I can't reuse mEditText in other dialogs, tempting though it is.

Once again, I've used an anonymous listener to respond to the positive button click, to perform the actual rename.

I've implemented a simple copy and paste mechanism to allow for file copies. The "Copy" is easy—I just grab the currently selected File and stick it into mClipBoard. But I wanted to make sure the user is sure this is what he or she wants to do, and I decided that trying to do these common tasks through onCreateDialog was going to be too cumbersome.

The reason to use onCreateDialog is that Android takes care of managing the dialog life cycle. However, it's not the only way to skin a cat. Listing 6-20 shows another approach.

Listing 6-20. Creating a Prompt Dialog on the Fly

```
public void promptMessage(String caption, Object message, String positive,
DialogInterface.OnClickListener onPositive, String negative, DialogInterface.OnClickListener
onNegative) {
    clearDialog();
    AlertDialog.Builder b = new AlertDialog.Builder(this);
    b.setTitle(caption);
    b.setMessage(message.toString());
    if (positive==null) positive="Yes";
    if (onPositive!=null) b.setPositiveButton(positive, onPositive);
    if (negative==null) negative="No";
    if (onNegative!=null) b.setNegativeButton(negative, onNegative);
    mDialog=b.create();
    mDialog.show();
}
```

This manages most of the boilerplate for building and showing a dialog, including clearing out any pre-existing dialogs. So, for example, the Paste command looks like Listing 6-21.

Listing 6-21. The Code for the Paste Dialog

```
promptMessage("Copy from "+mClipboard,"to "+mDestination, new OnClickListener() {

    @Override
    public void onClick(DialogInterface dialog, int which) {
        performCopy();
    }
});
```

This produces a dialog like Figure 6-9.

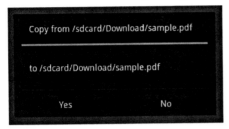

Figure 6-9. *The Paste dialog in action*

A Few Last Bits

Just a few last bits that I feel are valuable. Listing 6-22 shows a few behaviors worth noting.

Listing 6-22. Some Final Housekeeping

```
@Override
  protected void onStart() {
    super.onStart();
    ActionBar a = getActionBar(); // Actionbar doesn't seem to be available in
                                  // onCreate.
    if (a != null)
      a.setSubtitle(mCurrentDir.getAbsolutePath());
  }

  @Override
  protected void onDestroy() {
    clearDialog(); // Don't know if this is essential, but may as well be neat.
    super.onDestroy();
  }

  @Override
  public void onBackPressed() {
    if (mCurrentDir != null && mCurrentDir.getParent() != null) {
      setCurrentDir(mCurrentDir.getParentFile());
    } else {
      super.onBackPressed();
    }
  }
}
```

Default behavior for the back button is to just close the Activity. This is not terribly desirable here, so I overrode it to act the same as tapping the "parent" line.

Note that not all our dialogs are "managed." I added a clearDialog in onDestroy to make quite sure everything has been tidied up. Once again, I'm not completely sure it's required, but better safe than sorry.

Finally, I wanted to display the currently selected folder in the application bar's subtitle.

Interestingly, getActionBar returns a null in onCreate, so I put in an onStart method to populate it. ActionBar *is* available there.

Making It Better

This application could do more. Some obvious additions would be a Cut ➤ Paste as well as a Copy ➤ Paste function. Setting permissions may be desirable. *Hint: I've included a* chmod *method in* FileUtils. The performCopy feature handles copying folders, but it's a little basic at the moment, and could be much cleverer. It wouldn't be hard to add a "Share" menu option, or an "Edit." Really keen readers may wish to look at implementing FTP or LAN capability, but that's getting fancy. More to the point, this could be used as a basis for any application that finds the need to browse or manipulate files.

Summary

Above and beyond being a chapter about building a file explorer, this chapter covers quite a bit about resource handling, several different kinds of menus, and more ways of managing dialogs. We also show some cunning ways to manipulate files, and spend quite a lot of time on building your own ListActivity.

And then there's preferences, and how to build quite a nice preference editor with only a few lines of code. We even had a little play at Reflection.

So all in all, this little exercise has managed to roam far and wide, and touch on many aspects of Android programming—exploring in more ways than one.

CHAPTER 7

Contact Manager

And Other Potentially Useful Applications

Unlike the file explorer, which does not (as yet) come as a standard with Android, a contact manager is a pretty standard application. So rolling your own might not seem so useful.

Still, precisely because contact management is a core part of Android, learning how to manage, maintain, and update your contact list programmatically is a useful thing. Plus, this should give us a chance to refine our techniques even more.

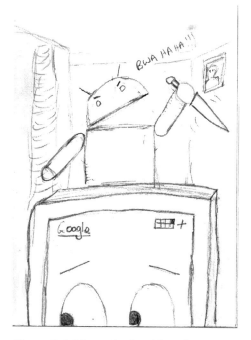

Figure 7-1. *It's good to be able to keep track of your friends . . .*

And Now for Something Completely Different

Before we plunge into the intricacies of contacts and cursors, a short detour. There is a project in the source file download called "Genma." It was not actually intended to be part of this book—just a quick program I threw together for my own amusement.

The concept was simple. There's a Japanese cartoon (known to the cognoscenti as *anime*) that my daughter has loved from an early age. This anime is called "Ranma ½," and one of the characters turns into a panda when splashed with cold water. He then communicates with signboards. Where he obtains the signboards is never adequately explained.

Anyway, my son suggested that a nice application for a tablet would be to be able to quickly type in a message and have it displayed in large letters. Apart from purely silly uses, this could be useful in a number of situations, including airports.

Not finding such an application readily available, I thought I'd just quickly throw one together. (The other, much longer, story about my panda costume I will leave to your imagination.) Indeed, it was the work of a few minutes to put something workable together.

However, after a while, I realized that getting it just so was going to involve going into unknown (and poorly documented) territory. Among other things, it prompted me to start putting together a common library, work out how to precisely calculate text sizes to maximize display area, and improve my dialog handling.

I also started exploring techniques for backward compatibility—how to take advantage of some Android features while still being able to run the application on a phone.

The Application

Figure 7-2 shows the basic screen layout. Very simply, a message is displayed in large letters on a screen, with a nice woodgrain background. The user can hit Edit to type in a new message. There is also list management, so you can have a list of preset messages for display.

The tricky bit turned out to be getting the largest text that would fit on the display. This is not a particularly well-documented part of Android (and I'm still not *completely* sure I've got it 100% right), but a solution was at last found.

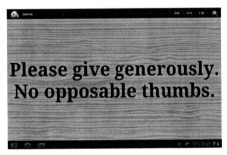

Figure 7-2. *Signboards, for fun and profit*

Anatomy of a Signpost

In a departure from my beloved LinearLayout, I thought I'd go for a simple FrameLayout. A FrameLayout will display a single view at a time—almost too simple. See Listing 7-1 for details.

Listing 7-1. The Genma Layout File

```xml
<?xml version="1.0" encoding="utf-8"?>
<FrameLayout xmlns:android="http://schemas.android.com/apk/res/android"
    android:orientation="vertical"
    android:layout_width="fill_parent"
    android:layout_height="fill_parent"
    android:id="@+id/root">
    <TextView
      android:id="@+id/textView1"
      android:layout_width="match_parent"
      android:layout_height="match_parent"
      android:background="@drawable/wood"
      android:text="Genma"
      android:duplicateParentState="true"
      android:textColor="#000"
      android:textStyle="bold"
      android:typeface="serif"
      android:gravity="center"
      android:textSize="64sp">
    </TextView>
</FrameLayout>
```

Obviously, most of the clever stuff went into the TextView. The background was as simple as setting the background attribute to a woodgrain bitmap.

Text color and style are fairly obvious. Android comes with three standard typefaces: Serif, Sans, and Monospace. I just stuck with the basics, but it's quite possible to include a custom font, which I'll look at later.

textSize was set to 64sp, which was the arbitrary placeholder size.

gravity is in fact quite an interesting attribute, in that it is how you handle the text justification. center by itself just centers the text horizontally and vertically, but you can define combinations of values to precisely control your text layout. gravity must be one or more (separated by "|") of the constant values shown in Table 7-1.

Table 7-1. Possible Flags for Gravity

Constant	Description
top	Push object to the top of its container, not changing its size
bottom	Push object to the bottom of its container, not changing its size
left	Push object to the left of its container, not changing its size
right	Push object to the right of its container, not changing its size
center_vertical	Place object in the vertical center of its container, not changing its size
fill_vertical	Grow the vertical size of the object if needed so it completely fills its container

Constant	Description
center_horizontal	Place object in the horizontal center of its container, not changing its size
fill_horizontal	Grow the horizontal size of the object if needed so it completely fills its container
center	Place the object in the center of its container in both the vertical and horizontal axis, not changing its size
fill	Grow the horizontal and vertical size of the object if needed so it completely fills its container
clip_vertical	Additional option that can be set to have the top and/or bottom edges of the child clipped to its container's bounds; the clip will be based on the vertical gravity: a top gravity will clip the bottom edge, a bottom gravity will clip the top edge, and neither will clip both edges.
clip_horizontal	Additional option that can be set to have the left and/or right edges of the child clipped to its container's bounds; the clip will be based on the horizontal gravity: a left gravity will clip the right edge, a right gravity will clip the left edge, and neither will clip both edges.

Unfortunately, no variation of fill did what I wanted it to, which was to adjust the text size to fill up the available space. The gravity property is probably intended for things other than text, which has its own special handling issues. Finding out how to make it perform this particular function took a considerable degree of trial and error. Listing 7-2 shows my eventual solution.

Listing 7-2. Resizing Text

```
void getBounds(TextPaint tp, String text, int maxwidth, Rect r) {
    float width = 0;
    int height = 0;
    int pos = 0;
    int len = text.length();
    float[] measured = new float[1];
    int lineHeight = (int) (tp.getTextSize()+ tp.getFontSpacing());
    while (pos < len) {
        int w = tp.breakText(text, pos, len, true, maxwidth, measured);
        width = Math.max(r.width(), measured[0]);
        height += lineHeight;
        pos += w;
    }
    r.set(0, 0, (int) (width), (int) (height));
}

protected void sizeText() {
    View root = findViewById(R.id.root);
    if (root != null) {
        int width = root.getWidth();
```

```
    int height = root.getHeight();
    int size = 16;
    if (width<=0 || height<=0) return;
    mText.setTextSize(size);
    String s = (String) mText.getText();
    Rect r = new Rect();
    TextPaint tp = mText.getPaint();
    while (true) {
      // tp.getTextBounds(s,0,s.length(),r);
      getBounds(tp, s, width, r);
      if (r.width() > width || r.height() > height)
        break;
      size += 1;
      mText.setTextSize(size);
    }
    mText.setTextSize(size - 1);
  }
}
```

Obviously, I wanted to tweak the size so that the message is as big as possible while still being visible on the screen. The first attempt was simply to set the text size of my TextView to be the same as the height of my display area. This turned out to work only if the text was not significantly longer that it was high, limiting my messages to about two characters long. Not as useful as you might think.

A NOTE ON FONT SIZES

The font size is given in terms of scaled density, or "sp". What this translates to is a size in pixels multiplied by a platform- (and screen density–) dependent scaling figure.

On tablets, this figure is normally 1.0 anyway, so a textSize of 64sp will translate to letters 64 pixels high . . . not taking into account line spacing and other imponderables.

On my phone, this scaling figure was 1.5, so a 64sp text = 1.5 * 64 = 96 pixels high.

You can find out your device's scaledDensity with a DisplayMetric, like so:

```
DisplayMetrics dm = new DisplayMetrics();
getWindowManager().getDefaultDisplay().getMetrics(dm);
actualHeight= mText.getTextSize()*dm.scaledDensity;
```

The next attempt was just a loop trying different text sizes until the size of the text I was trying to draw was either higher or longer than the space available, and then stepping back a pace.

The class to measure the size of your text is, rather counter-intuitively, TextPaint.

```
TextPaint tp = mText.getPaint();
```

TextPaint has quite a variety of text measuring functions, the obvious one being the following:

```
tp.getTextBounds(s,0,s.length(),rect);
```

This will fill in a Rect class with top, bottom, left, and right coordinates, and Rect has some helper methods to turn those into width and height. That approach worked okay, but getTextBounds was really designed for a single line of text. It did not cope well with line breaks, and made no allowance for word wrapping to take advantage of screen height.

getBounds (in Listing 7-2) makes use of TextPaint.breakText. This function will work to break up your sentence according to word boundaries and a maximum physical width. It also returns the actual width that it has calculated.

Working out the line height was, again, something of trial and error. I ended up going with TextPaint.getTextSize() + TextPaint.getLineSpacing().

It would appear that all these functions return pixels, rather than using scaledDensity, but don't quote me on that. The documentation is kind of fuzzy on that point. However, it all seems to work reliably.

Knowing When the View Is Available

Another element of trial and error was required to work out when to call sizeText to make sure the font was always the correct size. It turns out that none of the lifecycle events are particularly useful. However, onWindowFocusChanged does the job, as in Listing 7-3.

Listing 7-3. Capturing a Window Focus Event

```
@Override
public void onWindowFocusChanged(boolean hasFocus) {
  if (hasFocus) sizeText();
  super.onWindowFocusChanged(hasFocus);
}
```

Room for Improvement

The main loop of text sizing is a brute force approach, and could be cleverer, but since it seems fast enough for my purposes, I elected not to improve on it. That is one of the key rules about optimizing your code: make sure that what you are optimizing actually needs it.

> *"We should forget about small efficiencies, say about 97% of the time: premature optimization is the root of all evil."*

> —Donald E. Knuth

I'm not going to harp on about it, but the time to start optimizing a program is after you've got it working. But I digress.

There seems to be additional padding in the TextView control, so the eventual font is not quite as large as it possibly could be. Again, this started life as a quicky application. One day I will find out where this extra padding is coming from, and let you know.

Backward Compatibility

Backward compatibility in this case is as simple as setting a minimum SDK to something lower than your current SDK, and making sure you don't call the extra features if you don't need to. Listing 7-4 shows one approach.

Listing 7-4. Backward-Compatible Menus

```
@Override
public boolean onCreateOptionsMenu(Menu menu) {
  addAction(menu.add("Edit"));
  addAction(menu.add("Info"));
  addAction(menu.add("List"));
  menu.add("Edit List");
  menu.add("Add to List");
  return super.onCreateOptionsMenu(menu);
}

// This should work on phones AND tablets
  public static void addAction(MenuItem add) {
    if (Build.VERSION.SDK_INT>=11) {
      add.setShowAsAction(MenuItem.SHOW_AS_ACTION_IF_ROOM);
    }
  }
}
```

All I wanted was to make use of the ActionBar to display some of my menu options. To achieve this, I wrapped the items I wanted to appear on the bar in a call to addAction. This in turn checked the SDK level (by interrogating Build.VERSION.SDK_INT) and then called setShowAsAction only if it was running on a device that should support the additional code.

Another—possibly safer—approach is illustrated in Listing 7-5.

Listing 7-5. Backward-Compatible Menus Using Error Detection

```
public static void addAction2(MenuItem add) {
  try {
    add.setShowAsAction(MenuItem.SHOW_AS_ACTION_IF_ROOM);
  } catch (NoSuchMethodError ne) {
    // Just catch the error silently.
  }
}
```

This simply catches the error if there is one, and ignores it. I'm not fond of these structures as a rule—among other things, working out precisely what error conditions you need to trap can be tricky—but that is down to personal preference.

■ **Note** Error and Exception are actually siblings in the class hierarchy. Therefore a catch (Exception e) would, in fact, fail to catch anything in this case. This succeeded in driving me mad until I discovered this little behavior.

You may note that I'm using a simplified `menu.add` call compared to other examples. You don't actually need to stuff about setting IDs and so forth if you don't want to. You can just set the title. This is not recommended for large projects, because you are then relying on the title itself to identify which menu item was pressed. If you later change your mind about what to call the menu, you'll also have to change any references to that menu item. Still, I thought I should show you some options.

List Handling

Once again I used a `ListActivity`—they are pretty much the workhorse of the Android user interface. Figure 7-3 shows what it looks like.

This'll be about our third version of a list interface, so I'll only point out that I used an `ArrayAdapter` for the list. This is by far the simplest of the `ListAdapters`, maintaining its own list of objects and displaying the results in a simple `TextView`.

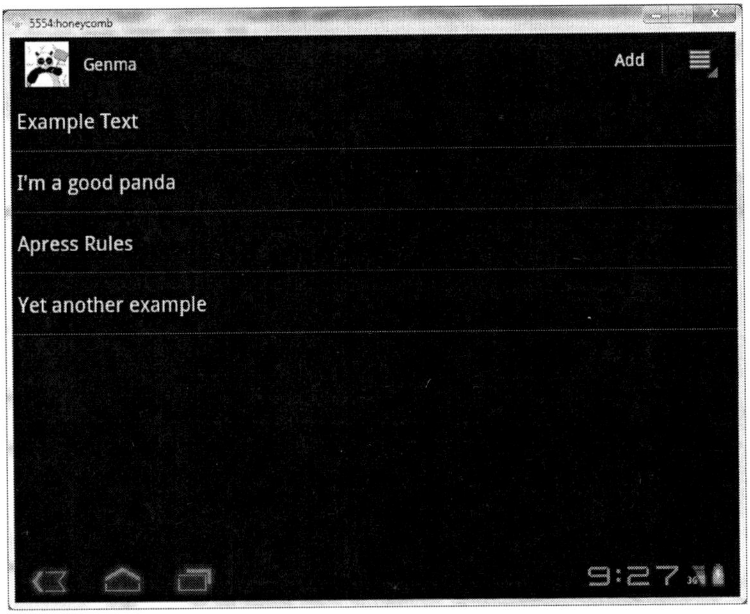

Figure 7-3. Genma handling lists

Saving the List

I'm using `SharedPreferences` to save the list and the currently displayed message. Listing 7-6 shows the code I'm using.

Listing 7-6. Storing a List in Preferences

```
mPreferences = PreferenceManager.getDefaultSharedPreferences(this);

public static List<String> loadList(SharedPreferences preferences) {
    List<String> result = null;
```

```
  int count = preferences.getInt("list.count", 0);
  if (count > 0) {
    result = new ArrayList<String>(count);
    for (int i = 0; i < count; i++)
      result.add(preferences.getString("list." + i, "empty"));
  }
  return result;
}

public static void saveList(List<String> list, SharedPreferences preferences) {
  SharedPreferences.Editor e = preferences.edit();
  int count = preferences.getInt("list.count", 0);
  for (int i = 0; i < count; i++) {
    e.remove("list." + i);
  }
  e.putInt("list.count", list.size());
  for (int i=0; i<list.size(); i++) e.putString("list."+i, list.get(i));
  e.commit();
}
```

Sadly there appears to be no handy routine to save an array or list to preferences, so I'm managing it a line at a time, which seems to work pretty well.

Reusing Your Libraries

At this stage, in our selection of projects, I notice that I'm starting to reuse code quite a bit. And that's as it should be, as a great deal of programming efficiency revolves around reuse of code.

Up until now I've just popped utility code in as and where I needed it, mostly to avoid unneeded complexity in my examples. But it's about time we started building a proper library of useful code, which I've done in BA3TPUtils.

Note that I've deliberately *not* set this up as an Android project. I have instead linked in an android.jar from android-sdk/platforms, for purposes of compilation. When you come to use this code, or indeed your own libraries, you may need to point this to wherever you've installed your android_sdk. You do this with Build Path ➤ Add External Archives.

To use this new library in other projects, we go to Properties ➤ Java Build Path ➤ Projects, and add BA3TPUtils in there.

Import and Export

Before we leave this little application, I got enthusiastic and included an import and export mechanism, to read and write my list as a text file. There are a few things worthy of note. One is the use of the Environment class to work out where the default Download folder is.

```
Environment.getExternalStoragePublicDirectory(Environment.DIRECTORY_DOWNLOADS);
```

There are a bunch of predefined public folders, as shown in Table 7-2.

Table 7-2. Predefined Public Folders

Constant	Description
DIRECTORY_ALARMS	Standard directory in which to place any audio files that should be in the list of alarms that the user can select
DIRECTORY_DCIM	The traditional location for pictures and videos when mounting the device as a camera
DIRECTORY_DOWNLOADS	Standard directory in which to place files that have been downloaded by the user
DIRECTORY_MOVIES	Standard directory in which to place movies that are available to the user
DIRECTORY_MUSIC	Standard directory in which to place any audio files that should be in the regular list of music for the user
DIRECTORY_NOTIFICATIONS	Standard directory in which to place any audio files that should be in the list of notifications that the user can select (not as regular music)
DIRECTORY_PICTURES	Standard directory in which to place pictures that are available to the user
DIRECTORY_PODCASTS	Standard directory in which to place any audio files that should be in the list of podcasts that the user can select (not as regular music)
DIRECTORY_RINGTONES	Standard directory in which to place any audio files that should be in the list of ringtones that the user can select (not as regular music)

So the export is easy.

For the import, I decided to get clever. FilePicker is a class I've created that builds a dialog box that displays files in a folder, and allows simple navigation—in short, Explorer in miniature.

A Last Note on Dialogs

It's worth a look at how I'm managing the text input dialog boxes. It's all very well managing dialogs through the onCreateDialog event, but it can easily get to be a pain when you start having more than a couple of dialogs.

As of SDK 8, showDialog and onPrepareDialog have an extra parameter, a Bundle. You can use it in showDialog to pass parameters to onPrepareDialog (see Listing 7-7).

Listing 7-7. Using Bundles to Pass Extra Arguments to Dialogs

```
if (menuname.equals("Edit")) {
  Bundle b = new Bundle();
```

```
   b.putString("text", value);
   showDialog(DIALOG_EDIT,b);
}

@Override
protected void onPrepareDialog(int id, Dialog dialog, Bundle args) {
  if (id==DIALOG_EDIT) {
    String text = null;
    if (args!=null) {
      text = args.getString("text");
    }
    mInput.setText(text);
  }
  super.onPrepareDialog(id, dialog, args);
}
```

Listing 7-7 shows how I'm populating a general-purpose input dialog each time it's called, with a Bundle containing the value I wanted displayed for editing.

Managing Contacts

Now for the actual contact manager (shown in Figure 7-4). It's not as pretty as I would have liked, but time got short on me. Plus we've already done several examples of list- and cursor-based applications. So rather than reinvent the wheel yet again, I've chosen to concentrate on some other quite useful aspects of programming in Honeycomb.

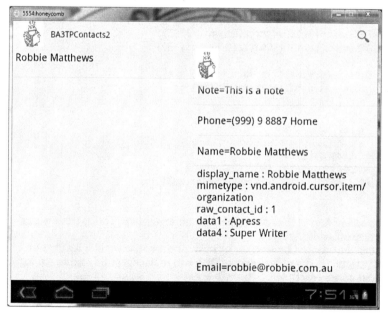

Figure 7-4. The contact manager in all its glory

The contact manager application looks a bit like Figure 7-4. Only I would expect more contacts to be available, it being quite tricky to import contacts into the emulator. This app will demonstrate adding, modifying, and deleting contact details. It also demonstrates the use of the search bar, and how to use a new Android feature introduced in Honeycomb, the Loader.

Loaders

Loaders will handle loading data asynchronously. It was always possible to do this using Java threads, but there was quite a bit of boilerplate and fiddling to get it working nicely. Loaders manage a lot of this for you. Let's have a quick look at how they work: check out Listing 7-8.

Listing 7-8. An Example of Loaders

```
public class LoaderListFragment extends ListFragment implements
    LoaderManager.LoaderCallbacks<Cursor> {
  public Loader<Cursor> onCreateLoader(int id, Bundle args) {
   if (id == CONTACT_GROUP) {
      return new CursorLoader(getActivity(),ContactsContract.Groups.CONTENT_URI, null,
         null, null, null);
    } else {
      return null;
    }
  }

  public void onLoadFinished(Loader<Cursor> loader, Cursor data) {
    int id = loader.getId();
    if (id==CONTACT_GROUP) {
      int title = data.getColumnIndex(ContactsContract.Groups.TITLE);
      int group_id = data.getColumnIndex(ContactsContract.Groups._ID);
      mGroups.clear();
      for (data.moveToFirst(); !data.isAfterLast(); data.moveToNext()) {
        mGroups.put(data.getInt(group_id),data.getString(title));
      }
    }
  }

  public void onLoaderReset(Loader<Cursor> loader) {
    if (loader.getId()==CONTACT_LOADER) mAdapter.swapCursor(null);
    else if (loader.getId()==CONTACT_DETAIL) mDetail.swapCursor(null);
  }
```

Listing 7-8 shows a slimmed down version of the code in the contacts program. This is what actually handles the necessary implementation of LoaderManager.

LoaderManager works on a pattern that should be familiar by now. Android uses callbacks in your program to manage the lifecycle of various Loaders. The Loaders then run in background and signal the main thread when the data is ready to be accessed.

The particular type of Loader I'm using is a CursorLoader. There are other types, but this is the one you're most likely to want to use.

Starting a Loader

You access the `Context`'s `LoaderManager` by calling `getLoaderManager()`, and you start a `Loader` running as follows:

```
getLoaderManager().initLoader(CONTACT_GROUP, null, this);
```

`CONTACT_GROUP` is a constant I defined earlier to uniquely identify which `Loader` we wanted to start. The second parameter is an optional `Bundle`, which is passed to the `onCreateLoader` method as args. The third parameter is a `LoaderCallbacks` listener . . . in this case, I've gone with my common pattern and made the `ListFragment` implement it.

The other useful `LoaderManager` method is `restartLoader`, i.e.:

```
getLoaderManager().restartLoader(CONTACT_DETAIL, null, this);
```

This will cause the `Loader` to start again, presumably with new parameters. `restartLoader` is very useful, because apart from anything else, it won't wait until the current `Loader` has finished to start again. This is not always an easy thing to manage neatly, so it's good that Android is doing the work for you. This will be particularly useful when I explain the use of the Search feature a little later in this chapter.

How a Loader Works

In Listing 7-8, I'm showing only the simplest of the three `Loaders` that I'm using in this application. It is just loading a `Map` of available contact groups for convenient display later on. It's almost overkill, but it does demonstrate what is going on.

A call to `LoaderManager.initLoader` (or `restartLoader`) will at some point result in a call to `onCreateLoader`. `onCreateLoader` will return a new `Loader`—in this case, the following:

```
return new CursorLoader(getActivity(),ContactsContract.Groups.CONTENT_URI,
 null, null, null, null);
```

`CursorLoader` takes as its arguments everything needed to make a query. The arguments (with the addition of an initial `Context` argument) are exactly as per a `ManagedQuery` or a `ContentResolver` query. This then goes off in the background, and when completely ready, calls `onLoadFinished` with the completed cursor.

In the case of `CONTACT_GROUP`, this is just used to populate a `Map`, but a more common use would be to assign to a `ListAdapter` for display purposes.

Finally, `onLoaderReset` is called when the `Loader` has finished for the day, to make sure that cursors can be freed up.

Why a Loader?

Users are an impatient lot. As a general rule, the less they have to wait for an application to respond to their demands, the happier they will be.

Queries take a finite time to run. In fact, most of the queries we are likely to make on an Android 3 tablet will be fast enough that user delay will be minimal, but `Loaders` take even that out of the equation.

Because the bulk of the work is taking place in a background thread, the foreground thread is free to respond to user actions promptly, so even if the actual processing is no faster, the apparent responsiveness is much snappier.

Responsiveness is good.

Responsiveness keeps the user happy.

Keeping the user happy is good . . . apart from anything else, the user might be you.

Back in the ancient days, when I was still programming on stone tablets, I found this out the hard way. Working out how to render a list in the background while still allowing the user to do stuff turned out to be the difference between a brilliant piece of software and an almost unusable pile of offal. I might add, I had to do this on a machine that would be considered underpowered to run a microwave these days, let alone a multi-user real-time dispatching system. And I didn't have the luxury of threads and other useful tools to achieve this . . . you kids don't know how lucky you are these days! (Old codger mode off.)

The Search Bar

As might be expected, Android has good support for search facilities. Heck, the phone versions of Android typically have a dedicated physical search button. Listing 7-9 shows one way of implementing this.

Listing 7-9. Implementing a SearchView

```
@Override
public void onCreateOptionsMenu(Menu menu, MenuInflater inflater) {
    // Place an action bar item for searching.
    MenuItem item = menu.add("Search");
    item.setIcon(android.R.drawable.ic_menu_search);
    item.setShowAsAction(MenuItem.SHOW_AS_ACTION_IF_ROOM);
    SearchView sv = new SearchView(getActivity());
    sv.setOnQueryTextListener(this);
    item.setActionView(sv);
}
```

The key here is the SearchView control. To quote the Android documentation, a SearchView is as follows:

> *A widget that provides a user interface for the user to enter a search query and submit a request to a search provider. Shows a list of query suggestions or results, if available, and allows the user to pick a suggestion or result to launch into.*

This can be associated with a MenuItem by means of MenuItem.setActionView, which allows you to provide your own View to display in place of the default Menu item. It should come out looking something like Figure 7-5.

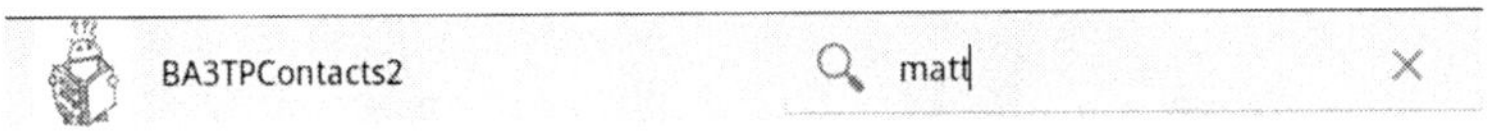

Figure 7-5. A SearchView in the ActionBar

You'll note setOnQueryTextListener setting a listener to respond to user-entered text changes. These are once again implemented in the main class, as per Listing 7-10.

Listing 7-10. Handling Search Requests

```java
public class LoaderListFragment extends ListFragment implements
    OnQueryTextListener, LoaderManager.LoaderCallbacks<Cursor>, OnItemClickListener {


  // Search Bar
  public boolean onQueryTextChange(String newText) {
    // Called when the action bar search text has changed. Update
    // the search filter, and restart the loader to do a new query
    // with this filter.
    mCurFilter = !TextUtils.isEmpty(newText) ? newText : null;
    getLoaderManager().restartLoader(CONTACT_LOADER, null, this);
    return true;
  }

  @Override
  public boolean onQueryTextSubmit(String query) {
    // Don't care about this.
    return true;
  }
```

OnQueryTextListener requires two methods, onQueryTextChange and onQueryTextSubmit. onQueryTextChange is called whenever the text changes, and onQueryTextSubmit is when the user actually hits Enter or the Search button. We could use onQueryTextSubmit to implement the search for contact details, but that would be boring.

Instead, we're going to respond to user input as they type, refining the query as they go. Done synchronously, this could be disastrously slow, but since we're doing all the actual querying in background, it's all transparent to the user. Let's look at what the CONTACT_LOADER (shown in Listing 7-11) is doing.

Listing 7-11. The Contact Loader

```java
  if (id == CONTACT_LOADER) {
    Uri baseUri;
    if (mCurFilter != null) {
      baseUri = Uri.withAppendedPath(ContactsContract.Contacts.CONTENT_FILTER_URI,
        Uri.encode(mCurFilter));
    } else {
      baseUri = ContactsContract.Contacts.CONTENT_URI;
    }

    // Now create and return a CursorLoader that will take care of
    // creating a Cursor for the data being displayed.
    String select = "(" + Contacts.DISPLAY_NAME + " is not null)";
    return new CursorLoader(getActivity(), baseUri,
        CONTACTS_SUMMARY_COLUMNS, select, null, Contacts.DISPLAY_NAME
          + " COLLATE LOCALIZED ASC");
  }
```

This is part of the onCreateLoader code. As you can see in Listing 7-10, when the user changes text in the SearchView, mCurFilter is set to the current search value.

Conveniently, ContactsContract offers a nice filter facility. This is accessed by building a Uri from ContactsContract.Contacts.CONTENT_FILTER_URI and whatever string you want to search for. This is clever enough to find what you're searching for in several areas, including first and last name.

So by building our query such that we use either the filter Uri or the plain one as needed, we can leverage quite a bit off built-in Android capabilities. This leveraging is quite noticeable at the other end of the Loader function, onLoadFinished. Listing 7-12 shows the complex nature of displaying our completed cursor.

Listing 7-12. Displaying a Completed Cursor Query

```
if (id==CONTACT_LOADER) {
  mAdapter.swapCursor(data);
}
```

As you can see: very, very complex.

I've already addressed ListAdapters at some length in previous chapters, so go check them out if you're not sure what's happening.

Contact Details

The contact API changed notably around Android 2.0. Whereas previously everything was handled using the Contacts class, now everything is handled by the ContactsContract class and its descendants and hangers-on.

A lot of the examples on the Web are still likely to show the old API. This still exists, but is maintained mainly for backward compatibility, and you are not encouraged to use it.

Now, instead of trying to keep everything on a Contact in the one record, now there are lots of different chunks of data that can be attached to a basic Contact. The relationship goes something like Table 7-3.

Table 7-3. The Relationship of Contact Records

Contact		
	Raw Contact 1	Data 1
		Data 2
		Data 3
	Raw Contact 2	Data 4
		Data 5

Each Contact can have one or more Raw Contacts, which in turn can have any number of data rows attached. A Contact is a top-level data construct, corresponding to an actual person or company. The Raw Contacts more or less correspond to the account the data is stored in, such as a Google Contacts entry, an e-mail address book, or even a phone SIM card. Each data row could be a phone number, an e-mail address, a postal address, a name, notes, a photo, or just about anything else you could think of that might be in an address book entry.

Table 7-4 shows a quick example of the sorts of data that might be stored, along with the class used for handling them.

Table 7-4. Some Common Contact Record Types

Class	Description
ContactsContract.CommonDataKinds.BaseTypes	The base types that all "Typed" data kinds support
ContactsContract.CommonDataKinds.CommonColumns	Columns common across the specific types
ContactsContract.CommonDataKinds.Email	A data kind representing an e-mail address
ContactsContract.CommonDataKinds.Event	A data kind representing an event
ContactsContract.CommonDataKinds.GroupMembership	Group membership
ContactsContract.CommonDataKinds.Im	A data kind representing an IM address
ContactsContract.CommonDataKinds.Nickname	A data kind representing the contact's nickname
ContactsContract.CommonDataKinds.Note	Notes about the contact
ContactsContract.CommonDataKinds.Organization	A data kind representing an organization
ContactsContract.CommonDataKinds.Phone	A data kind representing a telephone number
ContactsContract.CommonDataKinds.Photo	A data kind representing a photo for the contact
ContactsContract.CommonDataKinds.Relation	A data kind representing a relation
ContactsContract.CommonDataKinds.SipAddress	A data kind representing a SIP address for the contact
ContactsContract.CommonDataKinds.StructuredName	A data kind representing the contact's proper name
ContactsContract.CommonDataKinds.StructuredPostal	A data kind representing postal addresses
ContactsContract.CommonDataKinds.Website	A data kind representing a web site related to the contact

BA3TPContacts2 demonstrates several ways to access and update these data types. When you select a contact displayed in our main list, another Loader is started, loading up all the data rows it can find for the given contact (see Listing 7-13).

Listing 7-13. Querying Contact Details

```
if (id == CONTACT_DETAIL) {
    return new CursorLoader(getActivity(),ContactsContract.Data.CONTENT_URI, null,
        ContactsContract.Data.CONTACT_ID + "=" + mDetailId, null, null);
}
```

The various data rows are linked to the main contact by CONTACT_ID, and in Listing 7-13 I'm passing the value in mDetailId, which just happens to be set to the primary ID of the selected contact record.

Translating these records into something readable requires a bit of fiddling. I've provided some by no means complete examples in Listing 7-14.

Listing 7-14. Translating Contact Details into Something a Human Can Read

```
String getDataLine(Cursor c) { //Translate various contact data types.
    String type = columnData(c,ContactsContract.Data.MIMETYPE);
    if (type.equals(CommonDataKinds.Phone.CONTENT_ITEM_TYPE)) {
        return "Phone="+columnData(c,CommonDataKinds.Phone.NUMBER)+" "+getPhoneType(c);
    } else if (type.equals(CommonDataKinds.Email.CONTENT_ITEM_TYPE)) {
        return "Email="+columnData(c,CommonDataKinds.Email.ADDRESS);
    } else if (type.equals(CommonDataKinds.StructuredName.CONTENT_ITEM_TYPE)) {
        return "Name="+columnData(c,CommonDataKinds.StructuredName.DISPLAY_NAME);
    } else if (type.equals(CommonDataKinds.Nickname.CONTENT_ITEM_TYPE)) {
        return "Nickname="+columnData(c,CommonDataKinds.Nickname.DISPLAY_NAME);
    } else if (type.equals(CommonDataKinds.StructuredPostal.CONTENT_ITEM_TYPE)) {
        return "Address="+columnData(c,CommonDataKinds.StructuredPostal.FORMATTED_ADDRESS);
    } else if (type.equals(CommonDataKinds.Photo.CONTENT_ITEM_TYPE)) {
        byte[] b = c.getBlob(c.getColumnIndex(CommonDataKinds.Photo.PHOTO));
        ImageView iv = (ImageView) getActivity().findViewById(R.id.imageView1);
        if (b!=null) {
            iv.setImageBitmap(BitmapFactory.decodeByteArray(b, 0, b.length));
        } else {
            iv.setImageResource(R.drawable.icon);
        }
        return "Photo="+columnData(c,CommonDataKinds.Photo.PHOTO);
    } else if (type.equals(CommonDataKinds.Note.CONTENT_ITEM_TYPE)) {
        return "Note="+columnData(c,CommonDataKinds.Note.NOTE);
    } else if (type.equals(CommonDataKinds.GroupMembership.CONTENT_ITEM_TYPE)) {
        return "Group="+mGroups.get(columnDataInt↵
(c,CommonDataKinds.GroupMembership.GROUP_ROW_ID));
    } else if (type.equals("vnd.com.google.cursor.item/contact_misc")) {
        return "Misc";
    } else {
        return dumpDataLine(c);
    }
}
```

You can work out which sort of record a row is by looking at its ContactsContract.Data.MIMETYPE data field. By then comparing this value to the various common data types, you can work out how to display your data in a more or less pleasing fashion.

Most of the time, the most important chunk of data is returned in the general-purpose data column, DATA1. Each type will normally provide a more meaningful alias to this column, such as NUMBER for phone records, and NOTE for note.

Some record types return BLOBs (Binary Large Objects), which can contain raw binary data. For an example, you may wish to look at how I've managed Photo. The PHOTO field in this case contains a bitmap of a thumbnail of the attached photo, which I'm decoding and displaying in an ImageView at the top of the detail list.

GroupMembership returns the ID of a contact group. I use the previously acquired mGroups map to look up the title of the group rather than the rather uninformative ID.

I put in some special handling for vnd.com.google.cursor.item/contact_misc, since it kept coming up in my data and I couldn't find any information on what it did. This is not that much of a surprise, as you are free to make up your own data types, and thus should expect to come across unknown data types in any general querying application.

And finally, there is a default method that just returns any non-null column in the query, for unhandled data types.

I don't pretend that this list is comprehensive (or especially pretty), but I feel it points the way.

Editing Data

The contacts API also allows for adding, deleting, and updating contact details (see Figure 7-6). I've included examples of all of these actions. A simple click on a data row will pop up an edit window.

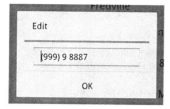

Figure 7-6. Editing a phone number

The code to edit (as shown below in Listing 7-15) is relatively simple, if somewhat bodgy.

Listing 7-15. Code to Edit Contact Data

```
private boolean isEditable(String type) {
  for (String s : editableTypes) {
    if (s.equals(type)) return true;
  }
  return false;
}

private void editRow(Cursor c) {
  mEditId = columnDataInt(c, ContactsContract.Data._ID);
  mEditCursor = c;
  Bundle b = new Bundle();
```

```
      b.putString("text",columnData(c,ContactsContract.Data.DATA1)); // Usually things↵
are in data1.
      getActivity().showDialog(0,b);
  }

  public void modifyData(String newValue) {
    if (mEditCursor==null) return;
    ContentValues values = new ContentValues();
    values.put(ContactsContract.Data.DATA1, newValue); // This is a bit quick and dirty
    Uri uri = Uri.withAppendedPath(ContactsContract.Data.CONTENT_URI,↵
String.valueOf(mEditId));
    try {
      getActivity().getContentResolver().update(uri, values, null,null);
    } catch (Exception e) {
      toast(e);
    }
    getLoaderManager().restartLoader(CONTACT_DETAIL, null, this);
  }
```

In Listing 7-15, I've made a couple of simplifying assumptions. For a start, I'm assuming that all the data types I want to edit are going to store the main field in DATA1. This is not a particularly *safe* assumption, so I've included a check so that it will call only the edit routine for a limited number of data types.

columnData is a handy helper method I've created to return the value of a column as a string, from the column name. I'm not quite sure why the Android Cursor doesn't do this automatically, as implementations of Cursor in other systems allow you to access columns directly via either column name or index. But they don't, so this supplies that facility.

Remember that all the data in the data rows are returned in a standard list of columns, DATA1 to DATA15. If you print out the value of CommonDataKinds.Phone.NUMBER, for example, you'll see it's actually "DATA1". I then throw up a dialog box to edit the data, which in turn calls modifyData with the new value.

Now, each row has a unique ID, *a.k.a.* ContactsContract.Data._ID. I'm loading this value into mEditId, so when I get to saving my changes I know which row to update.

There is a neat way to get a Uri as a direct reference to a data row. You do this by appending the _ID to ContactsContract.Data.CONTENT_URI. As a query, this will return a single row. As an update, this still refers to a single row, so all you need is to build a list of ContentValues, and pass it to getContentResolver.update().

Note the two null arguments in the update call. These are respectively a where clause and parameters for same, so you can in fact apply updates to multiple rows if you feel so inclined.

In this case, the Uri already uniquely identifies the row we want to change, so they can be left null.

Adding a Phone Number

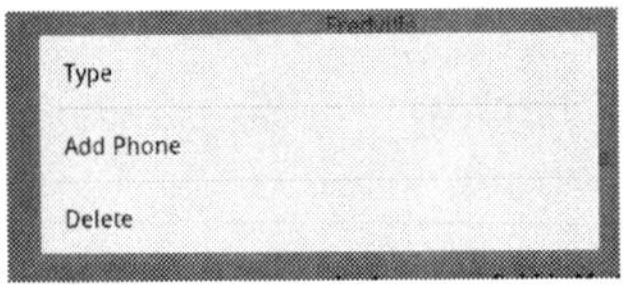

Figure 7-7. The Contact Context menu

I've implemented additional functions by way of a Context menu, as shown in Figure 7-5. Let's have a look at the Add Phone option (see Listing 7-16).

Listing 7-16. Code to Add a Phone Number

```
public boolean detailOption(MenuItem item) {
  AdapterView.AdapterContextMenuInfo info;
  try {
    info = (AdapterView.AdapterContextMenuInfo) item.getMenuInfo();
  } catch (ClassCastException e) {
    return false;
  }
  final Cursor c = mDetail.getCursor();
  final LoaderListFragment parent = this;
  c.moveToPosition(info.position);
  mEditId = columnDataInt(c, ContactsContract.Data._ID);
  if (item.getTitle().equals("Add Phone")) {
    ContentValues values = new ContentValues();
    long rawid = columnDataLong(c, Phone.RAW_CONTACT_ID);
    values.put(Phone.RAW_CONTACT_ID,rawid);
    values.put(Phone.NUMBER,"0400-999-999");
    values.put(Phone.TYPE, Phone.TYPE_MOBILE);
    values.put(Phone.MIMETYPE, Phone.CONTENT_ITEM_TYPE);
    try {
      ContentResolver cr = getActivity().getContentResolver();
      Uri result=cr.insert(ContactsContract.Data.CONTENT_URI, values);
      getLoaderManager().restartLoader(CONTACT_DETAIL, null, this);
      Log.v("Contacts2",result.toString());
      toast(result);
    } catch (Exception e) {
      Log.e("Contacts2","Insert",e);
      toast(e);
    }
    return true;
  }
  return false;
}
```

Listing 7-16 shows the basic requirements. Now, if you refer back to Table 7-2, you'll see that data rows are associated with Raw Contacts, so any new records added will need the Raw ID of the parent record. I'm pulling this from the currently selected record, neatly bypassing having to go and work out which Raw Contact to use (in situations where there is more than one to choose from).

We'll need a phone number, a phone type, and a MIME type. The rest is just a call to ContentResolver.insert.

Oh, and because I had issues myself getting this running, I refer you to the useful Log.e construction. This writes all the details of an exception to Logcat for later reference.

Changing Types

I've added code to allow you to select a phone type, i.e., Mobile or Home. Listing 7-17 shows how I've done this.

Listing 7-17. Code to Change a Type of a Phone Record

```
if (item.getTitle().equals("Type")) {
    ListPicker pick = new ListPicker(getActivity(), mPhoneTypes);
    pick.showDialog(new ListPicker.OnSelectedListener() {

        @Override
        public void onSelected(Object o) {
            ContentValues values = new ContentValues();
            values.put(Phone.TYPE,((PhoneType) o).type);
            Uri uri = Uri.withAppendedPath(ContactsContract.Data.CONTENT_URI, ↵
String.valueOf(mEditId)));
            getActivity().getContentResolver().update(uri, values, null, null);
            getLoaderManager().restartLoader(CONTACT_DETAIL, null, parent);
        }
    });
    return true;
}
```

The update is very similar to the update of the main data, except that I'm updating a different column.

You may be interested in my list selection method. In our continuing goal of building reusable code, I've created a variation of the FilePicker I developed for Genma to display a list of objects. Using objects rather than strings allows you to piggyback addition information. In this case, I've created an object to contain both the TYPE ID and a user readable title.

And Deleting

Finally, deleting some data (see Listing 7-18).

Listing 7-18. Deleting a Contact Record

```
if (item.getTitle().equals("Delete")) {
    String s = getDataLine(c);
    mBox.promptMessage("Delete",s,new DialogInterface.OnClickListener() {

        @Override
        public void onClick(DialogInterface dialog, int which) {
            Uri uri = Uri.withAppendedPath(ContactsContract.Data.CONTENT_URI, ↵
String.valueOf(mEditId)));
            try {
            parent.getActivity().getContentResolver().delete(uri,null,null);
            } catch (Exception e) {
                Log.e("Contact2","Delete",e);
                toast(e);
            }
        }
    });
}
```

I think by now the pattern is clear.

Summary

In this chapter, we've delved into a variety of aspects of Android programming. We've had a look at manipulating fonts and text, how to build an application that can take advantage of Honeycomb features but still run on older platforms. We've looked at a few different ways of throwing together menus (some of them quick and dirty, but still good to know). We've also had a pretty good look at contacts, how to read them and how to update them. Also, we had a good play with Loaders, the nice Android 3 classes that make asynchronously loading resources quick and painless.

And quick and painless is the way we like it, right?

CHAPTER 8

Dude, Where's My Car?

Adventures in GPS

Figure 8-1. Dude . . . where is my car?

One of the more interesting and useful capabilities that comes with almost every Android device is the Location options. Whether GPS or cell tower triangulation, these functions plus an Internet connection make it possible to use your Android device as a street directory, in-car navigation, or to keep track of your daily walk, or any number of other handy things.

In this chapter, we explore a little application I threw together that would make it easy to find my car in a large carpark. (Not just my car. Other people's cars too . . .) At the request of a friend who continually misses his bus stop, the same application will warn you when you're getting close to a given destination.

To get there, we explore the LocationManager, Services, Broadcast messages, Notifications, proximity alerts, and some simple 2D graphics.

Location Manager

Like many other services, you access the LocationManager through a call to getSystemServices, like so.

```
LocationManager lm = (LocationManager) getSystemService(Context.LOCATION_SERVICE);
```

This gives you a LocationManager, which is where most of the heavy lifting of finding out exactly where you are is done.

There are a couple of things worth realizing about the LocationManager. It provides a consistent interface between your code and the device's hardware. However, the implementation is entirely up to the platform provider, so you may get some different results on different platforms.

Location Providers

You may have several different means of determining your location. These are typically abstracted into three different types, as shown in Table 8-1.

Table 8-1. Location Providers

Type	Value	Description
LocationManager.GPS_PROVIDER	"gps"	Global positioning system; this is highly accurate, typically down to a few meters, but relatively expensive in terms of battery use, and it can take some time to acquire the satellites.
LocationManager.NETWORK_PROVIDER	"network"	Uses the cell phone network to triangulate on cell towers; this is not very accurate—down to 1 or 2 kilometers—but is quick to acquire and quite low in battery usage. This always assumes you have a phone in your device, though.
LocationManager.PASSIVE_PROVIDER	"passive"	This one's a special case. It's sort of a virtual provider. It'll pick up updates as they become available from either of the other two providers, but won't actually take responsibility for powering up either device.

In this case, because I want to know a fairly precise location, for most cases updating more or less in real time, I'm going to be concentrating on GPS.

BAT3PGps

I'm quite pleased with this little application. It works well, and demonstrates a lot of functionality. Once again, this is not a highly polished application, but I think it does what it's meant to do (see Figure 8-2).

Figure 8-2. BA3TPGps in action

Figure 8-2 shows my little GPS application in action. Note that I'm running it on my phone rather than the tablet the phone being more portable, but as designed it will work on either. The way it's meant to work is as follows:

You park your car, switch on the GPS (by hitting the GPS button), and then hit the Set Target button. This should memorize where you parked your car.

Once that is done, bringing up the BA3TPGps application will show you the direction and distance to your car . . . or indeed, any other target you may desire to set. It can keep a list of preset targets (i.e., bus stops or train stations), and can also be set to alert you when you get to within a preset distance of your destination.

░ **Reminder:** BA3TPGps uses the utilities library, and needs to be linked to BA3TPUtils. See Chapter 7 for more details.

A Class to Handle the Location Manager

The LocationManager is quite useful, but it does require a degree of boilerplate to get going.

For one thing, as discussed in the chapter about sensors, data is not always available on demand. You have to tell the LocationManager to start listening, which has the side effect of activating the underlying devices (and thus drawing power).

Then the Location Provider has to be given time to do its stuff . . . acquire satellites, work out cell towers, what have you.

Once they've got their act together, the LocationManager will send your application updates as they are available, by means of a Listener.

I've chosen to embed this into a separate class that does most of this work for you.

Listing 8-1. The LocationHandler Code

```
public class LocationHandler implements LocationListener {
  private final Context mContext;
  private final Map<String, Location> mLocationUpdates;
private final Map<String, String> mStatus;
  private final LocationManager mLocationManager;
  private final Geocoder mGeocoder;
  private LocationUpdater mUpdater;

  @Override
  public synchronized void onLocationChanged(Location location) {
    mLocationUpdates.put(location.getProvider(), location);
    if (mUpdater != null)
      mUpdater.locationUpdate(this, location);
  }

  @Override
  public void onProviderDisabled(String provider) {
  }

  @Override
  public void onProviderEnabled(String provider) {
  }

  @Override
  public void onStatusChanged(String provider, int status, Bundle extras) {
  }

  public LocationHandler(Context context) {
    mContext = context;
    mGeocoder = new Geocoder(mContext);
    mLocationManager = (LocationManager) mContext
        .getSystemService(Context.LOCATION_SERVICE);
    mLocationUpdates = new HashMap<String, Location>();
mStatus = new HashMap<String,String>();
  }

  public void shutdown() {
    stopLocating();
  }
```

```java
public void startLocating(int minUpdateTime, int minUpdateDistance) {
  for (String provider : mLocationManager.getAllProviders()) {
    mLocationManager.requestLocationUpdates(provider, minUpdateTime,
        minUpdateDistance, this, mContext.getMainLooper());
    Location loc = mLocationManager.getLastKnownLocation(provider);
    if (loc!=null) mLocationUpdates.put(provider, loc);
  }
}

public List<String> getProviders() {
  return mLocationManager.getAllProviders();
}

public Map<String, String> readStatus()
  return mStatus;
}
public Map<String, Location> readLocation() {
  return mLocationUpdates;
}

public synchronized void stopLocating() {
  mLocationManager.removeUpdates(this);
  mLocationUpdates.clear();
}

public List<Address> geocode(Double latitude, Double longitude,
    Integer maxResults) throws IOException {
  return mGeocoder.getFromLocation(latitude, longitude, maxResults);
}

public void setUpdater(LocationUpdater updater) {
  mUpdater = updater;
}

public static String getAccuracyName(int accuracy) {
  switch(accuracy) {
  case Criteria.NO_REQUIREMENT: return "No Requirement";
  case Criteria.ACCURACY_COARSE: return "Coarse";
  case Criteria.ACCURACY_FINE: return "Fine";
  default: return "N/A";
  }
}
```

```
public static String getPowerName(int power) {
  switch(power) {
  case Criteria.NO_REQUIREMENT: return "No Requirement";
  case Criteria.POWER_LOW: return "Low";
  case Criteria.POWER_MEDIUM: return "Medium";
  case Criteria.POWER_HIGH: return "High";
  default: return "N/A";
  }
}

public interface LocationUpdater {
  void locationUpdate(LocationHandler handler, Location location);
}

}
```

Listing 8-1 shows the LocationHandler class in full. In essence, it will manage starting and stopping all available providers and keeping an updated list of the most recent Location updates, and will optionally keep your application updated by means of the provided LocationUpdater interface.

The LocationHandler constructor takes a Context, since of course it does not have one of its own. From there, it finds the LocationManager and sticks that into a field for later use. It also grabs an instance of Geocoder. I didn't end up using this in the application, but it is a very useful utility class that can take a latitude and longitude and return a street address.

startLocating will lodge a requestLocationUpdates request for each available provider. This is overkill in this case, but it has the advantage of being generic and reusable. The parameters include a minimum distance (in meters) and time passed (in milliseconds). These are hints rather than firm settings, but you can use them to stop your application being flooded with messages.

If Location is your primary interest, though, you can leave both these settings at 0, and you'll be updated as fast as the underlying hardware can manage. This still does not flood you with data.

Of some interest is getProviders, which just returns a list of all the provider names. In practice, this will always turn out to be "gps," "network," and "passive," as per Table 8-1. You can find out details about each provider as needed: if it is enabled, a rough idea of power consumption and accuracy.

Table 8-2. Some Useful Properties of the Location Provider

Method	Information
LocationProvider.getAccuracy	Coarse or fine
LocationProvider.getPowerRequirement	Low, medium, or high
LocationProvider.hasMonetaryCost	Does it cost money to use?
LocationProvider.meetsCriteria	You can build criteria to search for your GPS requirements, such as desired accuracy and power use.
LocationProvider.requiresCell	Does it require access to a cell network?
LocationProvider.boolean requiresNetwork	Does it require access to the Internet?

Method	Information
LocationProvider.requiresSatellite	Does it require satellites?
LocationProvider.supportsAltitude	Can return altitude
LocationProvider.supportsBearing	Can return bearing (heading)
LocationProvider.supportsSpeed	Can return speed
LocationManager.isProviderEnabled	Is this particular provider enabled at present?

▨ **Note** Trap for young (and old) players. Even though my tablet has no cell connection at all, there is no indication that I don't have access to the "network" provider . . . above and beyond the fact that it never returns an actual location. A degree of programmer pragmatism is therefore a good idea.

In theory, you can also get status updates on the state of the various providers by means of the LocationListener.onStatusChanged event. In practice, this never seems to actually trigger . . . at least, not on any of the devices I've had a chance to test with. I suspect that this may be because the hardware vendors elected not to implement this functionality. It's not really important in the great scheme of things, but once again it points out the old adage: *the map is not the territory*. It's always wise to test your assumptions.

For enquiring minds, there *is* a separate LocationManager.GpsStatusListener that does appear to produce useful information, but I judged that to be outside the scope of this particular exercise (i.e., I ran out of time . . .).

You'll also note that the startListening method populates a Map entry for every provider, initially with the Locations retrieved from getLastKnownLocation. This last method is quite handy for presenting something quickly to the user that is at least vaguely sensible.

Location

All this mucking about setting up the various providers brings us to the end product: a Location. A Location contains all the information the provider has on where we are when it got its last fix. Table 8-3 shows some of the more interesting things that Location can tell us.

Table 8-3. *Useful Properties of a Location*

Method	Description
float bearingTo(Location dest)	Returns the approximate initial bearing in degrees East of true North when traveling along the shortest path between this location and the given location
float distanceTo(Location dest)	Returns the approximate distance in meters between this location and the given location
float getAccuracy()	Returns the accuracy of the fix in meters
double getAltitude()	Returns the altitude of this fix
float getBearing()	Returns the direction of travel in degrees East of true North
double getLatitude()	Returns the latitude of this fix
double getLongitude()	Returns the longitude of this fix
String getProvider()	Returns the name of the provider that generated this fix, or null if it is not associated with a provider
float getSpeed()	Returns the speed of the device over ground in meters/second
long getTime()	Returns the UTC time of this fix, in milliseconds since January 1, 1970
boolean hasAccuracy()	Returns true if the provider is able to report accuracy information, false otherwise
boolean hasAltitude()	Returns true if this fix contains altitude information, false otherwise
boolean hasBearing()	Returns true if the provider is able to report bearing information, false otherwise
boolean hasSpeed()	Returns true if this fix contains speed information, false otherwise

Apart from latitude and longitude, the two properties you are most likely to be interested in are getTime and getAccuracy. Time is important to tell us how up-to-date this reading is. A newer but less accurate Location may be more useful than an older but more accurate reading, for example.

Accuracy gives an indication of how precise this reading is. Depending on the quality of your hardware and how many satellites it can see, a GPS location can be accurate down to 2 meters. Network, on the other hand, is accurate to only about a mile or so . . . 1,700 meters is a typical accuracy where I live.

This figure means that you can be reasonably sure that you are somewhere within a circle of accuracy meters radius. If you've used Google Maps on your Android, you'll see this represented as a blue circle.

The Application

The first thing the user should do on starting the application is hit the GPS and Compass buttons. This will activate the location services, and also fire up the orientation sensors. This allows the application to show a simple compass rose that updates as the device moves, and also allows us to display distance and bearing of our previously selected target.

The Compass

We talked about how to calculate orientation way back in the chapter on sensors (Chapter 3), and the code I'm using here has been pretty much cut and pasted from that chapter. However, this time I'm displaying the results graphically.

Figure 8-3. Detail of the main display

I've started by popping an ImageView in the layout. I'm then generating a (very simple) compass rose making use of some very handy features of the canvas to rotate it to always point north. Then I'm mapping the bearing to Target as green dot.

Listing 8-2. Drawing the Compass Rose

```
// Graphical Display
public void drawCompass() {
    ImageView image = (ImageView) findViewById(R.id.imageView1);
    Bitmap b = Bitmap.createBitmap(image.getWidth(), image.getHeight(),
        Bitmap.Config.ARGB_8888);
    Canvas c = new Canvas(b);
    c.drawARGB(255, 255, 255, 255); // White fill.
    Paint p = new Paint();
    p.setARGB(255, 255, 0, 0); // Opaque RED
    int cx = b.getWidth() / 2;
    int cy = b.getHeight() / 2;
    c.drawCircle(cx, cy, cx, p);
    p.setARGB(255, 0, 0, 0); // Black;
    c.drawLine(cx, 0, cx, c.getHeight(), p);
    c.drawLine(0, cy, c.getWidth(), cy, p);
    p.setTextSize(c.getHeight() / 6);
```

```
      p.setTypeface(Typeface.DEFAULT_BOLD);
      p.setTextAlign(Align.CENTER);
      FontMetrics fm = new FontMetrics();
      Rect bounds = new Rect();
      p.getTextBounds("W", 0, 1, bounds);
      int lh = bounds.height();
      int north = (int) Math.toDegrees(mOrient[0]);
      c.rotate(-north, cx, cy);
      c.drawText("N", cx, lh, p);
      c.drawText("S", cx, c.getHeight() - fm.descent, p);
      c.drawText("W", p.measureText("W"), cy + (lh / 2), p);
      c.drawText("E", c.getWidth() - p.measureText("E"), cy + (lh / 2), p);
      p.setARGB(192, 0, 255, 0);
      Map<String, Location> locations = mLocationHandler.readLocation();
      if (locations != null && locations.containsKey("gps") && mTarget != null) {
        Location loc = locations.get("gps");
        int bearing = (int) bearing(new Target(loc), mTarget);
        c.rotate(bearing, cx, cy);
        c.drawCircle(cx, 8, 8, p);
      }
      image.setImageBitmap(b);
      updateInfo();
  }
```

Observe Listing 8-2. The first step for drawing the compass is getting a mutable bitmap to draw on. The mutable bit is important . . . many bitmaps that you acquire in Android (especially the R.drawables) are deliberately *immutable*. This uses the Bitmap factory method, createBitmap(), using the width and height of the target ImageView.

The next step is to create a Canvas to allow us to draw into the Bitmap.

Pretty much all actual drawing functions in Android make use of the Canvas class. The other class you'll be using a lot is the Paint class. Paint contains all the settings for your current graphic function, things like color, font, and line style. It's also the class you use for doing font measurement and suchlike . . . you may remember TextPaint from the previous chapter, which is a direct descendant.

You'll see a number of references to ARGB in this code. This stands for Alpha, Red, Green, Blue. These are all values from 0 to 255, and Alpha indicates transparency, where 0= completely transparent, and 255= completely opaque.

c.drawARGB(255, 255, 255, 255) is a handy function to fill in a background color (in this case, white).

I work out the center of the bitmap by simply dividing the width and height by 2, and storing the results in cx and cy respectively.

```
p.setARGB(255, 255, 0, 0); // Opaque RED
c.drawCircle(cx, cy, cx, p); // Draw as large a circle as will fit.
```

Now we start making use of Paint to define a red color, and then Canvas to draw a circle.

The next thing I do is set the height of the font (worked out through trial and error as 1/6 of the height of the compass), as well as other font attributes.

Then we obtain FontMetrics to give us an idea of how large our font actually is, so we can make the letters actually fit more or less neatly in the circle.

```
p.setTextSize(c.getHeight() / 6);
p.setTypeface(Typeface.DEFAULT_BOLD);
p.setTextAlign(Align.CENTER);
```

Worthy of note is that Text is drawn by default from the baseline, i.e., the bottom of the letter. It would also normally be drawn left justified, except that I've changed this to be *center* aligned.

What turned out to be a very useful feature for this particular purpose is the Canvas.rotate method.

```
c.rotate(-north, cx, cy);
```

This conveniently applies a rotation (in this case, negative North degrees) around a center point. This worked on the font as well, and made it *very* simple to implement. I then applied a counter rotation prior to drawing the bearing dot:

```
c.rotate(bearing, cx, cy);
c.drawCircle(cx, 8, 8, p);
```

It's worth noting that the rotations are additive, so I did not have to subtract the angle to North from my fresh rotation, as it had already happened. If you want to reset the rotation matrix back to normal, you can use Canvas.setMatrix(null). You may also want to play with Canvas.save and Canvas.restore to save and restore matrix (and clip) settings.

The final step is to tell the ImageView to display that bitmap, by using Canvas.setImageBitmap.

Bearing and Distance

Having got a location (and a pretty bitmap to display things on), we want to get a distance and a bearing. Now, I've already created a simple class called Target to conveniently contain Latitude and Longitude. Listing 8-3 shows an implementation of the Haversine formula to calculate distance, and the Great Circle bearing.

Listing 8-3. Formula to Calculate Distance and Bearing Between Two Points

```
public static double distance(Target from, Target to) {
  // Implementation of the 'haversine' formula
  // Returns distance in KM.
  long R = 6371; // radius of earth in km
  double dLat = Math.toRadians(to.latitude - from.latitude);
  double dLon = Math.toRadians(to.longitude - from.longitude);
  double lat1 = Math.toRadians(from.latitude);
  double lat2 = Math.toRadians(to.latitude);

  double a = Math.sin(dLat / 2) * Math.sin(dLat / 2) + Math.sin(dLon / 2)
      * Math.sin(dLon / 2) * Math.cos(lat1) * Math.cos(lat2);
  double c = 2 * Math.atan2(Math.sqrt(a), Math.sqrt(1 - a));
  double d = R * c;
  return d;
}

public static double bearing(Target from, Target to) {
```

```
        // Great circle bearing.
        double dLon = Math.toRadians(to.longitude - from.longitude);
        double lat1 = Math.toRadians(from.latitude);
        double lat2 = Math.toRadians(to.latitude);
        double y = Math.sin(dLon) * Math.cos(lat2);
        double x = Math.cos(lat1) * Math.sin(lat2) - Math.sin(lat1)
            * Math.cos(lat2) * Math.cos(dLon);
        double brng = Math.toDegrees(Math.atan2(y, x));
        return brng;
    }
```

Those of you with knowledge of trigonometry can observe and make knowing noises. Those who have been paying attention may wonder why I don't make use of the Location.distanceTo and Location.bearingTo methods. Ummm . . . because I didn't spot these functions until *after* I'd finished writing the code. So I've left them in anyway, dammit. Enjoy.

Are We There Yet?

This brings us to letting the user know when we've got to where we're going. I've put in no less than three different methods of alerting the user. First and simplest, just comparing distance in the update loop.

Listing 8-4. Alerting the User Using the Update Loop

```
        if (d <= location.getAccuracy()) {
            distance = "HERE! (" + d + "m)";
            if (mBuzz) {
                if ((now.getTime() - mLastBeep) >= 10000) { // Buzz every 10 seconds
                    mLastBeep = now.getTime();
                    mVibrator.vibrate(500);
                }
            }
        }
```

Listing 8-4 is included in updateInfo, which is called every time the application has something to tell the user. This is pretty much any time it gets a location update or the compass changes direction.

I simply compare the calculated distance to the target (d) to the accuracy of the last location fix. When we get to within that range (i.e., as close as is meaningful to the target), then I change the display to "HERE" and (if enabled) vibrate the phone.

I put in a timeout that stops the phone from vibrating more than once every ten seconds, because otherwise it just goes crazy.

Wakeup Calls

A friend of mine is continually missing his bus stop. It was with this in mind that I set up a "Wakeup" function. Basically, you tell the application to warn you when getting close to your target. This can be done through either the Preferences screen, or the Wake button on the main form.

We could just implement this in the same way I did the "vibrate-when-here" function, but one problem with using that approach is that an Activity will tend to fall asleep. This can be overridden using PowerManager to get WakeLocks. However, this is not an ideal solution as far as power usage goes. There are a few other ways of skinning this particular cat, though.

Services

Something that I've alluded to in the past is the existence of Services. A Service is like an Activity. The difference is that an Activity's prime role in life is to provide a user interface. A Service is designed to run in the background, even when the phone is "sleeping." The life cycle of a Service is simpler than an Activity . . . at its simplest, we get Table 8-4.

Table 8-4. Life Cycle of a Service

Method	Description
public void onCreate ()	Called by the system when the Service is first created
public void onDestroy ()	Called by the system to notify a Service that it is no longer used and is being removed
public int onStartCommand (Intent intent, int flags, int startId)	Called by the system every time a client explicitly starts the Service by calling startService(Intent)

I've created a NotifyService class to run in the background, responding to Location updates every 30 seconds or so until we get within range.

Listing 8-5. Notifying the User Using a Service

```
@Override
  public void onCreate() {
    mPreferences = PreferenceManager.getDefaultSharedPreferences(this);
    mPreferences.registerOnSharedPreferenceChangeListener(this);
    mNotificationManager = (NotificationManager) getSystemService(NOTIFICATION_SERVICE);
    mNotification = createNotify();
    loadPreferences();
    mLocationHandler = new LocationHandler(this);
    mLocationHandler.setUpdater(this);
  }

  @Override
  public int onStartCommand(Intent intent, int flags, int startId) {
    doNotify("Listening for Wakeup",false);
    mLocationHandler.startLocating(30000, 0);
    startForeground(NOTIFY_ID, mNotification);
    // If we get killed, after returning from here, restart
    return START_STICKY;
  }
```

Listing 8-6. The Code in MainActivity to Start the Service

```
  void doService(boolean onOff) {
    Intent background = new Intent(this, NotifyService.class);
    if (onOff) {
      startService(background);
```

```
    } else {
      stopService(background);
    }
  }
```

Listing 8-5 shows the first half of the puzzle. When `startService` is called (as shown in Listing 8-6), then `onCreate` is called if needed, followed by `onStartCommand`. Each time it is called, there is a new `startId`, which we don't care that much about in this situation.

`onStartCommand` just starts listening to the GPS, but specifically requests to be updated only every 30 seconds or so. This is an arbitrary figure, and is an attempt to keep battery use down. It's a figure that could usefully be parameterized.

The interesting part of this is the `startForeground` method. This does two things. Firstly, it gives priority to this `Service` so that it's less likely to get killed off by the system if resources are getting tight. Secondly, it pops up a notification in the status bar that lets the user know that something is happening, and secondarily allows the user to tap it to go back to our Activity. This brings us to notifications.

Notifications

Android has two main methods of communicating short messages to the user. The first is our much used `Toast` message. The second is the rather more complex `Notification`.

A Notification is displayed in the Android's Status bar, both as a small icon, and an option `TickerText` message. When the user clicks a `Notification`, a longer message can pop up. Also, you can store an `Intent` with the `Notification` that will get fired when the user taps the longer message. With the addition of some extra flags controlling behavior, the `Notification` is a useful and adaptable feature.

Listing 8-7. Creating a Notification in the NotifyService Class

```java
public static Notification createNotify() {
  return new Notification(android.R.drawable.ic_menu_rotate,"Wake Me↵
Up",System.currentTimeMillis());
}

public static void showNotify(Context context, Notification notify, String msg,↵
boolean sound) {
  Intent notificationIntent = new Intent(context, MainActivity.class);
  notificationIntent.setFlags(Intent.FLAG_ACTIVITY_NEW_TASK|Intent.FLAG_ACTIVITY_CLEAR_TOP);
  PendingIntent contentIntent = PendingIntent.getActivity(context, 0, notificationIntent,↵
0);
  notify.defaults &= (~Notification.DEFAULT_SOUND);
  if (sound) {
    String ringtone = PreferenceManager.getDefaultSharedPreferences(context).getString↵
("ringtone", "");
    if (ringtone.equals("")) {
      notify.defaults |= Notification.DEFAULT_SOUND;
    } else {
      notify.sound=Uri.parse(ringtone);
    }
  }
  notify.tickerText=msg;
  notify.setLatestEventInfo(context, "Dude", msg, contentIntent);
```

```
    NotificationManager nm =(NotificationManager) context.getSystemService↩
(NOTIFICATION_SERVICE);
    nm.notify(NOTIFY_ID, notify);
  }

  public void doNotify(String msg, boolean sound) {
    showNotify(this,mNotification,msg,sound);
  }
```

Listing 8-7 shows the creation and display of our Notify. First, you may note that I've set up createNotify and showNotify as static methods. This is because I wanted to reuse these Notifications later, and this seemed the simplest approach. createNotify() simply constructs a standard Notification object, using the following constructor.

```
Notification(int icon, CharSequence tickerText, long when)
```

This creates a Notification using an Icon resource, a tickerText message (displayed in the status bar when the Notification is displayed), and a timestamp.

░ **Note** This is a deprecated function. These days you are encouraged to use the Notification.Builder class instead, but see previous notes about my running out of time . . .

---

showNotify is rather more interesting. We start by building the Intent we want to fire when the user clicks the Notification. Pretty standard stuff—we're just going to pop up the main form.

PendingIntent is a lot like a normal Intent, with one or two important additions. Among other things, it's an object that gives other parts of the system temporary access to your security model. It gives the other application the permission to perform an Intent with the original application's permissions and identity. This is a bit like using sudo or setUID on a normal Linux system.

You can't construct it directly; you need to call one of getActivity, getBroadcast, or getService—thus:

```
    PendingIntent contentIntent = PendingIntent.getActivity(context, 0, notificationIntent,↩
  0);
```

This creates a PendingIntent that the Notification service can fire as if it were the original Context.

The rest of the code just sets up different parts of a Notification, of which the most important call is probably setLatestEventInfo. This should be called just about any time you intend updating a Notification.

Finally it calls NotificationManager.notify(NOTFIY_ID,notify) to actually display the Notification. The ID is a unique identifier for this particular Notification, and you can use it for updates and removals.

Here are things you can make your Notification do:

- Show a TickerText message in the status bar

- Vibrate (and define a vibrate pattern)

- Flash the LED a particular color and pattern

- Play a sound, either a default chime or a media Uri

- Show an Icon (possibly animated)

- Show an arbitrary View in the status bar

- Pop up with a detailed message with title and text, or a View of your own choosing

In this case, we're just going to play a sound and flash a message.

Listing 8-8. Tidying Up

```
@Override
public void onDestroy() {
  mPreferences.unregisterOnSharedPreferenceChangeListener(this);
  mLocationHandler.setUpdater(null);
  mLocationHandler.stopLocating();
  if (mNotification!=null) {
    String ns = Context.NOTIFICATION_SERVICE;
    NotificationManager mNotificationManager = (NotificationManager) getSystemService(ns);
    mNotificationManager.cancel(NOTIFY_ID);
    mNotification=null;
  }
  Toast.makeText(this, "service done", Toast.LENGTH_SHORT).show();
}
```

Listing 8-8 shows the last bit of the Service puzzle. Looking back at Listing 8-6, a Service can be manually stopped as well, using stopService. This will call the Service's OnDestroy method. Among just generally tidying up, this also explicitly cancels the Notification.

▓ **Note** Although a Service runs in the "background," it's still running in the main UI thread. This means if you have any lengthy processing to do, you should create a separate thread to do the work. As the Location.Listener works asynchronously, this isn't a problem, but I'll show you how to do a background thread sometime in the next chapter.

Proximity Alerts

There is another way of going about the "tell me when we're getting close" issue. LocationManager supports something handy called "proximity alerts." You request a proximity alert by calling addProximityAlert with a latitude, longitude, and distance. You also provide a PendingIntent (see the "Notifications" section) to be fired when the proximity alert goes off. Listing 8-9 shows the basic code to add a proximity alert to the MainActivity class.

Listing 8-9. Adding a Proximity Alert (in MainActivity)

```
public static final String PROXIMITY_EVENT = "com.apress.ba3tp.gps.Proximity";
```

```
private void addProximityAlert(double latitude, double longitude) {

    Intent intent = new Intent(PROXIMITY_EVENT);
    PendingIntent proximityIntent = PendingIntent.getBroadcast(this, 0, intent,
        0);
    IntentHolder.getInstance().setIntent(proximityIntent);
    mLocationManager.addProximityAlert(latitude, // the latitude of the central point of↵
the alert region
        longitude, // the longitude of the central point of the alert region
        mWarnDistance, // the radius of the central point of the alert region, in meters
        -1, // time for this proximity alert, in milliseconds, or -1 to indicate no expiration
        proximityIntent // will be used to generate an Intent to fire when entry to or exit↵
from the alert region is detected
        );

    IntentFilter filter = new IntentFilter(PROXIMITY_EVENT);
    registerReceiver(new ProximityIntentReceiver(), filter);
}
```

Note that we're using BroadcastReceiver, which (as you might imagine) is the
ProximityIntentReceiver class I created to receive Broadcast messages. Context.registerReceiver
registers a BroadcastReceiver with a given IntentFilter, so it'll fire up when the PROXIMITY_EVENT
intent is broadcast.

Listing 8-10. The ProximityIntentReceiver Class

```
public class ProximityIntentReceiver extends BroadcastReceiver {

    @Override
    public void onReceive(Context context, Intent intent) {

        String key = LocationManager.KEY_PROXIMITY_ENTERING;

        Boolean entering = intent.getBooleanExtra(key, false);
        IntentHolder.getInstance().setIntent(null);
        if (entering) {
            Log.d(getClass().getSimpleName(), "entering");
        }
        else {
            Log.d(getClass().getSimpleName(), "exiting");
        }
        Notification n = NotifyService.createNotify();
        n.flags |= Notification.FLAG_AUTO_CANCEL;
        NotifyService.showNotify(context, n, "Proximity Alert", true);
        // Remove alert.
        // Not sure this is completely necessary, but still...
        if (IntentHolder.hasIntent()) {
            LocationManager lm = (LocationManager) context.getSystemService↵
(Context.LOCATION_SERVICE);
```

```
        lm.removeProximityAlert(IntentHolder.getInstance().getIntent());
        IntentHolder.getInstance().setIntent(null);

    }
  }

}
```

Listing 8-10 shows the ProximityIntentReceiver class in its entirety. Note that I'm using exactly the same Notification that the NotifyService uses. This is why I implemented these as static methods, so I could reuse them even when I don't know for sure that the service has been started. The main difference is that I'm setting the "Auto Cancel" flag on this notification, as I just want it to go away when the user taps it.

Proximity Alert Pros and Cons

There are pros and cons to using proximity alerts. The obvious pro is that you're letting the OS do all the work, which is good. Someone else has spent time and effort working out the best way to hand off between the coarse and fine location providers, and the best way to preserve power.

The obvious con is exactly the same issue. You've handed off control to the OS, and letting someone else make your decisions. For example, the default behavior for proximity alerts is to check your location every four minutes. That's okay for a lot of applications, but even a slow bus can cover quite a distance in that time. The less obvious con is that there is a known bug/behavior with proximity alerts that can make them very difficult to turn off.

In theory, it's easy enough—just call removeProximityAlert with the same PendingIntent. What is not clearly documented—and part of the known problems—is what constitutes "Same"? Same identity? Same hashcode? Same name? Even hunting through the Android source code isn't much help, because this is part of the code designed to be supplied by the individual hardware vendors.

The safest option is to keep a copy of the PendingIntent as long as possible. The way I've chosen to do that is to create a singleton class to hang onto the PendingIntent. A "singleton" is a Java technique to create one, and only one, instance of a class. This will hang about until explicitly nulled out or the Java virtual machine ends. I don't know it's the perfect solution, but it's the best one I was able to come up with at short notice. Listing 8-11 shows the entire IntentHolder class.

Listing 8-11. Keeping a Static Instance of a Pending Intent

```
// This class just holds a static instance of a Pending Intent.
public class IntentHolder {
  private PendingIntent mIntent;
  private static IntentHolder mInstance=null;

  public static IntentHolder getInstance() {
    if (mInstance==null) {
      mInstance=new IntentHolder();
    }
    return mInstance;
  }

  public static boolean hasIntent() {
    return getInstance().getIntent()!=null;
```

```
  }

  public PendingIntent getIntent() {
    return mIntent;
  }

  public void setIntent(PendingIntent intent) {
    this.mIntent = intent;
  }

}
```

As you can see, it is not a complex class. As long as you call getInstance() to get your object, you should be fine. We could probably have achieved a similar result by just creating a static field in one of the other classes. This technique does allow for more flexibility in the long run, though.

Lists of Targets

Obviously, this application would be much more useful if I was able to store a list of Targets for later use. Well, that's pretty much what I've done. The list management code was lifted pretty much intact from the Genma application (see Chapter 7). The only real modifications were to store Targets rather than strings.

Listing 8-12. The Target Class

```
public class Target {
  double latitude;
  double longitude;
  private String mTitle;

  Target(double latitude, double longitude) {
    this.latitude = latitude;
    this.longitude = longitude;
  }

  Target(Location location) {
    this.latitude = location.getLatitude();
    this.longitude = location.getLongitude();
  }

  Target(String location) {
    setAsString(location);
  }

  public String getTitle() {
    if (mTitle == null)
      return latitude + "," + longitude;
    return mTitle;
  }

  public void setTitle(String title) {
```

```
    mTitle = title;
  }

  public String getAsString() {
    String s = latitude + "," + longitude;
    if (mTitle != null)
      s = s + "," + (mTitle.replace(",", ";"));
    return s;
  }

  public void setAsString(String location) {
    String[] parts = location.split(",");
    if (parts.length < 2)
      throw new IllegalArgumentException("Expected format lat,long[,title]");
    latitude = Double.valueOf(parts[0]);
    longitude = Double.valueOf(parts[1]);
    if (parts.length >= 3)
      mTitle = parts[2];
  }

  @Override
  public String toString() {
    return getTitle();
  }
}
```

Listing 8-12 shows the full Target class. This is a simple class that manages a latitude and longitude coordinate, and a title for public display. It has several constructors, including from Location and String.

I've given it getAsString and setAsString, to simplify saving it. The AsString property is simply the latitude and longitude, separated by commas. The title field is an optional third value.

Note the use of String.split as a quicky means of breaking up the incoming string into separate fields. Note also the slightly bodgy use of replace in the getAsString method to make sure there are no unwanted commas in the output string.

The toString() returns the title, which in turn returns the coordinates if no title has been set. With the title done that way, the list handling just had to be changed to use <Target> rather than <String> . . . a simple search and replace.

The hard bit was how to edit a three-value field. I could have been lazy and just let the user put in a three-value comma-separated string, but I decided to be a little bit cleverer than that.

The original add/edit functions in the list made use of an AlertDialog with an embedded EditText widget. It turns out you can embed even moderately complex layouts into your standard AlertDialog, very easily. First, I built a TableLayout in edittarget.xml.

Listing 8-13. EditTarget.xml

```
<?xml version="1.0" encoding="utf-8"?>
<TableLayout xmlns:android="http://schemas.android.com/apk/res/android"
        android:layout_width="match_parent" android:layout_height="match_parent">
        <TableRow android:id="@+id/tableRow1" android:layout_width="wrap_content"
                android:layout_height="wrap_content">
                <TextView android:layout_height="wrap_content" android:id="@+id/textView1"
                        android:text="Title" android:layout_width="wrap_content"></TextView>
                <EditText android:layout_height="wrap_content"
```

```
                        android:layout_width="match_parent" android:layout_weight="9"
                        android:id="@+id/eTgtTitle"></EditText>
            </TableRow>
            <TableRow android:id="@+id/tableRow2" android:layout_width="wrap_content"
                    android:layout_height="wrap_content">
                    <TextView android:layout_height="wrap_content" android:id="@+id/textView2"
                        android:text="Latitude" android:layout_width="wrap_content">
</TextView>
                    <EditText android:layout_height="wrap_content"
                        android:keepScreenOn="true" android:layout_width="match_parent"
                        android:layout_weight="9" android:id="@+id/eTgtLatitude"></EditText>
            </TableRow>
            <TableRow android:id="@+id/tableRow3" android:layout_width="wrap_content"
                    android:layout_height="wrap_content">
                    <TextView android:layout_height="wrap_content"
                        android:editable="true" android:id="@+id/textView3"
                        android:layout_width="wrap_content" android:text="Longitude">
</TextView>
                    <EditText android:layout_height="wrap_content"
                        android:layout_width="match_parent" android:layout_weight="9"
                        android:id="@+id/eTgtLongitude"></EditText>
            </TableRow>
</TableLayout>
```

Listing 8-13 shows the TableLayout. This is the first time I've used a TableLayout in this book, so it deserves a few words. Anyone familiar with HTML will have a good idea how a table is defined. You define a series of rows, with cells in each row. The TableLayout then takes care of making sure everything lines up neatly.

I'm using a combination of wrap_content and weight to make sure there is enough room for the caption in each column, while encouraging the actual EditText widget to take up as much space on the row as possible.

Listing 8-14. Code for ManageList

```java
@Override
  protected Dialog onCreateDialog(int id, Bundle args) {
    AlertDialog.Builder b = new AlertDialog.Builder(this);
    b.setTitle("List Manager");
    if (id==DIALOG_EDIT) {
      mEditTarget=getLayoutInflater().inflate(R.layout.edittarget, null);
      b.setView(mEditTarget);
      b.setPositiveButton("OK", new OnClickListener() {

        @Override
        public void onClick(DialogInterface dialog, int which) {
          Target newTarget = new Target(getEditString());
          if (mCurrent>=0) {
            Target oldTarget = mAdapter.getItem(mCurrent);
            mAdapter.remove(oldTarget);
            mAdapter.insert(newTarget, mCurrent);
          } else {
```

```
                mAdapter.add(newTarget);
            }
        }
    });
    return b.create();
    }
}
```

Listing 8-14 shows the onCreateDialog for the edit dialog. The interesting code is here:

```
mEditTarget=getLayoutInflater().inflate(R.layout.edittarget, null);
b.setView(mEditTarget);
```

This uses the default LayoutInflater to inflate the previous defined edit target, which is then embedded into the AlertDialog via the AlertDialog.Builder. This gives us something that looks like Figure 8-4.

Figure 8-4. What the target editor should look like

Listing 8-15 shows the code I use to populate and query the edit dialog.

Listing 8-15. Managing the Edit Dialog

```
protected String getEditString() {
    if (mEditTarget!=null) {
        EditText e1 = (EditText) mEditTarget.findViewById(R.id.eTgtTitle);
        EditText e2 = (EditText) mEditTarget.findViewById(R.id.eTgtLatitude);
        EditText e3 = (EditText) mEditTarget.findViewById(R.id.eTgtLongitude);
        return e2.getText().toString().replace(",",";")+","+
        e3.getText().toString().replace(",",";")+","+
        e1.getText().toString().replace(",",";");
    }
    return null;
}
```

```
protected void setEditTarget(Target value) {
  if (mEditTarget!=null) {
    EditText e1 = (EditText) mEditTarget.findViewById(R.id.eTgtTitle);
    EditText e2 = (EditText) mEditTarget.findViewById(R.id.eTgtLatitude);
    EditText e3 = (EditText) mEditTarget.findViewById(R.id.eTgtLongitude);
    e1.setText(value.getTitle());
    e2.setText(String.valueOf(value.latitude));
    e3.setText(String.valueOf(value.longitude));
  }
}
```

The only tricky bit was the quick and dirty use of `replace` to, again, make sure that there aren't any commas in the input field. I must admit, I was surprised at how simple it was to implement.

Where Was That Again?

Now, using latitude and longitude is all very well, and easily obtained from places like Google Maps. However, it's not a very intuitive way of doing things. Android has a number of ways of accessing maps. I decided it was beyond the scope of this exercise (I think I've made it clear by this time what that term means) to *select* a point from a map, but displaying a point is quite easy. In fact, this application demonstrates two simple means of bringing up a map.

Listing 8-16. Displaying Points on a Map

```
  } else if (id == MenuId.SHOW.getId()) {
      if (mTarget!=null) {
        Uri geo = Uri.parse("geo:"+mTarget.latitude+","+mTarget.longitude+"?z=18");
        Intent intent = new Intent(Intent.ACTION_VIEW,geo);
        startActivity(intent);
      }
  } else if (id == MenuId.SHOWMAP.getId()) {
    if (mTarget!=null) {
      try {
        Uri geo = Uri.parse("http://maps.google.com.au/maps?q=loc:"+mTarget.latitude↵
+","+mTarget.longitude+"&z=20");
        Intent intent = new Intent(Intent.ACTION_VIEW,geo);
        startActivity(intent);
      } catch (Exception e) {
        toast(e);
      }
    }
  }
```

The first uses the "Geo" `Uri`, a simple way of defining a geographic point. The "z" parameter indicates a zoom level. The zoom level is an exponential indicator, where 1=the entire earth, 2=1/2 the earth, 3=1/4 and so forth. The number 18, obtained by trial and error, is a comfortable level to display streets. Note that the geo `Uri` is still under development.

The second directly calls Google Maps, building an HTTP `Uri` and embedding the location. Note the "loc:" prefix, which tells Google to display a precise location. Without that prefix, Google will attempt to force the display to the nearest street address, not something you necessarily want to find in a car park.

Where to Go from Here?

I've already used this application in anger. It worked fine, although multi-story carparks turned out to be a problem, as GPS has issues when it can't see the sky. I will probably continue playing and expanding on it, and finding other ways to use it.

Some obvious suggestions for improvement would be an option for displaying different measurement systems. I come from a country that uses the metric system, so kilometers and meters are normal. It would be a trivial matter to include a conversion to miles and yards, for example.

The built-in compass has a tendency to jitter, probably because it doesn't *have* to be super accurate and therefore the hardware is no more expensive than it needs to be. It might be nice to put in an averaging algorithm to smooth things out.

Being able to pull up Google Maps to pick target locations would be nice. Google does provide an interface of their mapping functions. Check out `http://code.google.com/android/add-ons/google-apis/maps-overview.html` for details.

One of the reasons I elected not to play with this library is that you need to provide a unique key for each of your applications to access the mapping functions. This is not an onerous task, and is free, but adds complexity when trying to produce sample code.

The Wakeup function could do with being cleverer. For example, we could save power by using the coarse provider until we get into the general area, and only then firing up the fine provider.

The list goes on. I actively encourage you to take this base code and play with it, make it prettier and cleverer, make it sing.

Summary

So, in starting out to put together a simple demonstration of the Location services, we've actually managed to touch on quite a few new aspects of Android programming.

As well as the basics of `LocationManager`, we've covered some elements of building and using `Services`, `Notifications`, and `Broadcast` messages. We've also discovered a neat new way to implement complex edit boxes. And we also had a good play with proximity alerts, and, for good measure, taken a few tentative steps into the art of displaying maps.

Exciting, isn't it?

CHAPTER 9

Let the Games Begin!

Some 2D and 3D Graphical Game Techniques

In this chapter, I'm going to demonstrate the building blocks to put together a simple game, and go a little bit more into both 2D and 3D graphics.

Figure 9-1. Nothing like a friendly game . . .

Threads

However, here is a brief detour into the concepts of Threads. I've referred to them before, and if you aren't familiar with them, they can be a bit daunting. But have no fear—threading is actually one of the things Java does best.

A Thread is a bit like a lightweight process. This is the path your program is going down at any given moment. Threading allows your program to do two or more things at the same time, with the various Threads trading information only as needed.

Most of the time you are dealing with only one single Thread. This is the main user interface (UI) Thread, which everything we've done up till now has been running in.

This makes the programming nice and simple, but if you need to perform a lengthy process in your main Thread, the user interface will stop responding to the user. And slow responses make for unhappy users, which is bad.

The sort of real-time, continually updating graphical programming required by interactive games is best done in a separate Thread, which can trundle on at its own pace, doing all the game mechanics and rendering graphics as and when it can. In the meantime, the main UI Thread is sitting there, ready to respond to user input in a timely and cheerful manner.

Java Threads

Here is a very quick overview of Java Threads. There are two ways of implementing Threads. You can either create a subclass of Thread, or implement the Runnable interface. Listing 9-1 shows a simple demo showing both approaches.

Listing 9-1. An Example of Threading

```java
public class Main {

  /**
   * @param args the command line arguments
   */
  public static void main(String[] args) {
    Main me = new Main();
    try {
      me.dostuff();
    } catch (Exception e) {
      me.println(e);
    }
  }
}

  public void dostuff() throws Exception {
    println("Started.");
    BufferedReader inp = new BufferedReader(new InputStreamReader(System.in));
    MyThread thread1 = new MyThread();
    MyRunnable runner = new MyRunnable();
    Thread thread2 = new Thread(runner);
    thread1.start();
    thread2.start();
    println("Hit ENTER to finish. Q for a quick finish.");
    String s=inp.readLine();
    println("Stopping.");
    thread1.setRunning(false);
    runner.setRunning(false);
    if (s.toUpperCase().equals("Q")) {
      println("Wake up threads.");
      thread1.interrupt();
      thread2.interrupt();
    }
    thread1.join(); // Wait for threads to stop.
    thread2.join();
    println("Main Thread done.");
```

```
  }

  public synchronized void println(Object msg) {
    System.out.println(msg);
  }

class MyThread extends Thread {

  private boolean running;
  private int cnt;


  @Override
  public void run() {
    setRunning(true);
    while (running) {
      println("Thread 1: " + cnt++);
      try {
        sleep(2000);
      } catch (InterruptedException ex) {
        println("Thread 1 " + ex);
      }
    }
    println("Thread 1 done.");
  }


  public synchronized void setRunning(boolean onoff) {
    running=onoff;
  }
}

class MyRunnable implements Runnable {

  private boolean running;
  private int cnt;

  public void run() {
    setRunning(true);
    while (running) {
      println("Thread 2: " + cnt++);
      try {
        Thread.sleep(3000);
      } catch (InterruptedException ex) {
        println("Thread 2 " + ex);
      }
    }
    println("Thread 2 done.");
  }

  public synchronized void setRunning(boolean onoff) {
    running=onoff;
  }
```

```
    }
}
```

MyThread is a subclass of Thread, whereas MyRunnable implements the Runnable interface. The Thread for MyThread is simply constructed using new. The Thread to run MyRunnable is created by passing a Runnable to the Thread constructor. In each case, they provide a public void run() method, which is called by the new Thread once it starts running.

And the way to start a Thread running is to call the Thread.start() method. Calling run() won't do it for you: many's the time I've found that out the hard way, especially because it may appear to work at first. It'll be just running in the main Thread, though, and offer none of the concurrency that we are after.

Synchronizing Your Threads

Once your Thread is running, you need to be able to communicate with it, if only to make it stop. One of the issues that threading brings is that you lose control over the precise order that things happen. Two or more Threads may be trying to update the same data at exactly the same time, with unpredictable results. This is known as a "race condition."

Fortunately, Java offers the synchronized keyword. If multiple Threads attempt to call the same method at the same time, the synchronize feature makes sure they get access only one at a time. The others have to wait their turn. You can see examples of it in Listing 9-1, of particular use in the global println method.

Another possibly more useful version of synchronized is as part of a statement (see Listing 9-2).

Listing 9-2. Using synchronized in a Statement

```
public class SynchDemo {
    final List<String> things = new ArrayList<String>();

    int addString(String data) {
        synchronized(things) {
            things.add(data);
            return things.size()-1;
        }
    }

    String getString(int index) {
        synchronized(things) {
            return things.get(index);
        }
    }
}
```

Listing 9-2 shows a simple example of synchronized as a statement. When you synchronize an object, anything else attempting to synchronize the same object will wait until the first synchronize exits.

The object you are synchronizing with need not be the object actually being updated, but it is a common practice. It can be just about any object you care to name. The Java compiler may give you a warning if this object is not marked as final, though.

Another way of synchronizing Threads is to use the wait() and notify() functions, but I'll leave researching those as an exercise to the reader.

Stopping the Darn Things

Starting Threads is easy enough. Stopping them should be just as easy, right? Well, it's not hard, but does require a bit of thought.

There is a Thread.stop() method, but it's deprecated and you are heavily discouraged from using it. Java applets may come around to your house and beat you up if you persist. Also, every time you do, a fairy dies.

The preferred method is to set a flag that the Thread checks regularly, so that it exits the run loop. In Listing 9-1, I've given each of my Threads a running flag, and a function to set it. Once the running flag is clear, the Thread's main while loop will exit.

You may note the use of the join() method. This is called by one Thread to wait until another Thread has finished. This is good general practice, as your Thread may be busy doing something at the time, and needs time to finish off.

Now, for the purposes of this demonstration, I've put a sleep() in the Thread loops. This means that each Thread could wait two to three seconds before actually shutting down. This is not in itself a hardship, but what if your Thread is sleeping for minutes or hours?

You can wake them up by calling the Thread's interrupt() method. This will cause the sleeping Thread to immediately wake up, and also incidentally throw an InterruptedException. You could, if you liked, use this exception as a signal for the loop to exit instead of the flag. Interrupt() works on wait(), sleep(), and join(), and can also wake up a blocked I/O process (this last throws a ClosedByInterruptException). Note that this will work only on I/O channels that support the InterruptibleChannel interface, which is not all of them. You'll need to check the documentation for the fine detail.

Android Threads

Conveniently, Android has some additional support for when it comes to communicating between Threads. The Handler class provides a neat queued message mechanism, and Looper provides a handy method for processing same.

While you may not have explicitly used the Looper class yet, you have in fact been implicitly using one all along. As it happens, the main UI Thread is implemented using a Looper. That's what generates all the callbacks like onCreate, onClick, and so forth.

Knowing that it's there can make a lot more sense of what is going on sometimes.

Floater

When I say I've created a game, I may be being a little generous to myself. It's more like a visual toy (refer to Figure 9-2). I have a green dot floating over the screen. When I touch the screen, a red dot appears and attracts the green dot toward it. The green dot leaves a pleasant, luminescent trail behind it. That's pretty much it, but I spent hours playing with it the other day. I may be deranged . . .

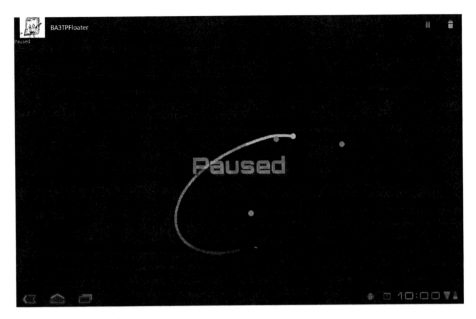

Figure 9-2. Floater in action

Right, let us look at the components that make this up. This is BA3TPFloater. In it, I demonstrate the following:

- Use of Threads
- The concept of a SurfaceHolder
- Use of a Handler (and, implicitly, a Looper)
- A different way of creating Menus
- Using custom fonts
- Assets
- Multitouch handling

Let's take it from the top.

SurfaceView

As you've probably guessed by the introduction to this chapter, we're going to be using Threads. It's generally accepted that the best way of doing anything real-time in Java is to use Threads. But anything on the screen is typically owned by the main UI Thread, and it's not generally a good idea to try to take control of its Views directly.

This is where the concept of SurfaceHolders comes in. A SurfaceHolder is a class that gives a Thread a separate part of the screen that it can directly update. And a SurfaceView is simply a View containing a

SurfaceHolder. Pretty much any graphics that you see on an Android screen that aren't more or less static will be implemented by SurfaceHolders. The Camera application is a prime example.

The bulk of BA3TPFloater is implemented in GameSurface (see Listing 9-3), which extends SurfaceView, and also defines and manages a Thread to do all the actual work.

Listing 9-3. The GameSurface Class

```
public class GameSurface extends SurfaceView implements SurfaceHolder.Callback,↵
OnTouchListener {
  private FloaterThread mThread;
  private TextView mTextView;
  private long universeClock = 0;
  private long lastInfo = 0;

  public static final int TRAIL_AGE = 6000;
  public static final long START_SPEED =100;
  public static final long GRAVITY =8000;
  public static final long UPDATE_RATE = 500; // Delay in MS between text updates


  class FloaterThread extends Thread {
    private SurfaceHolder mSurfaceHolder;
    private Handler mHandler;
    private Context mContext;
    private boolean mRun = false;

    public FloaterThread(SurfaceHolder surfaceHolder, Context context,
        Handler handler) {
      // get handles to some important objects
      mSurfaceHolder = surfaceHolder;
      mHandler = handler;
      mContext = context;
    }


    @Override
    public void run() {
      while (mRun) {
        Canvas c = null;
        try {
          c = mSurfaceHolder.lockCanvas(null);
          synchronized (mSurfaceHolder) {
            doMove();
            doDraw(c);
          }
        } finally {
          if (c != null) {
            mSurfaceHolder.unlockCanvasAndPost(c);
          }
        }
      }
    }
```

```
    }
  }

  public GameSurface(Context context, AttributeSet attrs) {
    super(context, attrs);
    // register our interest in hearing about changes to our surface
    SurfaceHolder holder = getHolder();
    holder.addCallback(this);
    setOnTouchListener(this);
    // Custom font.
    // create thread; it's started in surfaceCreated()
    // Note that the Handler we're constructing here runs in the original thread.
    mThread = new FloaterThread(holder, context, new Handler() {
      @Override
      public void handleMessage(Message m) {
        Bundle b = m.getData();
        if (b!=null) {
          if (mTextView!=null) {
            String info = b.getString("info");
            mTextView.setText(info);
          }
        }
      }
    });

    setFocusable(true); // make sure we get key events
  }

  @Override
  public void surfaceChanged(SurfaceHolder holder, int format, int width,
      int height) {
    mThread.setDimensions(width, height);

  }

  @Override
  public void surfaceCreated(SurfaceHolder holder) {
    mThread.setRunning(true);
    try {
      mThread.start();
    } catch (Exception e) { // Thread may still be running...
      Log.w("floater",e);
    }
  }

  @Override
  public void surfaceDestroyed(SurfaceHolder holder) {
    mThread.setRunning(false);
    boolean retry = true;
    // Hang about until thread has given up.
```

```
    while (retry) {
      try {
        mThread.join();
        retry = false;
      } catch (InterruptedException e) {
      }
    }
  }
}
```

Listing 9-3 is the cut-down framework. I've hidden most of the actual implementation of the game Thread, leaving only the basics.

It's important to realize that you don't get a Surface to actually draw on until the surfaceCreated event is called, so we use that to start the Thread running. The Surface remains available until the surfaceDestroyed event is called, so logically, that's where we shut the Thread down. These events are defined as part of the SurfaceHolder.Callback interface, which is why GameSurface implements it.

You rarely work directly with the SurfaceView; what you are really interested in is the SurfaceHolder (returned by SurfaceView.getHolder()).

GameSurface registers itself with the SurfaceHolder by calling addCallback(this). The rest of the GameSurface constructor deals with registering itself with several different UI callbacks, and creating FloaterThread. FloaterThread is constructed with a Context, a SurfaceHolder, and a Handler. The use of Context is fairly obvious, but while we're here let's have a look at the others.

Using Your SurfaceHolder

The key method for using SurfaceHolder is to call lockCanvas(). This returns a Canvas, which you can draw on. When you are done rendering the frame, you call unlockCanvasAndPost. This releases the Canvas back to the system, and actually makes your drawing visible.

Handlers

Once you start having a hard look around the Internet for sample code, you'll see Handler used quite a lot, usually without much explanation. The Handler, purely and simply, manages a message queue. This message queue is primarily used for Threads to talk to one another in a Thread-safe and synchronized fashion. One Thread can put a message into the queue, and the Handler in the other Thread can pull it out and look at it. While it would be easy enough to roll your own version of the mechanism, Handler is quite simple and versatile, and someone else has already done the hard yards for you.

```
    public void handleMessage(Message m) {
        Bundle b = m.getData();
```

You need to implement handleMessage, which is where you actually do the work of processing the message.

You can also send Runnable objects, which will be run in the destination Thread, but that's something we'll deal with later.

When you create a Handler, it automatically attaches itself to the current Thread. In this example, the Thread in question is still the main UI Thread. Now, a Handler does not exactly run by itself. Something has to be sitting on the other end, pulling things out. A very handy class to manage this is Looper (see Listing 9-4).

Listing 9-4. The Looper

```
Looper.prepare();
mHandler = new Handler() {
  public void handleMessage(Message msg) {
        // process incoming messages here
    }
};
Looper.loop();
```

The Handler will automatically associate itself with the current Thread's Looper, and the Looper will continually (and reasonably efficiently) pull messages off the queue and do things with them. When you're done with a Looper, call quit().

Now, where is the Looper for the Handler we created for GameSurface? Since we're running in the main UI Thread when we create the Handler, we end up automatically using the main Looper. The whole reason we are using the Handler/Looper combo here is to safely update the TextView on the main screen, which is running in a different Thread.

Using the Handler

So we've set up the Handler . . . how do we actually use it? Listing 9-5 shows the trick.

Listing 9-5. Using the Handler

```
private void sendMessage(Object info) {
  Message msg = mHandler.obtainMessage();
  Bundle b = new Bundle();
  b.putString("info", info.toString());
  msg.setData(b);
  mHandler.sendMessage(msg);
}
```

The only tricky bit is knowing where to get the Message object to send, which is to call the Handler's obtainMessage method. Into this you pop a Bundle, which can contain any amount of information.

Now, one of the nice things you can do is send a *delayed* message. You can use sendMessageAtTime, or sendMessageDelayed. This is one of the ways you can implement an efficient timing function.

Running the Game

The main run loop of the game Thread just calculates the game movement, and then draws the objects. I'm not going to spend a lot of time on the game mechanics. It's all basic stuff, and there in the code if you want to go looking. Instead, I'm going to focus on the Android-specific implementations.

Handling Input

When you touch the screen, a red dot appears and starts attracting the floating green dot toward it. I use a simple vector mechanism to control the object speed . . . each Attractor pulls the target toward it, the strength of the pull being the inverse of the distance.

One of the nice things that a tablet touch screen can do that a mouse can't is handle multi-touch. This means that you can touch the screen in more than one place at a time, and the application can respond to all those touches at once. This is how I managed to get multiple red dots on the screen at once. There are two parts receiving input events.

Listing 9-6. Responding to Touch Events

```
public class GameSurface extends SurfaceView implements SurfaceHolder.Callback,↵
 OnTouchListener {
// Some code

    setOnTouchListener(this);
// More code

@Override
  public boolean onTouch(View v, MotionEvent event) {
    int action = event.getActionMasked();
    if (action==MotionEvent.ACTION_DOWN || action==MotionEvent.ACTION_MOVE ||↵
action==MotionEvent.ACTION_POINTER_DOWN) {
       for (int i=0; i<event.getPointerCount(); i++) {
         mThread.setAttractor(i,(int)event.getX(i),(int) event.getY(i));
       }
    }
    return true;
  }
```

Observe Listing 9-6. You need to register an OnTouchListener with the View in question—in this case, the GameSurface itself. This will then respond to onTouch events.

A MotionEvent has a bunch of useful properties. The first thing you generally want to know is what is going on . . . is this a touch, a release, or a move? At its simplest, you are most likely to be interested in knowing if this was a MotionEvent.ACTION_DOWN, or a MotionEvent.ACTION_UP. You can do this by calling getAction(). From that, you can pull the X and Y pixel coordinates (relative to the view) as getX() and getY().

Multi-touch is a little more complex, because the second and subsequent finger returns a complex integer in getAction(), which includes both the action itself and an index indicating which pointer it was. getActionMask() masks out the additional pointer information, simplifying the interpretation.

You can then call getActionIndex() to pull which particular finger caused this event. More to the point, you can get a count of all the currently pressed points, and get each X and Y location using getX(int) and getY(int). I then use setAttractor on the Thread, which is a synchronized method to update a List of points. Oh, and you can use the Delete menu option to clear the dots if you like.

Custom Fonts

The default fonts that come with Android are pretty basic: Serif, Sans, and Mono (refer to Figure 9-3).

Figure 9-3. The built-in Android fonts

Mono can be safely considered a fixed-width version of Sans, and does not support bold or italic.

The Droid font took two years to develop, and is very carefully optimized to be readable on a small screen. For most practical purposes, these are fine, especially as Android allows for a degree of font decoration. As well as allowing the traditional bold and italic variations, you can easily adjust the font width and apply shading.

However, sometimes you need a different font, perhaps for rendering a word processor document, perhaps just because it looks nice. This turns out to be quite easy to do. Just get hold of a TrueType (TTF) or OpenType file (OTF) and drop it into the assets folder of your project. You can then load it into a Typeface class, assign it to a Paint class or TextView, and away you go!

The font I chose for this demonstration was Orbitron, an open source font from *The League of Movable Type*: www.theleagueofmoveabletype.com/. The particular file I used was orbitron-black.ttf, so loading it was a simple as Listing 9-7.

Listing 9-7. Loading a Custom Font from Assets

```
Typeface tf = Typeface.createFromAsset(getAssets(),"orbitron-black.ttf");
TextView tv = (TextView) findViewById(R.id.CustomFontText);
tv.setTypeface(tf);
```

Use to your heart's content. This does lead to the following question:

So What's an Asset?

It is frequently desirable to include support files in your application. Android has a special place to keep these files, stored in a compressed form as part of your APK file.

This is pretty much what happens with resources in your res folder, but there is a degree of complication with using resources. Apart from anything else, Android has some very specific ideas about what types of data should go where, and uses naming conventions to cope with different device configurations.

An asset can be any sort of file, including subfolders. You access them using an AssetManager. This is easy enough to come by, simply by calling the Context's getAssets() method. Tables 9-1 and 9-2 show the interesting bits of the AssetManager.

Table 9-1. Interest Bits of the AssetManager

Type	Method	Description
final String[]	getLocales()	Gets the locales that this asset manager contains data for
final String[]	list(String path)	Returns a String array of all the assets at the given path
final InputStream	open(String fileName)	Opens an asset using ACCESS_STREAMING mode
final InputStream	open(String fileName, int accessMode)	Opens an asset using an explicit access mode, returning an InputStream to read its contents; see Table 9-2.
final AssetFileDescriptor	openFd(String fileName)	Returns an AssetFileDescriptor, which in turn can be queried for a FileDescriptor

Table 9-2. Flags to Use When Accessing the AssetManager

Field	Description
ACCESS_BUFFER	Attempts to load contents into memory, for fast small reads
ACCESS_RANDOM	Reads chunks, and seeks forward and backward
ACCESS_STREAMING	Reads sequentially, with an occasional forward seek
ACCESS_UNKNOWN	No specific information about how data will be accessed

The most common way to use AssetManager is to call the open() method to return an InputFileStream. For that matter, many Android classes have methods to load directly from an asset.

For those classes that don't want to play directly with InputStreams or AssetManager, you can retrieve a FileDescriptor.

```
FileDescriptor fd = getAssets().openFd("myfile.txt").getFileDescriptor();
```

As a last resort, you can unpack it into a temporary file and use that.

■ **Tip** For strictly temporary files, the best place to store them can be found with getCacheDir().

Font Example

The actual example in the game is shown in Listing 9-8.

Listing 9-8. Using the Custom Font

```
private void showText(Canvas c,String msg) {
    if (myFont == null) {
        myFont = Typeface.createFromAsset(mContext.getAssets(),
            "orbitron-black.ttf");
        mFontPaint = new Paint();
        mFontPaint.setTypeface(myFont);
        mFontPaint.setColor(Color.YELLOW);
        mFontPaint.setAlpha(128);
        mFontPaint.setShadowLayer(4, 8, 8, Color.BLUE);
        mFontPaint.setTextSize(64);
    }
    Rect bounds = new Rect();
    mFontPaint.getTextBounds(msg, 0, msg.length(), bounds);
    int x =  (mWidth-bounds.width())/2;
    int y = (mHeight-(bounds.height()))/2 - (int) mFontPaint.ascent();
    c.drawText(msg, x, y, mFontPaint);
}
```

This produces something that looks like Figure 9-4.

Figure 9-4. What Listing 9-8 produces

First of all, the custom font is loaded into a Typeface object. To save re-creating it every time that routine is called, I also create a Paint object to hold things like the color and size.

This example sets the text color to yellow, and the alpha (transparency) to 50% so some of the background can be seen behind it. I also set up a blue ShadowLayer, offset right and down 8 pixels, with a 4-pixel blur radius, just to make it look a little prettier.

Finally I calculate the width and height of the text so I can center it in the view. Remember that the y coordinate of the drawText corresponds to the font baseline, so you have to subtract the ascent to precisely center it.

Menus: A Different Approach

Up until now I've used a fairly basic approach to menus, constructing them as needed in the onCreateOptionsMenu call. Well, you can also define a menu structure in an XML file. The easiest way do to this in Eclipse is New ➤ Android XML File ➤ Menu. The file I produced for BA3TPFloater is shown in Listing 9-9.

Listing 9-9. Defining a Menu Using XML

```
menu.xml
<?xml version="1.0" encoding="utf-8"?>
<menu xmlns:android="http://schemas.android.com/apk/res/android">
        <item android:icon="@android:drawable/ic_media_pause" android:id="@+id/menuPause"
                android:showAsAction="ifRoom" android:onClick="pauseClick"
                android:title="Pause"></item>
        <item android:id="@+id/menuClear" android:title="Clear"
                android:onClick="clearClick" android:icon="@android:drawable/ic_menu_delete"
                android:showAsAction="ifRoom"></item>
</menu>
```

Most of that should be reasonably self-evident by this time. You still need an onCreateOptionsMenu, but it will now look like Listing 9-10 created in MainActivity.

Listing 9-10. Using the XML Menu

```
@Override
public boolean onCreateOptionsMenu(Menu menu) {
    MenuInflater inflater = getMenuInflater();
    inflater.inflate(R.menu.menu, menu);
    return true;
}
```

It would be then quite easy to build an onOptionsItemSelected event as per Listing 9-11.

Listing 9-11. Using onOptionsItemSelected to Respond to the Menu

```
@Override
public boolean onOptionsItemSelected(MenuItem item) {
  int id = item.getItemId();
  if (id==R.id.menuPause) {
    // Do stuff
  } else if (id==R.id.menuClear) {
    // Do other stuff
  }
  return super.onOptionsItemSelected(item);
}
```

However, I've chosen to play with the onClick property. This behaves pretty much as per the Button onClick property we've used before in layouts. You need to create a method to respond to the clicks. These will look like Listing 9-12.

Listing 9-12. Using the MenuItem's onClick Property

```
public void pauseClick(MenuItem v) {
  mGame.togglePause();
}
```

213

```
public void clearClick(MenuItem v) {
  mGame.getThread().clearAll();
}
```

Again, the methods have to be public void, with a single parameter. The passed parameter is a
MenuItem, though, and not a View—something to watch out for.

Into the Third Dimension!

Since we're playing with graphics and game programming, let's have a look at 3D graphics. All Android
devices support the OpenGL libraries: specifically, OpenGL ES. OpenGL ES is a flavor specifically
designed for use on embedded devices.

Now, a tutorial on OpenGL programming is *absolutely* out of scope for this book. Whole books have
been devoted to this subject. (Apress has many fine examples. Feel free to seek them out and buy them.
This has been an entirely unpaid plug.)

The structure of BA3TPOpenGl is in general very similar to floater, except that Android provides
some classes that do quite a lot of the work for us. GLSurfaceView provides SurfaceView and its own
Thread handling already built-in, so we can focus on the actual graphics programming.

It's a Box

For the purpose of this demonstration, I've thrown together a texture mapped box with some basic
lighting (see Figure 9-5).

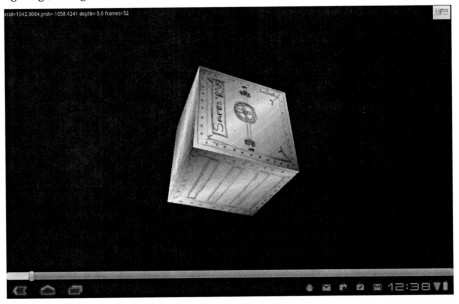

Figure 9-5. *A spinning box*

Figure 9-5 shows this demo in full flight. The SeekBar down at the bottom zooms in and out (more
accurately, adjusts the distance of the main object from the viewer), and the button called Lights turns

the lighting features on and off. Other than that, dragging your finger around the screen will cause the box to rotate in various directions. There is also a TextView to which I write various bits of information as I see fit.

Listing 9-13. The Skeleton of a GLSurfaceView Implementation

```java
public class GameSurfaceGl extends GLSurfaceView implements Renderer {


        public GameSurfaceGl(Context context, AttributeSet attrs) {
          super(context,attrs);
          init(context);
        }

        public GameSurfaceGl(Context context) {
                super(context);
                init(context);
        }


        private void init(Context context) {
                this.setRenderer(this);
                this.requestFocus();
                this.setFocusableInTouchMode(true);
// Intialize everything. GlSurfaceView requires a Rendered
// which we're implementing in this class.
// The request focus etc. are to make sure we receive input events.
        }

  public void onSurfaceCreated(GL10 gl, EGLConfig config) {
    // A surface is available. Here is where we do all the actual setup.
        }


        public void onDrawFrame(GL10 gl) {
// Do the drawing. GL10 contains bindings for the OpenGL libraries.
        }


        public void onSurfaceChanged(GL10 gl, int width, int height) {
// Something has changed. Recalculate your views
        }

        /**
         * Override the touch screen listener.
         *
         * React to moves and presses on the touchscreen.
         */
        @Override
        public boolean onTouchEvent(MotionEvent event) {

        }
```

Listing 9-13 is the bare skeleton of a GlSurfaceView with renderer. As you can probably tell, this doesn't actually do anything yet.

Generally speaking, you'll do general setup in the constructor. onSurfaceCreated is most likely where you'll set up specific OpenGL behavior.

onSurfaceChanged is a good spot to set up things like the ViewPort and Projection Matrix, because at that stage you'll know what size your screen is.

And finally, the onDrawFrame is where you do the actual drawing.

GlSurfaceView provides its own Thread to do the actual drawing in, and by default onDrawFrame will be called pretty much as soon as the system has finished displaying the previous frame. You can change this behavior if, for example, you don't feel the need to be continuously rendering. You can set GLSurfaceView.setRenderMode(RENDERMODE_WHEN_DIRTY), and then make GLSurfaceView.requestRender() when you want the frame redrawn.

Now, to set the whole thing in motion, you need an Activity to hold it (refer to Listing 9-14).

Listing 9-14. The MainActivity for the 3D Demo

```java
public class MainActivity extends Activity {

  private GameSurfaceGl surface;

  @Override
  protected void onCreate(Bundle savedInstanceState) {
    super.onCreate(savedInstanceState);
    setContentView(R.layout.main);
    surface = (GameSurfaceGl) findViewById(R.id.surface);
  }

  // Resume and pause have to be passed through to the GL Surface

  @Override
  protected void onResume() {
    super.onResume();
    surface.onResume();
  }

  @Override
  protected void onPause() {
    super.onPause();
    surface.onPause();
  }
```

Listing 9-14 once again shows the bare bones. The important thing that needs to be done is to call the Surface's onPause and onResume in the Activity's onPause and onResume. Let's get to some specifics.

Listing 9-15. Initializing the 3D Environment

```java
        private void init(Context context) {
                this.setRenderer(this);
                this.requestFocus();
                this.setFocusableInTouchMode(true);

                this.context = context;
```

```
                    ByteBuffer byteBuf = ByteBuffer.allocateDirect(lightAmbient.length * 4);

                    byteBuf.order(ByteOrder.nativeOrder());
                    lightAmbientBuffer = byteBuf.asFloatBuffer();
                    lightAmbientBuffer.put(lightAmbient);
                    lightAmbientBuffer.position(0);
                    // Set up some more stuff here…
            }
```

Listing 9-15 shows some key bits of the setup. First and foremost, you need to call setRenderer to tell the GlSurface how to render the screen. The setFocus stuff is to make sure that we get keystrokes and other useful events, which I'm not using in this example, but I feel it does no harm.

What might not be immediately obvious is the use of ByteBuffer and FloatBuffer. This structure preformats the Java floating point arrays into native data, which saves OpenGL having to do it on the fly. 3D graphics rendering is still among the most computationally expensive things you can ask a computer to do, so anything you can do up front to save time later is a good idea.

In this particular example, we're preprocessing the definitions of the various lights. Having said that, the use of these buffers *is* optional, but they do improve performance.

Listing 9-16. The onSurfaceCreated Event

```
public void onSurfaceCreated(GL10 gl, EGLConfig config) {
    // Set up various lights.
    gl.glLightfv(GL10.GL_LIGHT0, GL10.GL_AMBIENT, lightAmbientBuffer);
    gl.glLightfv(GL10.GL_LIGHT0, GL10.GL_DIFFUSE, lightDiffuseBuffer);
    // Position the light, and enable it.
    gl.glLightfv(GL10.GL_LIGHT0, GL10.GL_POSITION, lightPositionBuffer);
    gl.glEnable(GL10.GL_LIGHT0); // Enable Light 0

    // Settings
    gl.glDisable(GL10.GL_DITHER); // Disable dithering
    gl.glEnable(GL10.GL_TEXTURE_2D); // Enable Texture Mapping
    gl.glShadeModel(GL10.GL_SMOOTH); // Enable Smooth Shading
    gl.glClearColor(0.0f, 0.0f, 0.0f, 0.5f); // Black Background
    gl.glClearDepthf(1.0f); // Depth Buffer Setup
    gl.glEnable(GL10.GL_DEPTH_TEST); // Enables Depth Testing
    gl.glDepthFunc(GL10.GL_LEQUAL); // The Type Of Depth Testing To Do

    // Use nicest possible Perspective Calculations
    gl.glHint(GL10.GL_PERSPECTIVE_CORRECTION_HINT, GL10.GL_NICEST);

    // This is our opportunity to load textures and stuff.
    cube.loadGLTexture(gl, this.context);
}
```

If you're familiar with OpenGL, you should recognize the basic setup being done in Listing 9-16. If not, well, just hang on for the ride.

If onSurfaceCreated is called, you need to assume that all the OpenGL resources have been reset, and will need to be reloaded.

Listing 9-17. The onSurfaceChanged Event

```java
public void onSurfaceChanged(GL10 gl, int width, int height) {
  if (height <= 0) height = 1; // Avoid divide by zero.
  gl.glViewport(0, 0, width, height); // Reset The Current Viewport
  gl.glMatrixMode(GL10.GL_PROJECTION); // Select The Projection Matrix
  gl.glLoadIdentity(); // Reset The Projection Matrix

  // Calculate The Aspect Ratio Of The Window
  GLU.gluPerspective(gl, 45.0f, (float) width / (float) height, 0.1f, 100.0f);

  gl.glMatrixMode(GL10.GL_MODELVIEW); // Select The Modelview Matrix
  gl.glLoadIdentity(); // Reset The Modelview Matrix
}
```

Listing 9-17 sets a simple viewport and perspective. This method of setting the perspective would be of use only for a fixed position camera, but since that's what we're currently using, we may as well do it here.

Listing 9-18. The onDrawFrame Event

```java
public void onDrawFrame(GL10 gl) {
  // Clear Screen And Depth Buffer
  gl.glClear(GL10.GL_COLOR_BUFFER_BIT | GL10.GL_DEPTH_BUFFER_BIT);
  gl.glLoadIdentity(); // Reset The Current Modelview Matrix

  // Check if the light flag has been set to enable/disable lighting
  if (light) {
    gl.glEnable(GL10.GL_LIGHTING);
  } else {
    gl.glDisable(GL10.GL_LIGHTING);
  }

  // Drawing
  gl.glTranslatef(0.0f, 0.0f, z); // Move z units into the screen

  // Rotate around the axis based on the rotation matrix (rotation, x, y, z)
  gl.glRotatef(xrot, 1.0f, 0.0f, 0.0f); // X
  gl.glRotatef(yrot, 0.0f, 1.0f, 0.0f); // Y

  cube.draw(gl); // Draw the Cube

}
```

And Listing 9-18 shows the actual drawing. cube is a class that actually defines and draws the cube . . . all the vertices, faces, and textures are handled internally, as well as the actual drawing. This is all pretty straightforward OpenGL, and once again, beyond the scope of this exercise.

I have set up a Handler for the GlSurfaceView to talk back to the Activity, remembering that all the Rendering is taking place in its own Thread.

If you're interested, Listing 9-19 shows the full setup in MainActivity.

Listing 9-19. Setting Everything Up: The MainActivity onCreate Event

```
protected void onCreate(Bundle savedInstanceState) {
        super.onCreate(savedInstanceState);
        setContentView(R.layout.main);
        surface = (GameSurfaceGl) findViewById(R.id.surface);
        mText = (TextView) findViewById(R.id.textView1);
        surface.setHandler(new Handler() {
            public void handleMessage(android.os.Message msg) {
                Bundle b = msg.getData();
                if (b!=null && b.containsKey("text")) {
                  mText.setText(b.getString("text"));
                }
            }
        });
      mSeekBar = (SeekBar) findViewById(R.id.seekBar1);
          mSeekBar.setOnSeekBarChangeListener(new OnSeekBarChangeListener() {
            @Override
            public void onStopTrackingTouch(SeekBar seekBar) { }

            @Override
            public void onStartTrackingTouch(SeekBar seekBar) { }

            @Override
            public void onProgressChanged(SeekBar seekBar, int progress,
                        boolean fromUser) {
              surface.setZoom(progress);

            }
        });
}
```

I've set up the normal UI controls above and below the GameSurfaceGl, and the code in Listing 9-19 manages pretty much all the linking between one and the other.

More Interprocess Communication Options

A last little lagniappe: GlSurfaceView comes with a built-in link to the Render Thread. You can use queueEvent(Runnable) to have something run in the Render Thread, such as Listing 9-20.

Listing 9-20. Using a Runnable with Handler

```
    if (action==MotionEvent.ACTION_UP) {
    queueEvent(new Runnable() {

        @Override
        public void run() { // This will happen inside the render thread
          sendText("Up"); // Fairly pointless example...
        }
```

```
        });
    }
```

For this example, it really is as easy to just use synchronized methods, and even that is probably overkill. Still, when things are getting more complex, queueEvent could be quite useful.

Summary

So, in this chapter, we somewhat belatedly introduced Threads, and looked at using SurfaceViews to implement real-time graphics. I also showed off some ways of using custom fonts, and responding at a fairly low level to touch events, both single and multiple. We had a look at using Assets and the AssetManager. In passing, we touched on using an XML menu, and finally dipped our toes in the scary world of 3D graphics.

CHAPTER 10

Remind Me

Playing with Alarms and SMS

This particular application demonstrates alarms, sending and receiving SMS messages, and (as an added bonus) a quick look at Android's Text To Speech (TTS) capabilities. Oh, and we'll just quickly check out Android's implementation of SQLite. This application (BA3TPRemindMe) allows you to queue up SMS messages to be sent at a predetermined time. It's also clever enough to detect incoming SMS messages and, if they are appropriately tagged, read aloud the contents.

Figure 10-1. It takes a lot to wake up some people . . .

Alarms

In Android, an Alarm can be set to trigger an Intent at some later point. You can create an individual, one-off Alarm, or set an Alarm to repeat at regular intervals. Repeating Alarms can be set to go off at specific intervals, or according to some sensible pattern: on the quarter hour, for example. An Alarm can be made to wake up a sleeping Android device.

What an Alarm is *not* intended for is short-term timing events. For one thing, it is not guaranteed to be super accurate. For another, there is significant overhead setting and responding to Alarms. For short-term events where accuracy is needed, look at the Handler.sendDelayed methods.

It's probably no great surprise by now to find that Alarms are managed by an AlarmManager object, returned from getSystemService.

Pending Intents

Once again, we return to the world of the PendingIntent. You'll find yourself using PendingIntent pretty much any time you want the system to do something on your behalf—in this case, notifying you when an Alarm has gone off.

Listing 10-1. Creating an Alarm

```
public static final Uri REMIND_ME_URI = Uri.parse("alarm://com.apress.ba3tp.remindme");
    ContentValues cv = new ContentValues();
    AlarmManager am = (AlarmManager) getSystemService(ALARM_SERVICE);
    Intent intent = new Intent(this,WakeupHandler.class);
    intent.setData(Uri.withAppendedPath(REMIND_ME_URI, String.valueOf(lastId)));
    PendingIntent operation = PendingIntent.getBroadcast(this, PENDING_NOTIFY, intent, 0);
    am.set(AlarmManager.RTC_WAKEUP, cal.getTimeInMillis(), operation);
```

Listing 10-1 shows the basics of creating an Alarm. In this case, I'm using a BroadcastReceiver to respond to the Alarm, but I could have just as easily used a Service or an Activity. I'm also giving it a unique Uri . . . not strictly necessary, but useful for distinguishing it later. In fact, a unique Uri is an excellent idea, as it clearly indicates which Alarm you are dealing with.

One thing to be wary about with PendingIntents is that they may end up being reused, with unexpected results. For example, when I first tried this application, I managed to send 25 text messages to my wife's phone before I managed to switch the darn thing off.

AlarmManager.RTC_WAKEUP tells it what sort of Alarm we're making. RTC stands for Real Time Clock, and uses the time as returned from System.currentMilliseconds() as the unit of measure. The WAKEUP means that it will wake up the device if necessary. If you don't use a WAKEUP type of Alarm, it will wait to trigger until Android has woken up again.

cal is a Calendar object, which is a Java class for manipulating time and date, and which I'll explain more about later.

Stopping an Alarm

Sometimes, stopping an Alarm from going off is at least as important as setting one. You can use AlarmManager.cancel(PendingIntent) to clear an Alarm. This will clear an Alarm matching the passed Intent.

What is not immediately clear is what is intended by a *matching* Intent. This is a problem I found when playing with ProximityAlerts back in the chapter about GPS, and I wasn't completely happy about my solution then. I have since managed to find a more coherent explanation.

Matching PendingIntent

A matching PendingIntent is one in which the associated Intent.filterEquals(Intent) returns true. filterEquals compares the action, data, type, class, and categories for the two Intents . . . but *not* the extras.

To make life even more interesting, PendingIntent.getBroadcast, etc. will by default *reuse* a PendingIntent if it finds a match . . . but it won't update the extras in that Intent unless you explicitly tell it.

This caused me no end of problems trying to hunt down a bug with my BroadcastReceiver, because I was inadvertently changing (and in some cases, *not* changing) data in PendingIntents before they'd actually been used.

Table 10-1. The PendingIntent Flags

Flag	Description
FLAG_CANCEL_CURRENT	If the described PendingIntent already exists, the current one is canceled before generating a new one.
FLAG_NO_CREATE	If the described PendingIntent does not already exist, then simply return null instead of creating it.
FLAG_ONE_SHOT	This PendingIntent can be used only once.
FLAG_UPDATE_CURRENT	If the described PendingIntent already exists, then keep it but replace its extra data with what is in this new Intent.

Table 10-1 shows the different flags you can use in PendingIntent.getBroadcast, getService, or getActivity to control this behavior. I feel that the documentation for Android is a bit skimpy on this point. I had to work this out by trial, error, and Google. I can see why it would be useful, but the fact that the default behavior is to reuse objects without telling you is a bit of a trap for young players.

If in doubt, and you want to make sure this PendingIntent will not be reused, use FLAG_ONE_SHOT. If you want to update the underlying Intent and the changes you've made in Extras, use the FLAG_UPDATE_CURRENT to make sure your changes are applied. I found this out the hard way.

Sending SMS

You should by this time be detecting a pattern when I say that sending SMS messages is handled by an SmsManager. However, this time it's returned by SmsManager.getDefault() (See Listing 10-2).

Listing 10-2. Sending an SMS Using the SmsManager

```
void doSendSMS() {
  SmsManager sms = SmsManager.getDefault();
  try {
    sms.sendTextMessage(mPhone.getText().toString(), null, mText.getText().toString(),↵
null, null);
    toast("Sent.");
  } catch (Exception e) {
    toast(e);
  }
}
```

Listing 10-2 shows pretty much all you need to know about sending an SMS. The actual sendTextMessage command looks like this:

```
public void sendTextMessage (String destinationAddress, String scAddress, String text,↩
 PendingIntent sentIntent, PendingIntent deliveryIntent)
```

By and large, all you need to supply is a phone number for destinationAddress, and the text you need to send (160 chars max).

scAddress stands for the Service Center address, but I can't imagine there'd ever be a lot of use for it in normal operation.

sentIntent and deliveryIntent (if defined) will be triggered when the message is sent and delivered, respectively. For the purpose of this demonstration, I've left them as null, but I do make use of them in the full application for tracking statuses.

■ **Note** Sending SMS messages requires the android.permission.SEND_SMS permission.

There are some other methods that SmsManager supports, such as divideMessage and sendMultipartTextMessage for sending longer messages. There is another method, sendDataMessage, for sending binary data, but it's not at all clear what you'd use this for or how, so for the moment I'd be inclined to stay with sendTextMessage.

One other thing: There are two versions of SmsManager in the Android SDK. Make sure you use android.telephony.SmsManager, not android.telephony.gsm.SmsManager. If you accidentally import the latter, the compiler will throw deprecated warnings.

Receiving SMS

It turns out that receiving SMS updates is pretty easy. Once again, we look at BroadcastReceiver. All you really need to do is register a BroadcastReceiver filtered on the SMS_RECEIVED action in AndroidManifest.xml (refer to Figure 10-3).

Listing 10-3. Registering a Receiver in AndroidManifest.xml

```
<receiver android:name="SmsReceiver">
    <intent-filter>
        <action android:name="android.provider.Telephony.SMS_RECEIVED"></action>
    </intent-filter>
</receiver>
```

Listing 10-3 shows the entry in AndroidManifest.xml.

Listing 10-4. The SMSReceiver Class

```
public class SmsReceiver extends BroadcastReceiver {
  private SharedPreferences mPreferences;

  @Override
  public void onReceive(Context context, Intent intent) {
```

```
    mPreferences = PreferenceManager.getDefaultSharedPreferences(context);
    if (!mPreferences.getBoolean("tts", false))
        return;
// Actual SMS Handle code starts here
    Bundle bundle = intent.getExtras();
    Object messages[] = (Object[]) bundle.get("pdus");
    for (int n = 0; n < messages.length; n++) {
        SmsMessage smsMessage = SmsMessage.createFromPdu((byte[]) messages[n]);
        String body = smsMessage.getMessageBody();
// and ends here.
    if (body.startsWith("#SPEAK")) {
        Intent service = new Intent(context, SmsRecieveService.class);
        service.putExtra("tts", body.substring(6).trim());
        context.startService(service);
    }
  }
 }
}
```

Listing 10-4 shows the entire code for SmsReceiver. Whenever your Android device receives an SMS, the onReceive event is fired. The message(s) are returned as an array of byte arrays in "pdus" in Extras.

In case you're wondering, a PDU is a protocol description unit. This has a binary encoded form of the SMS message, including phone number and timestamp. This is not the easiest thing in the world to work with, which is why we use the SmsMessage.createFromPdu method to interpret it into something more useful.

In this case, I'm interested in the message body rather than anything else. If it starts with the tag "#SPEAK", then I send it to my Text To Speech service.

■ **Note** You need android.permission.RECEIVE_SMS to listen for incoming SMS messages.

Text To Speech

One of the cooler things about Android is the built-in Text To Speech (TTS) functionality, so I thought I'd include this in my demo.

Listing 10-5. The SMSReceiveService Class

```
public class SmsReceiveService extends Service implements OnInitListener {
  TextToSpeech mTts;
  boolean mTtsStarted = false;
  Queue<String> mMessages = new LinkedList<String>();

  @Override
  public void onCreate() {
    super.onCreate();
    mTtsStarted=false;
    mTts = new TextToSpeech(this,this);
```

225

```
  }

  @Override
  public void onDestroy() {
    mTts.shutdown();
    mTts=null;
    mTtsStarted=false;
    super.onDestroy();
  }

  @Override
  public int onStartCommand(Intent intent, int flags, int startId) {
    String msg = intent.getStringExtra("tts");
    if (msg!=null) {
      synchronized(mMessages) {
        mMessages.add(msg);
      }
      if (mTtsStarted) doSpeech();
    }
    return START_STICKY;
  }

  @Override
  public IBinder onBind(Intent intent) {
    // Not using this here.
    return null;
  }

  @Override
  public void onInit(int status) {
    mTtsStarted=true;
    doSpeech();
  }

  void doSpeech() {
    String msg;
    synchronized(mMessages) {
    while ((msg=mMessages.poll())!=null) {
      mTts.speak(msg, TextToSpeech.QUEUE_ADD, null);
    }
    }
  }
}
```

Listing 10-5 shows the TTS service in its entirety. In order to be used, TTS needs to be initialized. This takes a little time, so you need to set a Listener to know when it's ready. In the meantime, I've put the messages into a queue for later use.

Queues

There's a useful subset of `Collections` that are designed to make your life easier when it comes to queues. This is the `Queue` interface, and it offers methods to put things into the queue and pull them out again later. These methods are `add` and `poll`.

Most Queue implementations are First-In-First-Out (FIFO), but there is also `Stack`, which implements a Last-In-First-Out (LIFO) functionality. In this case, I want to queue up messages to be read in order, so I'm using `LinkedList`. `LinkedList` is an implementation of `List`, but it also implements `Queue`.

When the `Service` is started, I immediately create a `TextToSpeech` object.

```
mTts = new TextToSpeech(this,this);
```

This will not actually be available to use until I receive an `onInit` event from the `TextToSpeech` (which is part of the `TextToSpeech.OnInitListener` interface) . . . the `Listener` is the second parameter in the `TextToSpeech` constructor.

Whenever a message is received, I pop it into the `mMessages` queue for safekeeping. Then, if the flag has been set telling me the TTS service is ready, I pull these messages from my internal queue and add them to the TTS queue.

```
mTts.speak(msg, TextToSpeech.QUEUE_ADD, null);
```

Otherwise, I wait for the `onInit` and send them then.

When my `Service` is being destroyed, I'll call `TextToSpeech.shutDown()` to release any used resources.

Note the use of `synchronized` when I access `mMessages`. This is probably not needed, as the `Service` is going to be running only in the main UI `Thread`, but it's not going to hurt either.

SQLite

I've mentioned SQLite before, but so far haven't given any concrete examples (except in Python). Since I want to keep track of all the `Alarms` I'm creating, and since they are a bit complex to save in `SharedPreferences`, I thought now might be a good time.

According to the SQLite web site (`www.sqlite.org`), SQLite is as follows:

> *a software library that implements a self-contained, serverless, zero-configuration, transactional SQL database engine. SQLite is the most widely deployed SQL database engine in the world. The source code for SQLite is in the public domain.*

This makes it pretty much ideal for embedded devices. Android even uses it internally for all sorts of things.

A detailed treatise of SQL is beyond the scope of this book (well beyond). However, SQLite seems to tolerate most dialects of SQL, and supports most of SQL-92. It's also quite nippy, which is handy in a SQL database.

Creating a SQLite Database

The fiddliest bit about setting up a database can be making sure you have the right version of the various tables created. If you're developing a database, it's not uncommon to realize you need extra columns, or tables, or that you need to change some settings.

Keeping track of where you are can be difficult, especially when you get your application out there in the real world on multiple devices. What do you do then?

You can, obviously, write code to interrogate the database and make changes as needed. Android has provided a helper class to make this somewhat easier.

Listing 10-6. Using SQLiteOpenHelper

```java
public class AlarmDatabase extends SQLiteOpenHelper {

  public static final String DATABASE_NAME = "smsdb";
  public static final int DATABASE_VERSION = 4;
  public AlarmDatabase(Context context) {
    super(context, DATABASE_NAME, null, DATABASE_VERSION);
  }

  @Override
  public void onCreate(SQLiteDatabase db) {
    db.execSQL("create table alarms (_id integer primary key autoincrement," +
        "phone text,message text, trigger datetime, enabled boolean, status text,↵
lastupdate datetime)");
  }

  @Override
  public void onUpgrade(SQLiteDatabase db, int oldversion, int newversion) {
    if (newversion>oldversion) {
      db.execSQL("drop table alarms");
      onCreate(db);
    }
  }

}
```

Listing 10-6 shows a simple implementation of SQLiteOpenHelper. This tracks which version of the database you have, and works out if it needs to be created from scratch. Each time you change the format of the database, increment the DATABASE_VERSION. As you can see, I went through four versions in development before I was happy.

If it needs to be created, it will call the onCreate function, passing it an instance of the SQLiteDatabase to work with. In this case, I'm creating a single table ("alarms") using the SQL CREATE TABLE command. If it realizes that the version number has changed, onUpgrade is called. This time around, any data I might have stored is not particularly significant, so I just drop the "alarms" table and re-create with the new values.

However, you could use ALTER TABLE to add missing columns, or even issue commands to change data formats if needed.

Getting Your Database

Having created a SQLiteOpenHelper class, this is how you get your database to work with it:

```
SQLiteDatabase mDb = (new AlarmDatabase(this)).getWritableDatabase();
```

Obviously, there's a getReadableDatabase method as well.

You don't *have* to use SQLiteOpenHelper if you don't want to. SQLiteDatabase.openOrCreate() works fine, but you will still have to deal with creating your tables and so forth on your own.

Using Your Database

Having created your database, and opened it, it's pretty simple to use (see Table 10-2).

Table 10-2. Useful SQLiteDatabase Methods

Method	Description
void close()	Closes the database
int delete(String table, String whereClause, String[] whereArgs)	Convenience method for deleting rows in the database
void execSQL(String sql)	Executes a single SQL statement that is *not* a SELECT or any other SQL statement that returns data
long insert(String table, String nullColumnHack, ContentValues values)	Convenience method for inserting a row into the database
long insertOrThrow(String table, String nullColumnHack, ContentValues values)	Convenience method for inserting a row into the database
Cursor query(String table, String[] columns, String selection, String[] selectionArgs, String groupBy, String having, String orderBy, String limit)	Queries the given table, returning a Cursor over the result set
Cursor rawQuery(String sql, String[] selectionArgs)	Runs the provided SQL and returns a Cursor over the result set
int update(String table, ContentValues values, String whereClause, String[] whereArgs)	Convenience method for updating rows in the database

Table 10-2 shows the most common methods you are likely to call. Listing 10-7 shows how I'm using SQLite in my code.

Listing 10-7. Use of SQLite in the Alarm Demo

```
// Standard Date format
    static final SimpleDateFormat mSqlFmt = new SimpleDateFormat("yyyy-MM-dd HH:mm:ss");

// Insert
    ContentValues cv = new ContentValues();
    cv.put("phone", phone);
    cv.put("message", message);
    cv.put("trigger",mSqlFmt.format(cal.getTime()));
    cv.put("enabled", true);
    cv.put("status", "Pending");
    int lastId = (int) mDb.insert("alarms", null, cv);

// Update
    void updateStatus(int alarm_id, String msg) {
    ContentValues cv = new ContentValues();
    cv.put("status", msg);
    cv.put("lastupdate", MainActivity.mSqlFmt.format(new Date()));
    mDb.update("alarms",cv,"_id="+alarm_id,null);
    }

// Query
private void requery() {
    Cursor c = mDb.rawQuery("select * from alarms order by trigger", null);
    mAdapter.changeCursor(c);
    }

// Delete
        mDb.delete("alarms", "trigger<'"+MainActivity.mSqlFmt.format(new Date())+"'", null);
```

You may note that I've used rawQuery rather than query. query is actually a series of helper methods that, in the end, call rawQuery, and I'm actually more comfortable with straight SQL. There is no inherent virtue in going one way or the other; it's what works best for you.

You may also note that the insert function returns the most recent auto increment value.

The Application

The main screen for the actual BA3TPRemindMe application is shown in Figure 10-2. The layout for it looks like Listing 10-8.

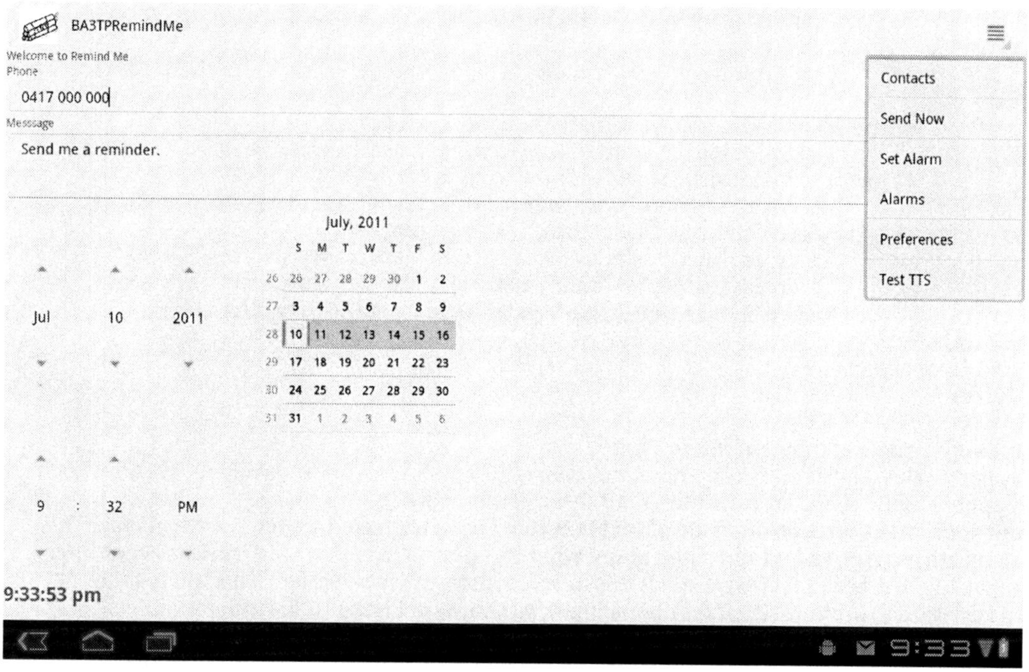

Figure 10-2. The BA3TPRemindMe main screen

Listing 10-8. Layout for the BA3TPRemindMe Main Screen

```xml
<?xml version="1.0" encoding="utf-8"?>
<ScrollView android:id="@+id/scrollView1"
        xmlns:android="http://schemas.android.com/apk/res/android"
        android:layout_width="match_parent" android:layout_height="wrap_content">
        <LinearLayout xmlns:android="http://schemas.android.com/apk/res/android"
                android:layout_width="fill_parent" android:layout_height="fill_parent"
                android:orientation="vertical" android:id="@+id/LinearLayout2">
                <TextView android:layout_width="fill_parent"
                        android:layout_height="wrap_content" android:text="@string/hello" />
                <TextView android:layout_height="wrap_content"
                        android:layout_width="wrap_content" android:id="@+id/textView1"
                        android:text="@string/phonelbl"></TextView>
                <EditText android:layout_height="wrap_content"
                        android:layout_width="match_parent" android:inputType="phone"
                        android:hint="Phone" android:id="@+id/ePhone"></EditText>
                <TextView android:layout_height="wrap_content"
                        android:layout_width="wrap_content" android:id="@+id/textView2"
                        android:text="@string/messagelbl"></TextView>
                <EditText android:layout_width="match_parent" android:id="@+id/eMessage"
                        android:hint="Message" android:includeFontPadding="true"
                        android:fadeScrollbars="true" android:scrollbars="vertical"
```

231

```
                            android:lines="3" android:minLines="3" android:layout_height=↵
"wrap_content"
                            android:inputType="textMultiLine|textCapSentences|textAutoCorrect">↵
</EditText>
                <DatePicker android:layout_height="wrap_content"
                        android:layout_width="wrap_content" android:id="@+id/eDatePicker" />
                <TimePicker android:layout_height="wrap_content"
                        android:layout_width="wrap_content" android:id="@+id/eTimePicker" />
                <DigitalClock android:layout_height="wrap_content"
                        android:layout_width="wrap_content" android:typeface="normal"
                        android:textStyle="bold" android:text="DigitalClock"
                        android:textSize="24sp" android:id="@+id/digitalClock1">↵
</DigitalClock>
        </LinearLayout>
</ScrollView>
```

There are a couple of things of interest here.

First, DatePicker and TimePicker. These are more or less standard Android widgets, yet they don't typically appear in the visual layout editor. I put these in manually.

I draw your attention to an attribute of EditText that I have neglected somewhat: inputType. This rather useful attribute gives Android a hint about what sort of data to expect, and it reacts accordingly. For example, in the ePhone EditText, I've set this to android:inputType="phone". This will tell the onscreen keyboard to optimize itself for phone input, as shown in Figure 10-3. Rather more interestingly, the eMessage EditText has it set to android:inputType="textMultiLine|textCapSentences|textAutoCorrect", telling Android that this is a MultiLine input, to capitalize sentences, and enable auto-correction.

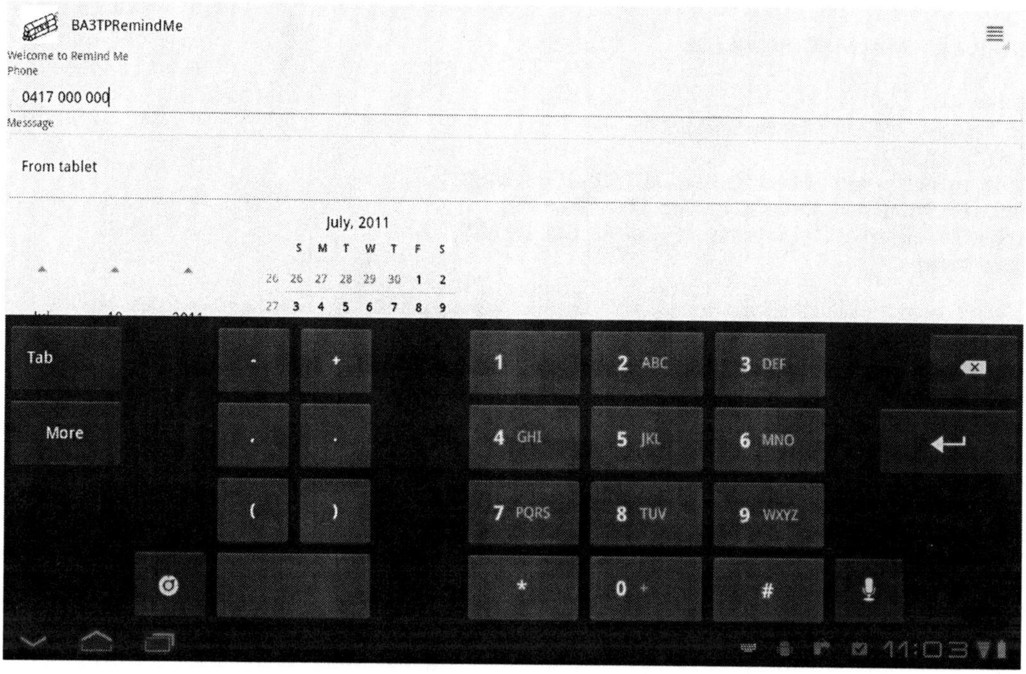

Figure 10-3. The onscreen keyboard for a phone inputType

Using the Application

It's pretty simple to use. Simply enter a phone number, a message to send, and a time and date to send it. Here are menu options:

- *Contacts*: Look up contacts for a phone number to send it to; if your device has a Search button, that will also look up contacts.

- *Send Now*: Send the SMS immediately

- *Set Alarm*: Send the message at the allocated time

- *Alarms*: View the status of the Alarms you've set

- *Preferences*: Preferences screen

- *Test TTS*: Will check that the Text To Speech function has been enabled on this device; if not, it will request a download of the needed files.

Contacts

There's a simple Intent to find a phone number from your contacts list (see Listing 10-9).

Listing 10-9. Searching the Contacts List

```java
@Override
public boolean onSearchRequested() {
    toast("Search");
    Intent intent = new Intent(Intent.ACTION_GET_CONTENT);
    intent.setType("vnd.android.cursor.item/phone");
    startActivityForResult(intent, REMIND_ME_GET_PHONE);
    return true;
}

@Override
protected void onActivityResult(int requestCode, int resultCode, Intent data) {
    switch(requestCode) {
    case REMIND_ME_GET_PHONE:
        if (data.hasExtra(Intent.EXTRA_PHONE_NUMBER)) {
            mPhone.setText(data.getStringExtra(Intent.EXTRA_PHONE_NUMBER));
            SharedPreferences.Editor e = mPreferences.edit();
            e.putString("phone", mPhone.getText().toString());
            e.commit();
        }
        break;
```

Listing 10-9 shows both the Intent to get the phone list, and the onActivityResult method to get the result. Note the onSearchRequested method. This will get triggered if your device has a Search button, which is a nice feature. The selected phone number is returned in EXTRA_PHONE_NUMBER.

Set Alarm

Listing 10-10 shows the code I use to actually set the Alarm.

Listing 10-10. Setting the Reminder Alarm

```java
void doSetAlarm() {
    Calendar cal = GregorianCalendar.getInstance();
    cal.set(mDate.getYear(),mDate.getMonth(),mDate.getDayOfMonth(),mTime.getCurrentHour(),↵
mTime.getCurrentMinute(),0);
    toast(cal.getTime());
    String message = mText.getText().toString();
    if (mUseTts) {
        message="#SPEAK "+message;
    }
    String phone = mPhone.getText().toString();

    ContentValues cv = new ContentValues();
    cv.put("phone", phone);
    cv.put("message", message);
    cv.put("trigger",mSqlFmt.format(cal.getTime()));
    cv.put("enabled", true);
    cv.put("status", "Pending");
```

```
  int lastId = (int) mDb.insert("alarms", null, cv);
  //int lastId = AlarmDatabase.getLastId(mDb);

  AlarmManager am = (AlarmManager) getSystemService(ALARM_SERVICE);
  Intent intent = new Intent(this,WakeupHandler.class);
  intent.setData(Uri.withAppendedPath(REMIND_ME_URI, String.valueOf(lastId)));
  intent.putExtra(WAKEUP_COMMAND,"sms");
  intent.putExtra(WAKEUP_EXTRA_PHONE, phone);
  intent.putExtra(WAKEUP_EXTRA_TEXT, message);
  intent.putExtra(WAKEUP_EXTRA_ALARM_ID,lastId);
  PendingIntent operation = PendingIntent.getBroadcast(this, PENDING_NOTIFY, intent, 0);
  am.set(AlarmManager.RTC_WAKEUP, cal.getTimeInMillis(), operation);
}
```

Let's see. The first thing we need to do is convert the date and time values in the Date and Time pickers into a Date. Sadly, the Time and Date pickers don't have a simple function to return a Date object. Fortunately, there is a Java class specifically designed to do just that, and this class is Calendar. Technically, it's a group of classes, but in practice everyone uses GregorianCalendar, since that's what is used pretty much everywhere.

Calendar has functions to manipulate dates in various ways. In this case, I just want to convert the human-readable year, month, day, hour, etc. into the internal system time. This is easily done with the Calendar.set method. The next thing I do is insert the Alarm into the database, which has the convenient side effect of returning a unique ID I can use to identify the Alarm.

▓ **Note** SQLite doesn't have a date type per se, but it can handle dates stored as either strings or numbers. It has a number of built-in date functions, but the simplest way for the moment is to treat the date as a string. mSqlDateFmt is defined as SimpleDateFormat("yyyy-MM-dd HH:mm:ss"), which will convert the date into a standard format string, and vice versa.

I've defined a handler to receive Alarm calls, in this case a BroadcastReceiver called WakeupHandler. Since the Alarm is defined as a PendingIntent, I could have implemented a Service or an Activity instead, but a BroadcastReceiver seemed easiest for this purpose.

I then put everything needed to send the SMS into the Intent extras. In this case, a command ("sms"), the phone number and message, and the ID. This last is not absolutely needed since it's already encoded in the Uri, but it doesn't hurt and makes debugging easier. Then I actually set the Alarm.

Listing 10-11. Responding to the Alarm

```
public class WakeupHandler extends BroadcastReceiver {
  public static final int NOTIFICATION_ID = 1001;
  private Context mContext;
  private SQLiteDatabase mDb;

  @Override
  public void onReceive(Context context, Intent intent) {
```

```
      mDb = (new AlarmDatabase(context)).getWritableDatabase();
      mContext = context;
      String cmd = intent.getStringExtra(MainActivity.WAKEUP_COMMAND);
      if (cmd == null) {
        toast("No command");
      } else {
        toast(cmd);
        int alarm_id = intent.getIntExtra(MainActivity.WAKEUP_EXTRA_ALARM_ID, 0);
        if (cmd.equals("sms")) {
          doSendSms(intent.getStringExtra(MainActivity.WAKEUP_EXTRA_PHONE),⏎
  intent.getStringExtra(MainActivity.WAKEUP_EXTRA_TEXT),
              alarm_id);
        } else if (cmd.equals("sent") || cmd.equals("delivered")) {
          int ret = getResultCode();
          doNotify("SMS "+cmd+" "+errmsg(ret));
          updateStatus(alarm_id,cmd+" "+errmsg(ret));
        }
      }
      mDb.close();
    }

    private String errmsg(int ret) {
      switch (ret) {
      case SmsManager.RESULT_ERROR_GENERIC_FAILURE: return "Failure";
      case SmsManager.RESULT_ERROR_NO_SERVICE: return "No Service";
      case SmsManager.RESULT_ERROR_NULL_PDU: return "Null PDU";
      case SmsManager.RESULT_ERROR_RADIO_OFF: return "Radio Off";
      case 0: return "OK";
      case -1: return "Done";
      default: return "Result="+ret;
      }
    }

    private Intent makeIntent(String msg, int id) {
      Intent intent = new Intent(mContext,this.getClass());
      intent.putExtra(MainActivity.WAKEUP_COMMAND, msg);
      intent.putExtra(MainActivity.WAKEUP_EXTRA_ALARM_ID,id);
      return intent;
    }

    private void doSendSms(String phone, String text, int id) {
      SmsManager sms = SmsManager.getDefault();
      try {
        doNotify("Alarm triggered");
        Intent sendIntent = makeIntent("sent",id);
        Intent deliveredIntent = makeIntent("delivered",id);
        PendingIntent sent = PendingIntent.getBroadcast(mContext, 0, sendIntent,⏎
  PendingIntent.FLAG_ONE_SHOT);
        PendingIntent delivered = PendingIntent.getBroadcast(mContext, 0,⏎
  deliveredIntent, PendingIntent.FLAG_ONE_SHOT);
```

```
        sms.sendTextMessage(phone, null, text, sent, delivered);
        updateStatus(id,"queued");
      } catch (Exception e) {
        toast(e);
      }
    }


    void updateStatus(int alarm_id, String msg) {
      ContentValues cv = new ContentValues();
      cv.put("status", msg);
      cv.put("lastupdate", MainActivity.mSqlFmt.format(new Date()));
      mDb.update("alarms",cv,"_id="+alarm_id,null);
    }


}
```

Listing 10-11 shows most of the WakeupHandler class, which does the bulk of the actual work.

The onReceive is set up to handle three different Intents, as differentiated by WAKEUP_COMMAND in extras. These can be "sms", "sent", and "delivered". "sms" comes from the Alarm itself, and tells the program to actually send the SMS. The other two come as status updates from the SMS subsystem, letting you know whether the SMS send worked. My service provider doesn't appear to support "delivered" as a status, so I'm not completely sure that it works. I left it in there for completeness as much as anything else.

Now, if you recall the previous discussions about PendingIntent and what constitutes a match, it may have made more sense to encode the behavior in the Intent's Data Uri, or possibly Categories. The design decision to use Extras was made before I'd quite come to grips with the way PendingIntent worked. In the end, I decided to leave things as they were, as it was simpler to read the extras Bundle. Just be aware that there are swings and roundabouts to any design decision.

I did also consider setting up a separate BroadcastReceiver just for the status messages, but in the end decided it added unnecessary complication and code duplication.

doSendSms does the work of actually sending the SMS, as well as setting up the previously mentioned Status Intents. It also calls updateStatus, which updates the status fields in the alarms table. When the SMS is actually sent, onReceive handles the updates by simply updating the alarms table.

"sent" messages have the result returned in the resultCode, which can be accessed by getResultCode(). errmsg() translates this code into something human-readable.

For "delivered", the raw PDU of the status report is in the extras ("pdu") tag. Theory says you could use SmsMessage to decode this, but I haven't been able to test.

The NOTIFICATION_ID is just set to an arbitrary integer, in this case 1001, and is used to distinguish between different notifications for the same application.

Alarms List

Listing 10-12. The Alarm List Manager

```
public class AlarmList extends ListActivity {
  SQLiteDatabase mDb;
  CursorAdapter mAdapter;
```

```java
@Override
protected void onCreate(Bundle savedInstanceState) {
  super.onCreate(savedInstanceState);
  mDb = (new AlarmDatabase(this)).getWritableDatabase();
  setContentView(R.layout.list); // All this to get empty data to show.
  registerForContextMenu(getListView());
  mAdapter = new CursorAdapter(this,null) {
    @Override
    public View newView(Context context, Cursor cursor, ViewGroup parent) {
      TextView result = new TextView(context);
      result.setTextSize(16);
      bindView(result,context,cursor);
      return result;
    }

    @Override
    public void bindView(View view, Context context, Cursor cursor) {

      StringBuilder sb = new StringBuilder();
      for (int i=0; i<cursor.getColumnCount(); i++) {
        sb.append(cursor.getColumnName(i)+" : "+cursor.getString(i)+"\n");
      }
      ((TextView) view).setText(sb.toString());
    }
  };
  setListAdapter(mAdapter);
  requery();
}

@Override
protected void onDestroy() {
  mDb.close();
  super.onDestroy();
}

private void requery() {
  Cursor c = mDb.rawQuery("select * from alarms order by trigger", null);
  mAdapter.changeCursor(c);
}
```

Listing 10-12 shows almost the entire code for the list manager. We use a CursorAdapter, which means overriding the createView and bindView, and then passing it a Cursor. The Cursor is the result of a SQLiteDatabase.rawQuery, which just lists the Alarms in order. The bindView, which actually populates the view, is a simple bit of code that reads each column and displays the name and values. A Cursor for CursorAdapter needs to include an "_Id" column, which needs to be a unique identifier for the row.

The only other thing to keep in mind is that, unlike some other queries we have used, SQLite Cursors will not automatically update when the underlying table changes. That is why requery is called what it is called. I call it whenever I do something to the table.

Listing 10-13. Manipulating the Underlying Alarms Table

```java
public boolean onOptionsItemSelected(MenuItem item) {
  int id = item.getItemId();
  switch (id) {
  case R.id.menuPurge:
    try {
      mDb.delete("alarms", "trigger<'"+MainActivity.mSqlFmt.format(new Date())+"'", null);
    } catch (SQLiteException e) {
      toast(e);
    }
    requery();
    break;
  }
  return super.onOptionsItemSelected(item);
}

@Override
public boolean onContextItemSelected(MenuItem item) {
  AdapterView.AdapterContextMenuInfo info;
  try {
    info = (AdapterView.AdapterContextMenuInfo) item.getMenuInfo();
  } catch (ClassCastException e) {
    return false;
  }
  int id = item.getItemId();
  switch(id) {
  case R.id.menuDelete:
    clearAlarm((int) info.id);
    mDb.delete("alarms", "_id="+info.id, null);
    requery();
    break;
  }
  return super.onContextItemSelected(item);
}

void clearAlarm(int id) {
  AlarmManager am = (AlarmManager) getSystemService(ALARM_SERVICE);
  Intent intent = new Intent(this,WakeupHandler.class);
  intent.setData(Uri.withAppendedPath(MainActivity.REMIND_ME_URI, String.valueOf(id)));
  PendingIntent operation = PendingIntent.getBroadcast(this, MainActivity.PENDING_NOTIFY, ↵
intent, PendingIntent.FLAG_NO_CREATE);
  if (operation==null) toast("Alarm intent not found");
  else {
    // Should match on Intent.
    am.cancel(operation);
    toast("Alarm cancelled.");
  }
}
```

Listing 10-13 shows the associated user interface logic that performs actions on this list.
AlarmList implements two user functions: Purge and Delete. Purge is implemented as a SQL
command to delete any Alarm that should have already gone off.

```
mDb.delete("alarms", "trigger<'"+MainActivity.mSqlFmt.format(new Date())+"'", null);
```

Note again the use of the standard date format, which among other things will compare sensibly to
other dates in the same format.

When it comes to Delete, this is implemented as a Context menu, which conveniently passes the
unique ID for the row. The Delete then becomes as simple as the following:

```
mDb.delete("alarms", "_id="+info.id, null);
```

Delete also attempts to clear the Alarm so that it doesn't go off any more, which brings us once again
to matching on PendingIntents.

I've made use of the PendingIntent.FLAG_NO_CREATE flag. This is not essential, but the result from
this can be used as an indicator of whether it actually found a match. If a match wasn't found, it's an
indication that the Alarm has already been triggered, or was cancelled some other way. Otherwise, it can
go ahead and cancel the Alarm.

Tip While debugging, you can find out the list of currently set Alarms by calling adb shell dumpsys alarm.

Testing TTS

Text To Speech is not normally installed out of the box on Android. Listing 10-14 shows the code used to
test that it has been installed, and to request an installation if it isn't there.

Listing 10-14. Testing If Text To Speech Is Installed

```
void doTestTts() {
  if (mTts!=null) {
    mTts.speak("Testing text to speech",TextToSpeech.QUEUE_FLUSH,null);
  } else {
    Intent checkIntent = new Intent();
    checkIntent.setAction(TextToSpeech.Engine.ACTION_CHECK_TTS_DATA);
    startActivityForResult(checkIntent, REMIND_ME_CHECK_TTS);
  }
}

@Override
protected void onActivityResult(int requestCode, int resultCode, Intent data) {
  switch(requestCode) {
  case REMIND_ME_CHECK_TTS:
    if (resultCode == TextToSpeech.Engine.CHECK_VOICE_DATA_PASS) {
      // success, create the TTS instance
      mTts = new TextToSpeech(this,this);
    } else {
```

```
      // Go fetch needed data
      Intent installIntent = new Intent();
      installIntent.setAction(
          TextToSpeech.Engine.ACTION_INSTALL_TTS_DATA);
      startActivity(installIntent);
      }
    break;
  }
  super.onActivityResult(requestCode, resultCode, data);
}

@Override
public void onInit(int status) {
//  mTts.setLanguage(Locale.US);
//  mTts.setPitch(0.8f);
//  mTts.setSpeechRate(1.2f);
    mTts.speak("TTS Loaded", TextToSpeech.QUEUE_FLUSH, null);
  }
```

How that works should be reasonably obvious by this time. Note that some of the other things you can do in the onInit event is to set things like the current language and pitch. Generally speaking, I found the defaults worked pretty well, but I left the commented-out code there as a guide.

Remember to go to Preferences to set TTS on, or it won't work. Oh, the first time I tried to use TTS in an application, I couldn't get it working. It took me a while to realize that the volume had been turned right down! This line tells Android to use the Volume buttons to control the application volume rather than the ringer volume.

```
setVolumeControlStream(AudioManager.STREAM_MUSIC);
```

Enhancing the Application

There are a few things that could be done to improve this program. For one thing, if the Android is switched off, any pending Alarms will be left in the database, but not be actually queued. It might be a good idea to listen for the Intent.ACTION_BOOT_COMPLETED broadcast, and either reset the Alarms or clear out the database.

It might be interesting to play with repeating Alarms, and also group lists for the messaging. You could also put in a facility to send e-mails as well as (or instead of) SMS. It would probably be a nice user feature to disallow setting an Alarm in the past, as it will never go off.

As a final thought, it's possible that Purge should explicitly cancel the old Alarms as well as remove them from the database. I leave this as an exercise for the reader.

Summary

So what have we learned today?

We've played with sending and receiving SMS messages, as well as Alarms. We've had a look at creating and manipulating a SQLite database. We've looked more at BroadcastReceivers and Services, and we've learned how to test, load, and use Text To Speech services.

Not a bad day's work, if you ask me.

CHAPTER 11

Everything Else

Advanced Techniques and Other Stuff

This chapter is a bit of a grab bag, for bits and pieces that I promised to get to and didn't, and some other bits that may have been a bit advanced for earlier chapters. Most of the examples for these have been thrown together into a grab bag application I've called BA3TPMisc.

Figure 11-1. Putting the pieces together

Timers

While Android has Alarms, these are fairly broad-stroke affairs, not really suitable for fine control. They don't promise a high degree of precision, and they carry a fair bit of overhead.

There are a number of methods of implementing fine timers, but the simplest is probably (non-intuitively) with the Handler. I've touched on Handler before, mostly in Chapter 9.. Now, as promised, how to use them as timers (shown in Listing 11-1).

Listing 11-1. Using Handler As a Timer

```
protected void onCreate(Bundle savedInstanceState) {
  super.onCreate(savedInstanceState);
  setContentView(R.layout.timers);
  mProgress = (ProgressBar) findViewById(R.id.progressBar1);

  mHandler = new Handler();

  // Stop spinner after 5 seconds.
  mHandler.postDelayed(new Runnable() {

    @Override
    public void run() {
      mProgress.setVisibility(View.INVISIBLE);
    }
  }, 5000);
```

Listing 11-1 shows part of the onCreate method for TimersActivity, which is part of the BA3TPMisc application. This will simply stop a progress bar spinner from spinning after five seconds.

The first thing of importance I do (after the basic setup boilerplate) is to create a Handler of my very own. A Handler's prime job is to manage passing messages to a given Thread. The Handler will automatically attach itself to the current Thread's Looper. In this case, the current Thread is the main UI Thread, which means it already has a Looper running, so we don't have to make our own.

The nice thing about using a Handler is that all the received messages are processed in the target Thread, in a known order, so you have a lot fewer concurrency problems to deal with. For that very reason, it's not advisable to pass lengthy processes to the Handler, precisely because you *are* running them in the main Thread. The lengthy processing should have already been done in the Thread that is calling Handler.

Now, there are two main groups of methods in Handler, post and send. send will send a message, which will require a handleMessage method to be defined. We covered those in Chapter 9. . post will send a Runnable, which the Looper will execute.

▪ **Reminder** A Runnable is a class that implements the Runnable interface, which defines a single method: public void run().

In normal circumstances, the message will be processed in the same order it was posted, but you can also tell it to process at a given time.

postDelayed/sendDelayed will be delivered after a user-defined number of milliseconds has passed. postAtTime/sendAtTime trigger at an absolute time, but the time is the time returned from SystemClock.uptimeMillis(). This returns milliseconds since boot, not counting time spent in deep sleep.

The first of my timers uses postDelayed to run an anonymous Runnable after 5,000 milliseconds/5 seconds. Let's look at a few other options in Listing 11-2.

Listing 11-2. Using Handler.PostDelayed

```
In onCreate:
------------
    mToggle = (ToggleButton) findViewById(R.id.toggleButton1);
    mToggleTick.retrigger=true;
    mToggleTick.doTimer();
-----------
  // Toggle the toggle button every second.
  private class ToggleTick implements Runnable {
    boolean retrigger=false;
    @Override
    public void run() {
      mToggle.setChecked(!mToggle.isChecked());
      if (retrigger) doTimer();
    }

    public void doTimer() {
      mHandler.postDelayed(this,500);
    }
  }
}
```

In Listing 11-2, I'm creating a repeating timer that will toggle a toggleButton at regular intervals. For neatness as much as anything, I'm implementing this as a class, which simply retriggers itself each time. You'll note that I've added a retrigger field. This will allow me to stop the darn thing if I need to.

Listing 11-3 shows a simple real-time clock.

Listing 11-3. Implementing a Real-Time Clock

```
    private ClockTick mClockTick = new ClockTick();
    private SimpleDateFormat mDateFmt = new SimpleDateFormat("hh:mm:ss");

    @Override
    protected void onCreate(Bundle savedInstanceState) {
...
      mClockTick.retrigger=true;
      mClockTick.doTimer();
...
    }

  // Toggle the toggle button every second.
  private class ClockTick implements Runnable {
    public boolean retrigger;

    @Override
    public void run() {
      mRadio.setChecked(!mRadio.isChecked());
      mRadio.setText(mDateFmt.format(new Date()));
      if (retrigger) doTimer();
    }
```

```
  public void doTimer() {

    long nextTime = SystemClock.uptimeMillis() + 1000;
    nextTime = (nextTime/1000) * 1000; // Force it to trigger on the actual second.
    mHandler.postAtTime(this, nextTime);
  }
}
```

The difference between Listing 11-2 and Listing 11-3 is that I use the postAtTime method, rounding to the nearest full second. This should mean that the clock updates in a nice, regular fashion.

Listing 11-4. Using Handler.postAtTime with a Token

```
// Just tick up the progress bar.
  mHandler.postAtTime(new Runnable() {

    @Override
    public void run() {
      mHorizontal.incrementProgressBy(1);
      if (mHorizontal.getProgress()<mHorizontal.getMax()) {
        mHandler.postAtTime(this,"progress",SystemClock.uptimeMillis()+200);
      }
    }}, "progress", SystemClock.uptimeMillis()+200);
```

Listing 11-4 shows yet another way of creating a repeating time, this time entirely inline. This one will keep updating a horizontal progress bar until it is full, and then stop. You'll notice that I'm using postAtTime rather than postDelayed, and that a third parameter has snuck in. This is because there are two different forms of postAtTime (and sendAtTime):

```
postAtTime(Runnable r, long uptimeMillis)
postAtTime(Runnable r, Object token, long uptimeMillis)
```

The second has this mysterious additional parameter, token. token turns out to be a tag that can be used to identify and manipulate messages in the Handler queue. This becomes useful when it comes to the subject of the next section.

Stopping Gracefully

Anytime you start playing with Threads and similar toys, you need to keep in mind stopping them in a graceful fashion. The same is true with timers. Listing 11-5 shows a few different approaches.

Listing 11-5. Stopping Gracefully: A Few Techniques

```
  @Override
  protected void onDestroy() {
    // Shutting down the timers. Probably not needed in this demo.
    mToggleTick.retrigger=false; // Just setting a flag to stop Runnable from↵
retriggering itself.
    mHandler.removeCallbacks(mClockTick);  // Actually removing the Runnable from the queue.
    mHandler.removeCallbacksAndMessages("progress"); // Use the token method to↵
identify things to remove.
```

```
    super.onDestroy();
}
```

To be completely honest, I'm not sure what happens to timers when an Activity shuts down.

It's always a good idea to shut your stuff down as cleanly as possible. The first and simplest is to just set a flag. mToggleTick will stop retriggering itself because I've turned off the retrigger flag. A safer way would be to call the Handler's removeCallbacks method, which will yank the queued Runnable out of the queue, thus making quite sure it doesn't run.

But the timer in Listing 11-4 is implemented entirely in anonymous declarations. I don't have a reference to it to remove it. Fortunately, I had the forethought to include a token object (in this case, the String "progress") when I queued it, so I can call removeCallBacksAndMessages, which will remove every appropriately tagged message or callback.

■ **Tip** Here is something I had to look up: to make a progress bar a horizontal bar rather than the default spinner, set the style to: style="?android:attr/progressBarStyleHorizontal". *ADT 12 and up offers this as a default widget.*

Doing Things in Background

Given the importance of not blocking your main UI Thread, wouldn't it be nice if there was a class that handled it all for you? Not terribly surprisingly, Android offers just such a class, and it is known as AsyncTask. Every time you use AsyncTask, you'll need to subclass it. As a bare minimum, you'll want to override doInBackground. This will give you a class that will run something in background, with its own Thread. This is not terribly useful in itself, given how easy it is to create your own Thread. What is useful is if you override a few more methods. Table 11-1 shows the key methods you'll want to override.

Table 11-1. The Important AsyncTask Methods to Override

Method	Description
abstract Result doInBackground(Params... params)	Override this method to perform a computation on a background Thread
void onPreExecute()	Runs on the UI Thread before doInBackground
void onPostExecute(Result result)	Runs on the UI Thread after doInBackground
void onProgressUpdate(Progress... values)	Runs on the UI Thread after publishProgress is invoked
void onCancelled(Result result)	Runs on the UI Thread after cancel is invoked and doInBackground has finished

The sequence of calls goes as follows:

1. onPreExecute is called in the foreground Thread, and is used for setup.

2. doInBackground is called in the background Thread, and will run cheerfully in background until told to stop.

3. onProgressUpdate runs in the foreground Thread, and is called when you call publishProgress from the background Thread.

4. onPostExecute is called with the result of the doInBackground call, and it, too, runs in foreground.

And onCancelled will be called instead of onPostExecute if cancel has been called.

WHAT'S WITH "..."?

Java has a cute feature that is referred to as varargs. If you see something like myMethod(String… params), it tells you that the params argument is actually an array. You can treat it as String[] when reading it.

Where it differs from a straight array is that Java will build the array for you if required. You could thus call it like the following:

```
myMethod("Argument 1","Argument 2","Argument 3","ad nauseam");
```

In fact, you can continue adding arguments until you get bored. You can also build and pass your own array.

It's just a little syntactic sugar to make your life easier.

Let's have a look at how this works in practice (refer to Listing 11-6).

Listing 11-6. Using AsyncTask

```
public class AsynchActivity extends Activity {

    TextView mProgress;
    Button mOk;
    MyAsynchTask mTask;

    @Override
    protected void onCreate(Bundle savedInstanceState) {
        super.onCreate(savedInstanceState);
        setContentView(R.layout.asynch);
        mProgress = (TextView) findViewById(R.id.eProgress);
        mOk = (Button) findViewById(R.id.btnOk);
    }

    public void clickOK(View v) {
        v.setEnabled(false); // Stop doubling stuff up.
```

```
    mTask = new MyAsynchTask();
    mTask.execute("/sdcard");
}

public void clickCancel(View v) {
  if (mTask!=null) {
    mTask.cancel(true);
  }
}
```

Listing 11-6 shows the framework for our test, which looks a little like Figure 11-2.

Figure 11-2. What Listing 11-6 should produce

When OK is pressed, an AsyncTask is created and then executed. In the demo, it will run through all the files on the SDCard, returning the number of files and total size. This will typically take several seconds at least . . . if you have a crowded disk, possibly much longer. The code that does the deed is here:

```
mTask = new MyAsynchTask();
mTask.execute("/sdcard");
```

▪ **Note** Each instance of AsyncTask created will execute only once. You'll get an exception if you try to execute it twice.

Let's have a look at the beast itself in Listing 11-7.

Listing 11-7. The Overridden AsyncTask

```
class MyAsynchTask extends AsyncTask<String, String, String> {

  @Override
  protected void onCancelled(String result) {
    mOk.setEnabled(true);
    mProgress.setText("Cancelled:"+result);
    super.onCancelled(result);
  }
```

```java
@Override

protected void onPostExecute(String result) {
  mOk.setEnabled(true);
  mProgress.setText("Done: "+result);
  super.onPostExecute(result);
}

@Override
protected void onPreExecute() {
  mProgress.setText("Starting...");
  super.onPreExecute();
}

@Override
protected void onProgressUpdate(String... values) {
  if (values.length>0) {
    mProgress.setText(values[0]);
  }
}

private void recurseFiles(File file, long totals[]) {
  if (file.isDirectory()) {
    File[] files = file.listFiles();
    if (files==null) return;
    publishProgress(file.getName());
    for (File f: files) {
      if (isCancelled()) break; // Breaking out.
      recurseFiles(f,totals);
    }
  } else {
    totals[0] += 1;
    totals[1] += file.length();
  }
}


@Override
protected String doInBackground(String... params) {
  // This is where all the work actually happens.
  long totals[] = new long[2];
  if (params.length<1) {
    return "No parameters supplied.";
  }
  try {
    File start = new File(params[0]);
    recurseFiles(start,totals);
  } catch (Exception e) {
    return e.toString();
  }
```

```
        return "Files: "+totals[0]+" Size: "+totals[1];
    }
}
```

This will simply update a TextView with information as we go along, as you can see in onProgressUpdate.

onPreExecute is called first, and can be used to initialize things.

Then doInBackground is called. Here, I'm recursing through the file structure on the SDCard and adding them up in the totals array—the file count goes in totals[0] and the combined size goes in totals[1].

And once we're done, the result returned from doInBackground is passed to onPostExecute. But I may wish to cancel the background task, which is done using cancel.

```
cancel(boolean mayInterruptIfRunning)
```

The Boolean parameter indicates whether cancel should issue an interrupt as part of the cancellation.

In doInBackground, isCancelled() should be checked regularly to see whether the background task should stop.

If the AsyncTask is stopped with a cancel, then instead of onPostExecute being called when doInBackground finishes, onCancelled is called.

▨ **Note** onCancelled has two forms: onCancelled() and onCancelled(Result). The latter is the preferred form, in that the result of doInBackground is passed to it. However, this form is available only in API 11 or later, something to keep in mind if writing backward-compatible code.

So what's with this String,String,String thing?

```
class MyAsynchTask extends AsyncTask<String, String, String>
```

Rather cleverly (I think), AsyncTask supports a template, which tells it what type of data to use. The first argument is the type of the parameter passed in execute. The second argument is the type of data used for the progress reports. The third argument is the type of data returned by doInBackground.

I used Strings for it all in my demo, but you could easily use something else, e.g., an int value to update a progress bar.

Asking for Directions

Many chapters ago, I promised to show how to use a dialog in a modal fashion . . . in other words, behaving like Delphi or Visual Basic. This will pop up a yes/no dialog, and wait on the result. This approach is really only meaningful from within a separate Thread like AsyncTask. And I may have mentioned, it's not that trivial to set up . . . although, once you've done it, you can always build your own utility class for later.

The approach I've found is used internally for SL4A, so I know it works. It's probably not the only method, but let's go with it for the moment. Let's have a look at some of the components needed to pull this off (see Listing 11-8).

Listing 11-8. Accessing the Main Thread

```
// Cunning bit of code to run something in the main thread.
public static void runInMainThread(Context context,final Runnable task) {
  Handler handler = new Handler(context.getMainLooper());
  handler.post(new Runnable() {
    @Override
    public void run() {
      task.run();
    }
  });
}
```

The first thing to remember is that UI components have to run in the UI Thread. Listing 11-8 shows one way to achieve this.

Earlier in this chapter we looked at Handler, and post. The default behavior when creating a Handler is for it to latch onto the Looper attached to the current Thread, but you can tell it to use a different Looper. In this case, new Handler(context.getMainLooper()) creates a Handler linked to the main Looper. This means that we can then pass a Runnable and have it run in the main Thread.

That makes it a straightforward task to show a dialog, but how do we go about waiting for the result? This leads us to some of the more interesting Java classes to do with concurrency.

Listing 11-9. Using Future to Wait for a Result

```
public class FutureResult implements Future<Boolean> {

  private final CountDownLatch mLatch = new CountDownLatch(1);
  private volatile Boolean mResult;

  public void set(Boolean result) {
    mResult=result;
    mLatch.countDown();
  }

  @Override
  public boolean cancel(boolean mayInterruptIfRunning) {
    return false;
  }

  @Override
  public Boolean get() throws InterruptedException {
    mLatch.await();
    return mResult;
  }

  @Override
  public Boolean get(long timeout, TimeUnit unit)
```

```
      throws InterruptedException {
    mLatch.await(timeout,unit);
    return mResult;
  }

  @Override
  public boolean isCancelled() {
    return false;
  }
  @Override
  public boolean isDone() {
    return false;
  }
}
```

Listing 11-9 shows a class I created that implements the Future interface. A Future represents the result of an asynchronous computation, with standard methods for checking whether the computation is complete and so forth.

FutureEvent is a simple class that contains a Boolean, and controls access to it.

The class that does most of the important work here is CountDownLatch. Anything calling the CountDownLatch.await() method will wait there until the countdown equals 0. In this case, we want the background Thread to wait only until the main Thread has finished its work, so we set the CountDownLatch to 1.

Calling FutureEvent.get() will wait until something else has called FutureEvent.set(), making it ideal for this task.

Listing 11-10. Displaying a Dialog and Waiting for the Result

```
public boolean askProceed(final Context context) {

  final FutureResult mResult = new FutureResult();

  runInMainThread(context, new Runnable() {
  @Override
  public void run() {
    AlertDialog.Builder builder = new AlertDialog.Builder(context);
    builder.setTitle("Demo Dialog");
    builder.setMessage("This will wait until a response is offered.");

    DialogInterface.OnClickListener buttonListener = new DialogInterface.OnClickListener() {
      @Override
      public void onClick(DialogInterface dialog, int which) {
        boolean result = (which==DialogInterface.BUTTON_POSITIVE);
        mResult.set(result);
        dialog.dismiss();
      }
    };
    builder.setNegativeButton("No", buttonListener);
    builder.setPositiveButton("Yes", buttonListener);
```

```
       builder.setOnCancelListener(new DialogInterface.OnCancelListener() {

         @Override
         public void onCancel(DialogInterface dialog) {
           mResult.set(false);
           dialog.dismiss();
         }
       });
       builder.show();
     }
   });
     try {
       return mResult.get();
     } catch (InterruptedException e) {
       return false;
     }
   }
 }
```

Listing 11-10 shows the code to build and display a dialog, and wait for the result.

Building a dialog should be a familiar task by now. What this does is display the dialog in the main Thread, and the wait for mResult to be set, at which point the result can be returned to the calling program. The complexity of the setup is more than made up for with the ease of use:

```
ret=askProceed(mContext);
```

Obviously, this is a stripped-down example. askProceed could take more parameters to give you more options with your dialog, and FutureEvent could be modified to contain something more than just a Boolean.

The Download Manager

If you've used Android for any length of time, you'll notice that downloads tend to happen in a separate Thread, with handy notifications when it's done. As of API 9, this is fairly easy to arrange, using the DownloadManager. You obtain a DownloadManager in the usual way:

```
dm = (DownloadManager) getSystemService(DOWNLOAD_SERVICE);
```

With the DownloadManager, you can enqueue download requests, and receive notifications when it's done. It also offers convenient methods to query the current status of downloads, and access a screen to manage downloads (see Figure 11-3).

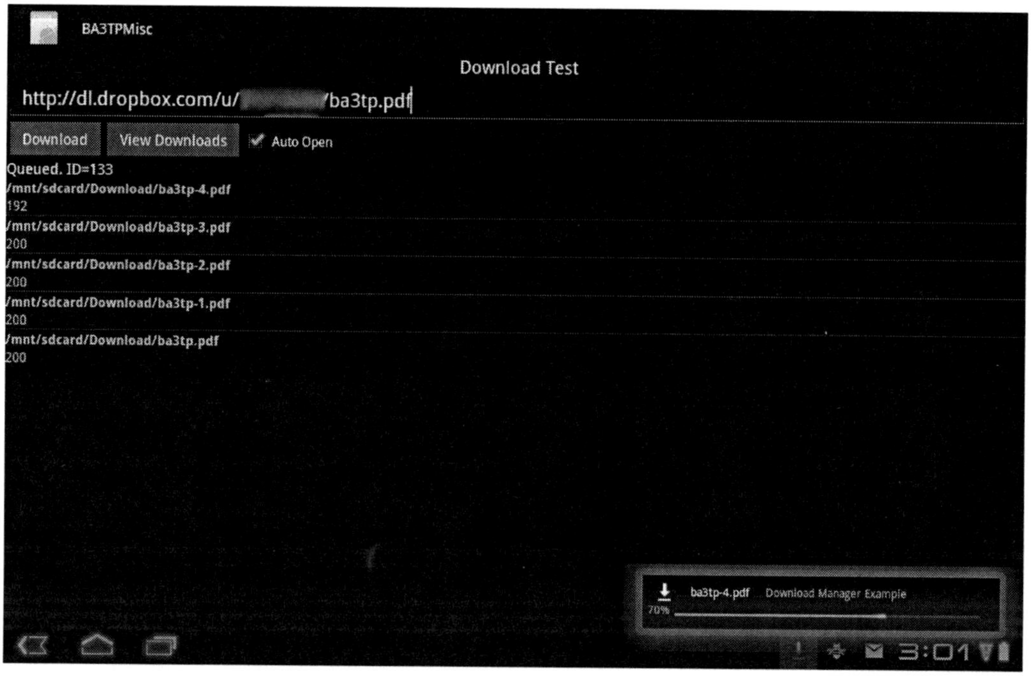

Figure 11-3. Using the Download Manager

Figure 11-3 shows the example in action. What you see on the screen is an EditText with an input type of textUri. Under the buttons, I've put an info bar to display stuff, and under that I've popped in a ListView showing the current status of downloads.

Listing 11-11. Starting a Download Using the Manager

```
public void clickDownload(View v) {
  try {
    Uri source = Uri.parse(mUrl.getText().toString());
    DownloadManager.Request r = new DownloadManager.Request(source);
    r.setDescription("Download Manager Example");
    r.setDestinationInExternalPublicDir(Environment.DIRECTORY_DOWNLOADS,↵
source.getLastPathSegment());
    long id=dm.enqueue(r);
    Toast.makeText(this, "download queued", Toast.LENGTH_SHORT).show();
    mInfo.setText("Queued. ID="+id);
    IntentFilter filter = new IntentFilter(
        DownloadManager.ACTION_DOWNLOAD_COMPLETE);
    registerReceiver(new BroadcastReceiver() {

      @Override
      public void onReceive(Context context, Intent intent) {
        Toast.makeText(context, intent.toString(), Toast.LENGTH_SHORT).show();
```

```
        long fileId = intent.getLongExtra(DownloadManager.EXTRA_DOWNLOAD_ID, -1);
        mInfo.setText(intent.toString()+" fileId="+fileId);
        requery();
        if (fileId>=0 && mAutoOpen.isChecked()) {
          try {
            Intent di = new Intent(Intent.ACTION_VIEW);
            Uri download = dm.getUriForDownloadedFile(fileId);
            String mimetype = dm.getMimeTypeForDownloadedFile(fileId);
            di.setDataAndType(download, mimetype);
            startActivity(di);
          } catch (Exception e) {
            Toast.makeText(context, e.toString(), Toast.LENGTH_SHORT).show();
          }
        }
      }
    }, filter);
  } catch (Throwable e) {
    Toast.makeText(this, e.toString(), Toast.LENGTH_SHORT).show();
  }
}
```

Listing 11-11 shows pretty much all you need to know to operate the DownloadManager. You start off by creating a request:

```
DownloadManager.Request r = new DownloadManager.Request(source);
```

source is a Uri, and you could just stop right there if you wanted to. DownloadManager will do something sensible with your download. However, I've decided to add a description, and also tell it explicitly where I want the destination file stored.

```
r.setDestinationInExternalPublicDir(Environment.DIRECTORY_DOWNLOADS,↩
 source.getLastPathSegment());
```

getLastPathSegment() will pull out the last segment of a Uri, which, most of the time, corresponds to the actual file name you're trying to save. setDestinationInExternalPublicDir will build a destination file out of one of the standard download areas and a file name. It will also take steps to not overwrite an existing file, appending a -1 or -2, etc. until you get a unique file.

After all that, you can queue the requested download using DownloadManager.enqueue(). This returns a long ID, which can be used to keep track of the download.

Once again, you could just stop there with the sense of a job well done, but I've decided to get a little fancy. When the download is complete, the DownloadManager will issue a DownloadManager.ACTION_DOWNLOAD_COMPLETE broadcast message. I'm going to create a BroadcastReceiver on the fly to respond to this message.

```
long fileId = intent.getLongExtra(DownloadManager.EXTRA_DOWNLOAD_ID, -1);
```

When it does respond, the download file ID will be returned in DownloadManager.EXTRA_DOWNLOAD_ID. I then attempt to view the just downloaded file, using dm.getUriForDownloadedFile(fileId) and dm.getMimeTypeForDownloadedFile(fileId) to build a view Intent and calling startActivity.

Querying Your Downloads

You can also get a Cursor containing the current state of the downloads by using DownloadManager.query, as demonstrated in Listing 11-12.

Listing 11-12. Querying the DownloadManager

```
    String[] columns = {DownloadManager.COLUMN_LOCAL_FILENAME,DownloadManager.COLUMN_STATUS};
    int[] fields = {android.R.id.text1,android.R.id.text2};
    mAdapter = new SimpleCursorAdapter(this, android.R.layout.two_line_list_item, null,↵
columns, fields);
    mList.setAdapter(mAdapter);
    requery();
  }

 public void requery() {
    DownloadManager.Query query = new Query();
    mAdapter.swapCursor(dm.query(query));
  }
```

DownloadManager.query is called with a DownloadManager.Query object to define the actual query that you desire. I've just left it open, but you can call setFilterById(long... ids) and setFilterByStatus(int flags) on the Query object to narrow down your results.

I've just thrown this into a very simple ListView. The fields returned from the query are shown in Table 11-2, with the STATUS flags listed in Table 11-3.

Table 11-2. Columns Returned from a DownloadManager Query

Column	Description
COLUMN_DESCRIPTION	The client-supplied description of this download
COLUMN_ID	An identifier for a particular download, unique across the system
COLUMN_LAST_MODIFIED_TIMESTAMP	Timestamp when the download was last modified, in System.currentTimeMillis()
COLUMN_LOCAL_FILENAME	The pathname of the file where the download is stored
COLUMN_LOCAL_URI	Uri where downloaded file will be stored
COLUMN_MEDIAPROVIDER_URI	The Uri to the corresponding entry in MediaProvider for this downloaded entry
COLUMN_MEDIA_TYPE	Internet Media Type of the downloaded file
COLUMN_REASON	Provides more detail on the status of the download

Column	Description
COLUMN_STATUS	Current status of the download, as one of the STATUS_* constants
COLUMN_TITLE	The client-supplied title for this download
COLUMN_TOTAL_SIZE_BYTES	Total size of the download in bytes
COLUMN_URI	Uri to be downloaded

Table 11-3. Possible Values of Status

Status	Description
STATUS_FAILED	Download has failed.
STATUS_PAUSED	Download is waiting to retry or resume.
STATUS_PENDING	Download is waiting to start.
STATUS_RUNNING	Download is currently running.
STATUS_SUCCESSFUL	Download has successfully completed.

Finally, there is a quick and easy way to see and otherwise manipulate the downloaded files, as shown in Listing 11-13.

Listing 11-13. Viewing the Downloads

```java
public void clickView(View v) {
    Intent intent = new Intent(DownloadManager.ACTION_VIEW_DOWNLOADS);
    startActivity(intent);
}
```

This will pop up a window a lot like Figure 11-4.

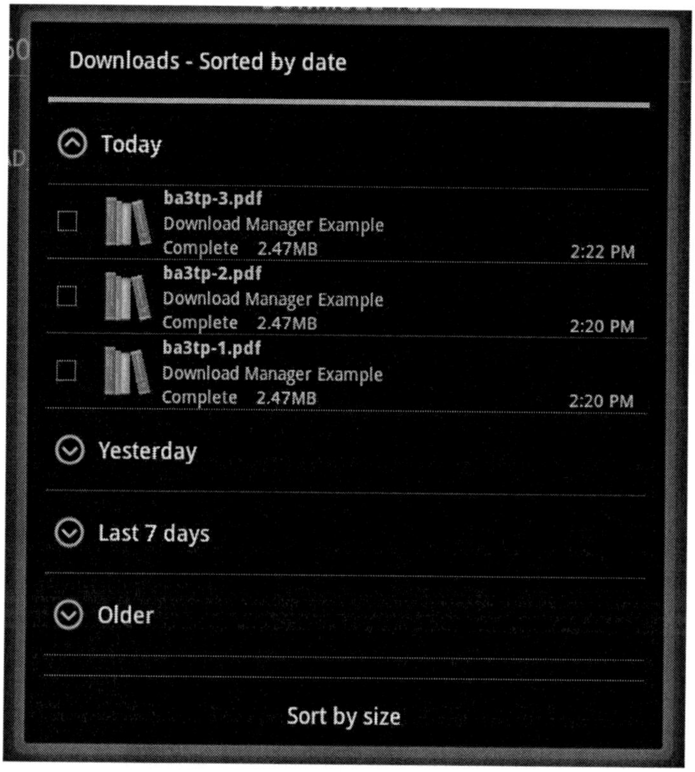

Downloads - Sorted by date

Today

ba3tp-3.pdf
Download Manager Example
Complete   2.47MB   2:22 PM

ba3tp-2.pdf
Download Manager Example
Complete   2.47MB   2:20 PM

ba3tp-1.pdf
Download Manager Example
Complete   2.47MB   2:20 PM

Yesterday

Last 7 days

Older

Sort by size

Figure 11-4. The Download Manager screen

Animations

Android supports a frankly astonishing number of types of animations, whether it be cartoon-style sprites or complex transformations. These can be used to give your interface more sparkle, or just because you like pretty things. I've included a simple example of a "tweening" animation, which will rotate and scale a single image. Listing 11-14 shows the animation activity in its entirety.

Listing 11-14. Using Animation

```
public class AnimateActivity extends Activity implements AnimationListener {
  View mImage;
  Animation mSpinzoom;
  Animation mFadeAway;


  @Override
  protected void onCreate(Bundle savedInstanceState) {
    super.onCreate(savedInstanceState);
    setContentView(R.layout.animate);
```

```
    mImage = findViewById(R.id.imageView1);
    mSpinzoom = AnimationUtils.loadAnimation(this, R.anim.spinscale);
    mFadeAway = AnimationUtils.loadAnimation(this, R.anim.fadeaway);
    mSpinzoom.setAnimationListener(this);
    mFadeAway.setAnimationListener(this);
  }

  void reset() { // Reset our image back to normal.
    mImage.setScaleX(1);
    mImage.setScaleY(1);
    mImage.setVisibility(View.VISIBLE);
  }

  public void clickAnimate(View v) {
    reset();
    mImage.startAnimation(mSpinzoom);
  }

  @Override
  public void onAnimationEnd(Animation animation) {
    if (animation==mSpinzoom) {
      mImage.setScaleX(10); // Maintain size we ended up...
      mImage.setScaleY(10);
      mImage.startAnimation(mFadeAway);
    } else if (animation==mFadeAway) {
      mImage.setVisibility(View.GONE); // And make it go away.
    }
  }

  @Override
  public void onAnimationRepeat(Animation animation) {
  }

  @Override
  public void onAnimationStart(Animation animation) {
  }

}
```

Defining an Animation

There are a number of predefined Android animations you can use. These include fade_in, fade_out, slide_in_left, and slide_out_right. It's probably more fun to define your own, and the easy way to do that is to create a New Android XML ➤ Animation, which will be placed in res ➤ anim. These animation files offer considerable flexibility. Listing 11-15 shows one I prepared earlier.

Listing 11-15. An Animation Definition

```
res/anim/spinscale.xml:
<?xml version="1.0" encoding="utf-8"?>
```

```
<set xmlns:android="http://schemas.android.com/apk/res/android"
        android:shareInterpolator="false"
        android:interpolator="@android:anim/accelerate_interpolator">
        <scale
          android:fromXScale="1.0"
          android:toXScale="10.0"
          android:fromYScale="1.0"
          android:toYScale="10.0"
          android:pivotX="50%"
          android:pivotY="50%"
          android:duration="2000" />

        <rotate
          android:fromDegrees="0"
          android:toDegrees="180"
          android:pivotX="50%"
          android:pivotY="50%"
          android:duration="2000" />
    <rotate
      android:interpolator="@android:anim/bounce_interpolator"
      android:startOffset="2000"
          android:fromDegrees="0"
          android:toDegrees="180"
          android:pivotX="50%"
          android:pivotY="50%"
          android:duration="2000" />
</set>
```

This is more complex than it needs to be, but I got excited.

A set contains a number of transformations, which can be applied either simultaneously or sequentially depending on your settings. What this does is describe an animation that will scale the original item by starting at 1 and going up to 10 times its original size.

pivotX and pivotY describe the position to scale from—in this case, the center of the image—and duration tells it how long to take (in milliseconds). At the same time, and over the same period, the first rotate transformation will be rotating the image 180 degrees. The second rotate kicks in after a time delay of 2,000 milliseconds (as defined by startOffset) and applies a counter-rotation back to the right side up.

Interpolating . . . in Public, No Less

Note the interpolators I used. The transformation command tells the animation what to do to the object it is animating, and how long to take.

The default behavior is to smoothly and evenly proceed from one state to the next, but that can look boring. An interpolator describes the rate at which the transformation proceeds. The accelerate_interpolator starts slow and speeds up. There's a decelerate_interpolator too. bounce_interpolator gets quickly to the end of the transformation, and then bounces back a few times. Very pretty.

Loading Your Animation

There is, fortunately, a utility class to make loading your animation easy.

```
mSpinzoom = AnimationUtils.loadAnimation(this, R.anim.spinscale);
```

This translates your animation file into an animation class. Note that if you've made an error, this is where it will find it.

Applying the animation is very simple indeed:

```
mImage.startAnimation(mSpinzoom);
```

And the animation will start playing.

Something to bear in mind: when the Animation has finished playing, the View in question will pop back to its original state. If this is not what you want, you need to detect that the Animation has finished, and do something with your image to make it match the new state. This is done by adding an AnimationListener to the Animation:

```
mSpinzoom.setAnimationListener(this);
```

In this case, when the animation is done, I use setScaleX and setScaleY to make the View match the scaled image.

But we're not done! I decided that just spinning, scaling, and bouncing weren't enough, so as soon as the first animation ends, I kick off a new one. Listing 11-16 shows a different animation, fadeaway.

Listing 11-16. A Fade Animation

```
res/anim/fadeaway.xml:
<?xml version="1.0" encoding="utf-8"?>
<alpha xmlns:android="http://schemas.android.com/apk/res/android"
  android:fromAlpha="1.0"
  android:toAlpha="0.0"
  android:duration="3000" >
</alpha>
```

This is a simple animation that fades away to total transparency over the course of three seconds. It does this by adjusting the alpha of the object, from 1.0 (fully opaque) down to 0 (completely transparent). If you look back at Listing 11-16, the very last thing that I do with my image is set the visibility to GONE once fadeaway has finished its work.

There is, in fact, quite a bit more to animations, but hopefully this will get you started. The Android web site has quite a few examples to play with, too.

USB

One of the shiny things that Honeycomb tablets can do that the older OSs can't is handle USB hosting. Android 3.0 had fairly basic USB hosting, with only a fairly small number of devices supported. Keyboards and simple USB drives were about the limit.

However, Android 3.1 (at time of writing, fresh out of the box) comes with much better USB support. This includes mouse support (very cute!) and a much wider range of drive-like devices it will talk to. I can now directly transfer files from my Android tablet to my Android phone via USB. Previously I had to either use Bluetooth (which is very slow for large files) or plug into a computer.

Programming Your USB

Yes, you can now write a USB driver for your device. For complex things like disk drives, you shouldn't need to worry, but there are a host of small, simple USB devices out there.

For testing purposes, I dug up a cheap roll-up USB piano keyboard, just to see how hard it would be. (If you are interested, it's the Dream Cheeky Rollup Keyboard, available from www.dreamcheeky.com.) In fact, it was remarkably simple (see Listing 11-17).

Listing 11-17. A Simple USB Activity

```java
public class UsbActivity extends Activity {
  ListView mList;
  UsbManager mUsbManager;
  UsbEndpoint mUsbEndpoint;
  MyReceiver mReceiver = new MyReceiver();
  UsbDeviceConnection mConn = null;
  Handler mHandler;
  TextView mInfo;
  static public final int VENDOR_ID = 6465; // These work for my test USB music keyboard.
  static public final int PRODUCT_ID = 32801; // You'll need to change for your own device.
  @Override
  protected void onCreate(Bundle savedInstanceState) {
    super.onCreate(savedInstanceState);
    setContentView(R.layout.usb);
    mList = (ListView) findViewById(R.id.listView1);
    mInfo = (TextView) findViewById(R.id.eInfo);
    mUsbManager = (UsbManager) getSystemService(USB_SERVICE);
    mHandler = new Handler();
    clickList(null);
  }
}
```

As you can probably see with Listing 11-17, we use UsbManager, obtained in the usual fashion.

■ **Note** UsbManager is available only for Android 3.1 and up . . . API 12. This example will not work on 3.0 or before.

This application will list the available USB devices, and detect if a device is removed. It will also enable you to read from a USB device (as long as it is simple), but you will need to set the vendor and product IDs to match your device. Fortunately, you can use the listing function to work out what these are.

Listing 11-18. Obtaining a List of USB Devices

```java
public void clickList(View v) {
  Map<String, UsbDevice> mylist = mUsbManager.getDeviceList();
  List<String> values = new ArrayList<String>(mylist.size());
```

```
if (mylist != null && mylist.size() > 0) {
  for (String key : mylist.keySet()) {
    StringBuilder b = new StringBuilder();
    UsbDevice device = mylist.get(key);
    b.append(device.toString() + "\n");
    for (int i = 0; i < device.getInterfaceCount(); i++) {
      UsbInterface usbint = device.getInterface(i);
      b.append("  " + usbint + "\n");
      for (int j = 0; j < usbint.getEndpointCount(); j++) {
        UsbEndpoint endpoint = usbint.getEndpoint(j);
        b.append("    " + endpoint + "\n");
      }
    }
    values.add(b.toString());
    if (device.getVendorId() == VENDOR_ID
        && device.getProductId() == PRODUCT_ID) {
      if (mConn == null) {
        try {
          UsbInterface usbi = device.getInterface(0);
          mUsbEndpoint = usbi.getEndpoint(0);
          mConn = mUsbManager.openDevice(device);
          if (mConn.claimInterface(usbi, true)) {
            startComms();
          } else {
            closeConn();
          }
        } catch (Exception e) {
          toast(e);
        }
      }
    }
  }
} else {
  values.add("No USB devices found.");
}
```

Listing 11-18 shows the guts of the program. This gets a list of attached devices by calling UsbManager.getDeviceList(). This will return a list of UsbDevices, or null if none are attached.

Each UsbDevice has one or more UsbInterfaces, and each UsbInterface has one or more UsbEndpoints.

Now, the main part of this loop is building a list to be displayed to the user. However, I decided that just listing the devices was boring. If you look, you can see the code looking for a specific vendor and product. These are hardwired at present. It may make more sense to make them configurable, but I'll leave that as an exercise for the reader.

Setting up a connection to a USB means you need to locate a specific UsbInterface. In the case of my test device, it has only one interface, and only one UsbEndpoint.

Having located the device you want, and worked out which interface you want, the following lines of code will establish a connection.

```
mConn = mUsbManager.openDevice(device);
if (mConn.claimInterface(usbi, true)) {
```

claimInterface returns true if it succeeds, at which point you can start talking to the device.

At this point, there are a couple of different ways of transferring data. I chose to use bulkTransfer. But since that is a blocking call, it should be carried out in a separate Thread.

Listing 11-19. Using a Thread to Read from the USB Port

```
private void startComms() {
  Thread comms = new Thread(new MyComms());
  comms.start();
}

class MyComms implements Runnable {

  @Override
  public void run() {
    byte[] buffer = new byte[8]; //Happen to know max size for this device is 8
    while (mConn!=null) {
      int len=mConn.bulkTransfer(mUsbEndpoint, buffer, buffer.length, 10000); // Wait↵
10 seconds
      if (len>0) {
        StringBuilder sb = new StringBuilder();
        for(int i=0; i<len; i++) {
          sb.append(String.format("%02x", buffer[i]));
        }
        final String s = sb.toString();
        mHandler.post(new Runnable() {

          @Override
          public void run() {
            mInfo.setText(s);
          }});
      }
    }
  }

}
```

Listing 11-19 shows the Thread that listens to the incoming data. Now, I also hard-coded the incoming buffer size to 8. It would make more sense to use the result from UsbEndpoint.getMaxPacketSize(). Still, it does allow me to keep things clear.

The roll-up piano has a very basic interface. It just streams the state of all the pressed keys in an 8-byte bitmap. This means I'm only ever really interested in the latest data, so that's all I display (as a hex string).

Responding to USB Events

It's all very well talking to USB devices, but you also need to know when they are plugged in and removed. It turns out that responding to an unplugged device is quite easy (see Listing 11-20).

Listing 11-20. Knowing If Your USB Has Been Unplugged

```
registerReceiver(mReceiver, new IntentFilter(
    UsbManager.ACTION_USB_DEVICE_DETACHED));

class MyReceiver extends BroadcastReceiver {

  @Override
  public void onReceive(Context context, Intent intent) {
    Toast.makeText(context, intent.toString(), Toast.LENGTH_SHORT).show();
    closeConn();
    clickList(null); // Refresh the list.
  }
}
```

As shown in Listing 11-20, it's just a matter of listening out for a
UsbManager.ACTION_USB_DEVICE_DETACHED broadcast.

You'd think you could do the same thing with a UsbManager.ACTION_USB_DEVICE_ATTACHED message,
but it turns out to be a little more complex. You need to have something like Listing 11-21 in
AndroidManifest.xml.

Listing 11-21. Responding to a USB Device Being Plugged In

```
        <activity android:name="UsbActivity">
            <intent-filter>
                <action android:name="android.hardware.usb.action.USB_DEVICE_ATTACHED">↵
</action>
            </intent-filter>
                    <meta-data android:name="android.hardware.usb.action.USB_DEVICE_ATTACHED"
                    android:resource="@xml/device_filter" />
        </activity>
```

Listing 11-22. A Simple Device Filter

```
res/xml/device_filter.xml
<?xml version="1.0" encoding="utf-8"?>

<resources>
    <usb-device vendor-id="6465" product-id="32801" />
</resources>
```

You will also need an XML file like Listing 11-22 to define the usb-device filter. I've set this to
specifically look for my vendor and product ID, but you can set it for general classes, and you could put
in a range of IDs. This has the advantage of automatically starting the Activity when you plug it in. It
gives you the ability to write and distribute a specific driving application. The final result looks like
Figure 11-5.

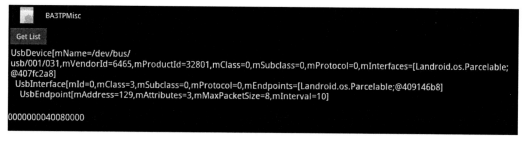

Figure 11-5. The USB example in action

That row of numbers down at the bottom corresponds to the map of the pressed keys. So, given Android's media capabilities, it would not take terribly long at all to turn this into a rather cool portable piano app.

Summary

This last chapter has been very much a grab bag of random techniques, things that turned up or were mentioned in other chapters but it didn't make sense to put there. Lots of it had to do with Threads and other multi-processing functions. We played with Handlers, using them for timers and many other useful things. We looked at the very useful background task manager, AsyncTask, and how to use the DownloadManager. We dipped our toes in the turbulent waters of animation. And finally, for the mad hackers among you all, we played with the brand new, shiny USB interface.

And Finally

It's been an interesting trip. I learned a lot writing this book, and I certainly hope you learned at least something reading it. There's a lot more stuff you can do with Android, but I hope this will have given you a nice solid grounding to move on with. Hope to see you again some other book.

Android: onward and upward!

The End

Index